W9-CDZ-122

Confucianism, Law, and Democracy in Contemporary Korea

CEACOP East Asian Comparative Ethics, Politics and Philosophy of Law

Series editors: Philip J. Ivanhoe, Chair Professor of East Asia Comparative Philosophy and Religion and Director of the Center for East Asian and Comparative Philosophy (CEACOP) at City University of Hong Kong; Sungmoon Kim, Associate Professor of Political Theory at City University of Hong Kong; Erik Lang Harris, Assistant Professor of Philosophy at City University of Hong Kong

This series features path-breaking and field-defining works in East Asian comparative philosophy with a special interest in works of normative and applied ethics, political theory and philosophy of law. The series is published in partnership with the Center for East Asian and Comparative Philosophy (CEACOP) at City University of Hong Kong.

Titles in the Series

Confucianism, Law, and Democracy in Contemporary Korea, edited by Sungmoon Kim

Confucianism, Law, and Democracy in Contemporary Korea

Edited by Sungmoon Kim

ROWMAN & LITTLEFIELD

INTERNATIONAL

London • New York

Published by Rowman & Littlefield International, Ltd.
Unit A, Whitacre Mews, 26-34 Stannary Street, London SE11 4AB
www.rowmaninternational.com

Rowman & Littlefield International, Ltd. is an affiliate of Rowman & Littlefield
4501 Forbes Boulevard, Suite 200, Lanham, Maryland 20706, USA
With additional offices in Boulder, New York, Toronto (Canada), and London (UK)
www.rowman.com

Copyright © 2015 by Sungmoon Kim and contributors

All rights reserved. No part of this book may be reproduced in any form or by any
electronic or mechanical means, including information storage and retrieval systems,
without written permission from the publisher, except by a reviewer who may quote
passages in a review.

British Library Cataloguing in Publication Information Available
A catalogue record for this book is available from the British Library

ISBN: HB 978-1-7834-8223-8
ISBN: PB 978-1-7834-8224-5

Library of Congress Cataloging-in-Publication Data

Confucianism, law, and democracy in contemporary Korea / edited by Sungmoon Kim.
pages cm. — (East Asian comparative ethics, politics and philosophy of law)
Includes bibliographical references and index.
ISBN 978-1-78348-223-8 (cloth : alk. paper) — ISBN 978-1-78348-224-5 (pbk. : alk. paper) —
ISBN 978-1-78348-225-2 (electronic)
1. Korea (South)—Politics and government—21st century. 2. Law—Korea (South) 3. Democracy—
Korea (South) 4. Confucianism—Korea (South) I. Kim, Sungmoon.
DS923.25.C66 2015
320.95195—dc23
2014047245

∞™ The paper used in this publication meets the minimum requirements of American
National Standard for Information Sciences Permanence of Paper for Printed Library
Materials, ANSI/NISO Z39.48-1992.

Printed in the United States of America

Contents

Introduction

Sungmoon Kim

For the past two decades, comparative political theory has grown into a recognized subfield in both political science and philosophy; nevertheless, scholars in both fields still are rarely interested in how political theory as a set of normative arguments and prescriptions engages dialectically with the actual social, legal, and political realities of a particular polity. Often what we find in the existing literature is a cross-cultural methodology,[1] a global philosophy,[2] or a pure conceptual or historical analysis,[3] but never a political theory that has imbibed and seeks systematically to account for concrete, contemporary human experiences, practices, and aspirations. This problem is especially serious in the scholarship on Confucian political theory and philosophy, first because of the dominance of pure textual studies in the current practice of theorization and second, and more importantly, because of the scarce attention on the part of contemporary scholars to how modern East Asians are still and complexly conditioned by traditional Confucian norms, habits, and mores, despite drastic social, economic, and political changes in their lives, and how to evaluate and further give a normative expression to such ongoing modern *Confucian* practices whose outlook is distinct not only from Western-style liberal democracy but also from traditional Confucianism practiced in premodern East Asia. Even when scholars engage in the practical questions of Confucian political theory such as the institutions of Confucian democracy or a new Confucian constitutional order, their proposals tend to be speculative, abstract, and sometimes merely assertive, having little relevance to East Asia's existing social, legal, and political conditions.[4]

All the more problematic is that increasing interest in Confucian constitutionalism and democracy notwithstanding, disciplinary barriers still prove too formidable to allow scholars in various academic disciplines such as political science, philosophy, and law to engage in a productive dialogue. For

instance, political theorists often forget that the notion of Confucian constitutionalism was coined by a group of legal scholars and discuss it without
adequate consideration of its legal implications while legal scholars rarely
pay attention to the normative dimension of Confucian constitutionalism and
its broader social and political context. Likewise, though philosophers are
often preoccupied with the abstract construction of a normatively attractive
vision of Confucian democracy, their relative ignorance of specific legal and
political institutional configurations of past Confucian and present republican
regimes prevents them from developing a more socially relevant Confucian
philosophical theory.

Taken together, the chapters in this volume aim to contribute to what can
be called *rooted Confucian political and legal theory* by focusing on one
particular East Asian society of the Confucian heritage—South Korea (here-
after Korea)—whose traditional society was the most Confucian among premodern East Asian countries (including China)[5] and still remains, albeit
arguably, the most Confucian in its legal, political, and cultural practices.[6]
Korea offers an interesting case for thinking about Confucian democracy and
Confucian constitutionalism because it is one of the rare East Asian countries
whose fully entrenched liberal-democratic institutions are not only compatible with but in a profound sense undergirded by the Confucian *habit of the
heart*—positive or negative—which exerts a profound influence on the people's legal, social, political, and even economic practices.[7] That is, the case
of Korea challenges the stark philosophical or rhetorical binary of "East
versus West" or "Confucian democracy versus liberal democracy," to which
many Confucian political philosophers subscribe, and encourages them (and,
more importantly, citizens in East Asia) to think about ways to develop
democratic institutions and constitutional practices in a Confucian cultural
and societal context. The Korean case provides us with important insights
into ways that the institutional hardware of liberal democracy and democratic
constitutionalism can be compatible with Confucian cultural software—
namely, Confucian legal and political reasoning and practices.

My claim that this book contributes to Confucian political and legal theory, however, does not mean that the contributors in this volume are unani-
mously sanguine about the possibility of Confucian constitutional democracy
as a normative vision for the future of Korean democracy and constitutionalism. In fact, one of the distinct features of this volume is that rather than
assuming or arguing for the normative attractiveness, even supremacy, of
Confucian democracy or Confucian constitutionalism purely on philosophical grounds, as many do in Confucian political theory, and advocating traditional, fully comprehensive Confucianism without qualification, the contributors identify the Confucian elements in the existing laws (including the
constitutional law) as well as in current political culture and practices. They
carefully examine what elements could underpin a distinctively Korean-Con-

fucian style of constitutional democracy that is nevertheless liberal in its political orientation and what elements should be removed or critically re-vamped to make Confucian culture compatible with democratic constitution-alism, at the heart of which are moral principles such as individual dignity and political equality (including, prominently, gender equality).

Another distinctive feature of this volume is that it pays special attention to the fact of pluralism, which increasingly characterizes Korean (and East Asian for that matter) social and political life. Unlike most of the literature in Confucian political theory, which either completely bypasses this important question or merely asserts that Confucian democracy or constitutionalism is compatible with value pluralism without advancing a compelling argument for such a claim, some of the contributors in this volume show how key political rights such as religious freedom and freedom of association are (or should be) actually practiced under the Korean-Confucian cultural and con-stitutional framework or in what direction Confucianism has to be reformed to make room for these rights and freedoms. The questions they raise in-clude: to what extent and under what conditions are religious and associa-tional freedoms protected and whether (and how) Confucian culture con-strains or is compatible with these important liberal rights. As such, the chapters in this volume together wrestle with the practical meaning of liberal rights under Korean-Confucian societal culture and attempt to illuminate ways in which traditional Confucianism, which is androcentric, patriarchal, and undemocratic, has been and can further be transformed through legal and political processes into a new Confucianism that supports democratic legal and political practices in contemporary Korean society.

In the opening chapter entitled "Conceptualizing Korean Constitutionalism: Foreign Transplant or Indigenous Tradition?,"[8] Chaihark Hahm challenges the conventional wisdom that constitutionalism is a new phenomenon in Korea, which began with the establishment of the Constitutional Court, one of the most important achievements of the successful democratization in the late 1980s. Hahm reinterprets the political discourse of the Chosŏn dynasty as a form of constitutional discourse, thus demonstrating Korea's long con-stitutional tradition. In light of this traditional discourse, he explores contem-porary Korean constitutionalism, the constitutional norms of which are sup-ported by Confucian political traditions and cultural values. Hahm does not present what contemporary Korean constitutionalism looks like or how a modern Korean constitutionalism that is predicated on traditional Confucian values and practices can be compatible with Korea's democratic and pluralist societal context. Rather by aiming to re-appropriate the sources of constitu-tional norms in traditional Korea in the service of a contemporary Korean constitutionalism that is culturally relevant, Hahm raises an important nor-mative question—what Korean constitutionalism should be like in the culturally Confucian and politically democratic societal context—not only for legal scholars but also for political theorists and philosophers. In a sense, the subsequent chapters in the volume can be considered rejoinders, positive or negative, to Hahm's historical interpretation and normative suggestion.

Hahm begins his chapter by redefining the very concept of "constitutionalism." His strategy of conceptual redefinition is twofold. On the one hand, Hahm defines constitutionalism *negatively* by understanding it as "the idea of opposing arbitrary or absolute power." Here Hahm's strategy is to show that if traditional Confucian Korean politics was not marked by despotism or tyranny or if premodern Koreans developed a way to restrain the ruler's otherwise absolute power and its arbitrary exercise, then we can conclude that there must have been some "constitutional" measures in Confucian Korea, some codified practice that accomplished the functional role that explicit historical constitutions have filled. In the fourth section of his chapter, Hahm argues that Confucian ritual codes and norms (*ye* 禮; *li* in Chinese) played an important constitutional role by constraining the ruler's political power and disciplining his bodily movement and psychological temperament.[9] On the other hand, Hahm broadens the definition of constitutionalism beyond its usual referent of legal limitations on government powers by making various forms of political institutions, practices, and discourse integral to constitutionalism, thereby redefining constitutionalism as "a combination of both external incentive structure as well as internal, educative, processes of character formation." Once again, in Hahm's judgment, Confucian ritual practices performed this *formative* dimension of constitutionalism remarkably well during the Chosŏn dynasty. Understanding constitutionalism in this broad sense, Hahm then argues that at the core of constitutionalism is the normative force of *tradition* as the basis of "constitutional conventions" and illustrates in the remainder of the chapter how Confucian ritual discourses provided traditional Koreans with a "constitutional culture" in which the interpretive nature of the Confucian constitutional discourse occasionally gave rise to "disagreements" among its participants. According to Hahm, with four major sources of constitutional authority—the way of the former (sage-)kings, ancestral precedents, Zhu Xi's orthodoxy, and the laws and institutions of the current Chinese court—constitutional adjudication was not necessarily straightforward but the participants in the Confucian constitutional discourse were nevertheless able to manage a principled constitutional culture by virtue of intensive interpretative deliberations as shown in the famous Ritual Controversy (*yesong* 禮訟) among scholar-officials in the seventeenth century. Hahm concludes this rich chapter by arguing that contemporary Korean constitutionalism will be given a firmer cultural grounding when the formative or educative aspect of Confucian ritual practices (*ye*) is retrieved and translated into the modern context.

In her chapter "Confucianism That Confounds: Constitutional Jurisprudence on Filial Piety in Korea," Marie Seong-Hak Kim grapples with the same issue Hahm raises, namely "constitutionalism in the Korean context," from the perspective of the constitutional jurisprudence on penal provisions that involve the Confucian ideal of filial piety. Kim argues that the recent Korean Constitutional Court's decision that affirmed Articles 224 and 235 in the Criminal Procedure, which prohibit descendants from filing a complaint against their lineal ascendants, proves "the powerful presence of the Confucian ideology in Korean law and society." The Court's decision shows that Korea, constitutionally committed to liberal democracy, is still deeply predicated on Confucian ethics and moral norms to which filial piety is central. Kim's concern in the paper, however, is not merely to expose the Confucian elements deeply entrenched in the Korean legal system. Rather, her goal is to investigate whether the constitutional jurisprudence of the relevant penal provisions that uphold filial piety over one of the basic constitutional rights—the right to be heard at the criminal proceedings—makes sense in contemporary Korean legal and social contexts.

To do so, Kim first conducts a historical analysis of the origin of filiality-based criminal jurisprudence by examining traditional Confucian legal practices during the Chosŏn dynasty and shows that they were not so much designed or practiced so as to promote love and harmony among the close blood relations, as has been understood by the Constitutional Court, but to preserve the hierarchical order within the family, and by extension, the political order; this is why Chosŏn legal codes emphasized the supreme moral (and legal) significance of filial piety. After revealing that the Chosŏn models of Articles 224 and 235 were indeed grounded on the double notions of subordination to the political order and the perpetuation of the family order, as illustrated by the casual juxtaposition between loyalty (*ch'ung*) and filial piety (*hyo*), Kim then discusses whether it is justifiable to continue this type of legal practice in modern Korea, where "few would contend with a straight face that laws demanding unconditional subordination to the ruler are consistent with a liberal and democratic constitution based on popular sovereignty." Kim challenges the Court's decision by drawing attention to the fact that with the enactment of special law on sexual crimes and domestic violence in 1997, allowing lineal descendants to file complaints against the lineal ascendants, Korean legal consciousness no longer perceives filial piety as an absolute virtue, always trumping other important legal considerations. In the end, Kim does not deny the existence of the general norm of filial piety even among the contemporary Koreas, but she feels strongly that there should be a new legal and normative framework in which traditional Confucian values are not in conflict with liberal-democratic constitutional ideals.

Hahm's invitation to search for a Korean-style constitutionalism that is culturally relevant in the Korean Confucian context sounds both sensible and

timely, but it can be seen as anachronistic for some, especially Korean wom-
en who have suffered great injustice under traditional Confucianism's patriarchal, patrilineal, and androcentric social and political institutions, including
the notorious family-head system. The family-head system institutionalized
traditional Confucianism's male-centered worldview in a powerful way by
relegating women to mere members of the family, led by the family-head,
typically a father, as well as by defining their legal (and ritual) status purely
as someone's wife, daughter, mother, or daughter-in-law, where *someone*
refers exclusively to the head of the family. In "Locating Feminism beyond
Gender and Culture: A Case of the Family-Head System in South Korea,"
Hee-Kang Kim explores a fresh way to understand the public controversy
surrounding the Korean Constitutional Court's decision that found the family-head system stipulated in the Civil Code unconstitutional from the larger
philosophical framework of the relationship between gender and culture.
Contrary to the dominant view that sees the case in terms of "gender versus
culture," Kim proposes to see it (especially the feminist position in the case,
often understood as "liberal") as a series of dialectical and discursive processes in which gender equality, the core feminist value, is re-appropriated
and reinforced with reference to the very Confucian value of the family.

Kim begins her chapter by taking issue with the perceived "dilemma"
between gender and culture. The dilemma arises because while defenders of
gender equality tend to understand gender equality as a universal value applicable uniformly to diverse cultures, proponents of cultural relativism deny
this universalist assumption of gender equality, believing that the norms of
gender equality are fundamentally rooted in particular cultures, each having
its own norms regarding gender. In other words, the dilemma is that while
cultural sensitivity leads to moral indifference, cultural insensitivity leads to
universalizing essentialism. In Kim's view, the Court's decision and the
Korean National Assembly's subsequent legislation to abolish the family-
head system should not be understood from this oppositional view between
gender and culture. Nor should the decision be deemed as a victory of liberalism over Confucianism. First, Kim points out that what motivated Korean
feminists in their years-long struggle to abolish the family-head system was
not so much their desire to mechanistically apply the universal (liberal) norm
of gender equality to Korean society at the expense of its cultural specificity
but their passionate commitment to realizing gender equality by distinguish-
ing the authentic Korean Confucian family structure, unadulterated by Japanese colonialism, from the one imposed by the colonial power, which remade
the Korean family-head system, originally a ritual institution mainly for ancestor worship, into a legal organization modeled after the Japanese family.
Kim then argues that once the family-head system is disentangled from its
colonial legacies, it is no longer an object to be overcome but something to
be reformed from within, from the ethical perspective of Confucianism itself,

on which (or on a particular interpretation of which) the institution was traditionally justified. According to Kim this is exactly what Korean feminists did: while struggling to reform the Korean family structure in a way that enhances gender equality, they did not deny core Confucian values. In fact, they argued that the rearrangement of the family structure through the abolishment of the family-head system would help to better preserve the family, the core institution of Confucianism, without making it a center of various forms of injustice. In this way, Kim claims, Korean feminists were able to reform Korea's patriarchal and heavily unjust family structure by reconstructing and re-identifying Confucian culture rather than abandoning it *in toto* in favor of Western liberalism.

Sungmoon Kim further grapples with the question of gender equality in Korea's modern democratic and yet Confucian cultural context. He begins his chapter "Civil Confucianism in South Korea: Liberal Rights, Confucian Reasoning, and Gender Equality" by raising the following questions: Are Confucian values really incompatible with liberal-democratic values and institutions as most Koreans (and East Asians for that matter) believe, for whom Confucianism is nothing more than a relic of the old regime and the very source of its downfall? Can liberal democracy be attained only if Confucian values are superseded by liberal rights and the social values affiliated with them? If, nevertheless, Koreans are still deeply soaked in Confucian values and practices, even when they subscribe to different moral systems and religious faiths as private individuals and are formally committed to the liberal-democratic constitution, how do they negotiate their Confucian habits of the heart and the formal liberal-democratic constitutional structure? In this chapter, Kim examines how cultural negotiations between traditional Confucian values/practices and liberal rights/values actually take place in democratic Korea by focusing on one of the landmark decisions made by the Supreme Court in 2005, in which the Court ruled that women are entitled to formal membership with all the accompanying rights and privileges of their paternal clan organization (*chongjung* 宗中), overturning a 1958 decision that admits only adult men as legitimate members.

Instead of understanding this case as the clash between progressive liberalism and archaic patriarchal Confucianism, Kim argues that a close examination of the Court's jurisprudence reveals that what appears to be a liberal victory was indeed morally motivated as well as justified by Confucian moral reasoning. Kim shows that the Court, particularly its majority opinion, held the view that in the present case, in which the Confucian customary practice was found at odds with the constitutional principles of gender equality and individual dignity, the latter can be promoted not by simply abolishing male-centered Confucian customs and imposing liberal norms but by allowing women to fully participate in ritual activities and rightfully exercise the virtue of filial piety, from which they have been systemically excluded.

One of Kim's central claims is that though the Court's majority and minority opinions seem to track political liberalism and liberal pluralism respectively, liberal jurisprudence is severely limited and ultimately inadequate for coming to terms with the Court's jurisprudence, which relies heavily on Confucian moral reasoning. Thus Kim argues that in order to make coherent sense of Korea's culture-related legal practices in which traditional Confucianism is reinvented into a new mode of Confucianism that is plausible under democratic and pluralistic social circumstances—what Kim calls *civil Confucianism*, it is necessary to develop a fresh normative framework that is neither purely liberal nor traditional Confucian.

While the chapters so far (though Marie Kim is somewhat ambiguous in this regard) are generally sanguine about the possibility of Confucian constitutionalism and democracy in democratic Korea, the following three chapters express varying degrees of skepticism.

In "Qualitative Defects of Korean Constitutional Democracy and Political Rationalism as a Confucian Legacy," Bi Hwan Kim turns Chaihark Hahm's main thesis upside down by claiming that constitutionalism was completely alien to Confucian Korea during the Chosŏn dynasty because of the dynasty's strong subscription to *political rationalism* deeply embedded in Song-Ming Neo-Confucianism, the version of Confucianism which became Chosŏn's state ideology. By "political rationalism" Kim, drawing on Michael Oakeshott and Pierre Rosanvallon, means "an attitude or consciousness that views politics as a kind of technique to apply pre-conceived rational principle(s) mechanistically to specific situations without considering their contingent character" (n1). Kim's chapter is mainly historical-descriptive as much of it is concentrated on how political rationalism, as he understands the term, has unfolded throughout Korea's history, beginning in the mid-sixteenth century when a group of orthodox Neo-Confucians seized political power and embarked upon (in Kim's view) the most rationalist form of politics in Chosŏn history, thus laying the rationalist foundation for subsequent Korean politics. Kim's chapter is normative-evaluative as the author reconstructs Korean political history from the perspective of political rationalism, of which he is quite critical, and explores a Korean democratic constitutionalism that is non-rationalist and yet possibly predicated on some Confucian virtues.

Kim begins his chapter by attributing the current crisis of Korean democracy, characterized by political polarization and antagonism, mutual hatred and exclusion, intolerance, and a live-and-let-die attitude, to a particular mode of political consciousness and attitude—namely, political rationalism—formed during the mid-Chosŏn period when orthodox Cheng-Zhu Neo-Confucianism attained political hegemony. Though later, more practical, Confucianism, such as the Practical Learning (*shirak* 實學) of the eighteenth and nineteenth century, is often contrasted to more metaphysics-oriented orthodox Neo-Confucianism, Kim argues that notwithstanding some notable differences between orthodox and practical Neo-Confucianisms in terms of substantive philosophical content, political rationalism, whose defining characteristic is a deductive mode of thinking at the expense of concrete political reality, still remains intact in the latter version(s) of Confucianism. He asserts that this paradigmatic political consciousness and attitude did not undergo any meaningful change even during the modern period of political reforms after the Western impact. Central to Kim's claim is that political rationalism has been reinforced since the establishment of the modern Korean state—by imposing Cold War liberalism (which understands liberal values purely as the antithesis of what communism stands for) (the First Republic), by driving state-led economic developmentalism (the Third and Fourth Republic), and by combining an authoritarian government with extreme privatization of public resources and assets (the Fifth Republic)—and the situation has not been ameliorated even after recent democratization. In Kim's judgment, democratic governments are still driven by the political engineering of a handful of political elites, who draw their political legitimacy purely from electoral procedures, thus failing to construct a viable democratic constitutional system. Kim concludes that in order to consolidate Korean constitutional democracy, "the strong rationalist attitude toward politics must be somehow checked or moderated by a totally different kind of political consciousness" and promoting "a more flexible empirical mindset" geared toward political compromises and deliberation. Though Kim is largely ambivalent about traditional Confucianism's democratic implications, he seems to be somewhat sanguine about the possibility that certain Confucian virtues can be highly conducive to the construction of a deliberative constitutional culture in Korean society.

In "Confucianism and the Meaning of Liberalism in the Contemporary Korean Legal System," Junghoon Lee echoes Bi Hwan Kim's overall negative view of Confucianism (especially its political impact in traditional and contemporary Korea) by showing how during the colonial period *Confucian rationalism* (as Kim calls it) further deteriorated into *Confucian statism*, a political ideology in which the private is subsumed by the public that is directly identified with the interest of the state. In this provocative chapter, Lee raises a serious question about recent attempts among Confucian political theorists to construct and present Confucian communitarianism as an alternative to liberalism. Lee argues that the Korean search for Confucian communitarianism as an alternative to liberalism, to which Korea is now constitutionally committed, is anachronistic because, historically speaking, Korea has never experienced liberalism, properly understood, and accordingly so-called "liberal problems" such as family disintegration, human alienation, and the destruction of the environment cannot be attributed to liberal-

ism. Such problems, argues Lee, existed even before liberalism was introduced in Korea.

According to Lee, since the Chosŏn dynasty, in which Neo-Confucianism
became firmly entrenched as state ideology, the political form Confucianism
took in Korea has been not so much Confucian communitarianism but Confucian statism and it is this particular, quite pathological, form of Confucianism that not only gave rise to most "liberal problems" but, more importantly,
prevented liberalism from being properly understood and practiced. Lee
traces the root of Confucian statism to the Confucian notions of the public
and the private and argues that Confucianism's dichotomous, almost zero-
sum, understanding of the two and extreme exaltation of the former (directly
equated with the state) over the private allowed no room for individual
autonomy and freedom, the central value of liberalism. The radical absence
of moral individuality in Confucianism, Lee further claims, made Confucian
communitarianism impossible in the Confucian world because communitarianism is inconceivable without positing the existence of moral individuality.
Lee then discusses how a particular version of Confucian statism, developed
by Meiji Japan, profoundly influenced a group of modern Korean intellectuals and political leaders who otherwise struggled to build the Korean state as
a modern liberal constitutional state. For these early adopters, liberalism,
often interpreted in mediation of theories of state organism and social evolution, was rarely understood as the political philosophy of individualism; it
was primarily understood as a particular form of government, of which an
individual is merely a part. Confucianism played a crucial role in facilitating
this anti-liberal "liberalism" to take a root in modernizing Korea. In Lee's
view, nothing fundamental has changed, even after Korea's heroic democratization. Through an analysis of the jurisprudence of the Korean courts in
several representative legal cases involving the freedoms of religion and
conscience, Lee shows that the Korean courts, still heavily influenced by
Confucian statism, tend to give far more moral weight to the interests of the
state than to those of individuals even when they acknowledge the citizenry's
constitutional rights to such freedoms. This problem has been worsened in
Korea because religious groups themselves are striving for a close relationship with the state, the constitutional principle of the Wall of Separation
notwithstanding, instead of trying to regulate their internal affairs autonomously. Lee concludes his chapter by stressing that it is only when the
Korean courts are fully committed to liberalism that the long tradition of
Confucian statism can finally be overcome and individual rights and freedoms better protected.

The six chapters discussed so far all revolve around the question of
whether or not ideas such as "Confucian constitutionalism," "Confucian democracy," or "Confucian communitarianism" are feasible in contemporary
Korean legal, political, and social contexts. Those who are sanguine about

the feasibility of these reformed modes of Confucianism in contemporary democratic and pluralist Korea are by no means oblivious to the elements of political rationalism or Confucian statism in the way traditional Confucianism has historically unfolded in Korea (and beyond) but they are convinced that given the powerful cultural hold of Confucianism on Korean law and politics, especially the family-oriented and filiality-centered ethics in which Koreans are deeply soaked, the right way to think about Korean constitutionalism and democracy is to productively engage with them, rather than opt for a wholesale Western liberalization. Except for Junghoon Lee, critics of Confucianism, too, seem to embrace this sort of political prescription, even while being wary of some negative aspects of Confucianism that have bedeviled Korean politics and jurisprudence. None of these critics (even including Lee) seem to find Confucian values such as filial piety, respect for elders, and harmony within the family particularly problematic or dangerous *per se*, as they are the values to which the Korean constitution is indirectly committed (as Marie Kim's chapter powerfully shows); they are only worried, and rightly so, about the ways in which these values are manipulated in the service of top-down political engineering or illiberal statism.

Then, what theoretical implications can we draw from these chapters focused on Korea for a more general discussion of Confucian constitutionalism or democracy? Fred Dallmayr's contribution, focusing on the recent Chinese debate on Confucian constitutionalism, encourages us to revisit the earlier chapters from a broader theoretical standpoint as well as reflect upon the Chinese debate against the backdrop of concrete legal and political conditions. Though Dallmayr himself does not engage with the Korean case(s) directly, I hope that readers will grasp the crucial relevance of the Korea-focused chapters to the Chinese debate presented in this chapter.

Dallmayr begins his chapter entitled "Confucius for Our time: Reflections on Politics, Law, and Ethics" by presenting three modes of the recent Confucian revival: a minimalist (which limits Confucian teachings to private family life only), a maximalist (which erects Confucianism into an all-embracing or totalizing ideology governing politics and society), and a hybrid or in-between mode (focused on limited constitutional reform coupled with personal and civic education). After critically examining the core claims of Confucian maximalism by Chinese scholars such as Jiang Qing and Kang Xiaoguang, Dallmayr espouses the third, most self-limited, mode of Confucian revival in East Asia with a special focus on ethical and civic education that enables citizens in East Asia to constrain the political power of the ruler (or the ruling elites).

Dallmayr is deeply worried that the maximalist revival of Confucianism is likely to establish Confucianism as a state religion, thereby making it a dominant political ideology or comprehensive worldview. The problem is that this sort of maximalist Confucianism is hard to reconcile with the modern condition of moral pluralism as well as the modern principles of personal freedom and equality before the law, which define the core features of modern nation-states in contemporary East Asia. More attractive in Dallmayr's view are modern Confucian constitutional reforms suggested by philosophers such as Joseph Chan, Chenyang Li, and Tongdong Bai, who advocate a moderate version of Confucian perfectionism that not only is compatible with moral pluralism but also embraces some key democratic institutions, most notably competitive election. This does not mean that Dallmayr agrees fully with these moderate Confucian constitutionalists. While appreciating these scholars' less maximalist leanings, Dallmayr has some serious concerns about their positive attachment to so-called "meritocracy," a political rule by a select minority of elites who purportedly possess virtues and abilities. Dallmayr has no objection to the claim that political leadership must be meritorious but he is not convinced that constitutional or legal orders by themselves provide adequate safeguards against the corruption of power; "as good Confucians, they [advocates of Confucian meritocracy] must also realize that merit and virtue are not created by constitutional or legal provisions but have to be fostered independently or at least in tandem with social or public institutions [such as royal lectures during the traditional Confucian period in China]." In this regard, Dallmayr argues, the basic insight of democracy with regard to human fallibility and political accountability should not be readily dismissed as a "Western" import and Confucian meritocracy's predisposition toward self-selection and top-down imposition should be counterbalanced with the role of civic education in a social or political body conceived as an ethical community.

Dallmayr's critique of maximalist Confucianism echoes strongly with the concerns raised by Junghoon Lee and Bi Hwan Kim. As we have seen, what Lee and Kim call Confucian rationalism and Confucian statism respectively are the maximalist modes of Confucianism and their criticisms of these modes of Confucianism have an important philosophical basis, as Dallmayr clearly shows. At the same time, Dallmayr's endorsement of moderate Confucian constitutionalism undergirded by democracy and civic education has strong resonance with the normative prescriptions suggested by Chaihark Hahm, Marie Kim, and especially Sungmoon Kim, who espouse a version of Confucianism—what Sungmoon Kim calls *civil Confucianism*—that is democratic and civil. Seen in this way, the chapters on Korea offer an important empirical basis against which to explore Confucian constitutionalism and democracy in China and East Asia that is not only philosophically attractive but also practically relevant in East Asia's increasingly democratic and pluralist societal contexts.

Finally, Hwa Yol Jung, in his "On Confucian Constitutionalism in Korea: A Metacommentary," which serves as an epilogue for this volume, revisits the very notion (and practice) of Confucian constitutionalism and encourages us to problematize the fundamental premises of the Western idea of constitutionalism—namely, possessive individualism and rights talk—from the Confucian (or more broadly "Sinic") relational ontology as well as its ethics of responsibility. Though like Hahm, Jung is interested in developing a constitutionalism (or a mode of constitutional thinking) in the context of Korea's Confucian culture, his overtly philosophical project is radically different from Hahm's (and others' in part I of this volume) jurisprudential project in that he wants to displace the existing Western conception of constitutionalism with the Confucian ethics of responsibility that derives from the Confucian relational ontology of "Interbeing."

Jung's argument is subtle and complex. On the one hand, Jung extols Hahm's jurisprudential "cultural hermeneutics," finding it exemplifying what he calls a "transversal approach," at the center of which is the Sinic logic of *yin* and *yang*, or "unfinalizable dialogism," to put it in another way. On the other hand, however, Jung feels that Hahm's idea of Confucian constitutionalism, insofar as it is a sort of (West-inspired) democratic constitutionalism, does not take democracy's "*of* and *by* the people" elements seriously in its overemphasis of "*for* the people." In Jung's view, Hahm does not give sufficient attention to constitutionalism's central concerns—the separation of powers and the checks and balances between the powers. Jung then takes issue with the Western (mainly liberal) notion and practice of constitutionalism, premised on the assumption of possessive individualism and the absolute right of the individual, by examining various liberal constitutional thinkers, most notably John Locke and Ronald Dworkin, and presents an "ethics of responsibility," a la Emmanuel Levinas, as the most fundamental philosophical as well as practical alternative to rights talk and a rights-based constitutionalism. Jung's core argument is that there is a remarkable similarity between Confucian (or generally Sinic) relational ontology and thinking, focused on what Pierre Bourdieu calls "the performative magic of the social," and Levinas's ethics of responsibility, at the core of which are self-transcendence as opposed to self-absorption, self-affirmation, and care for others. Jung concludes that "the heteronomic ethics of responsibility opens a new threshold of philosophizing politics for generations yet to come."

Although Jung does not connect his later argument about relational ontology and ethics of responsibility directly with his earlier critique of Hahm's notion of Confucian constitutionalism and Western (particularly American-style) constitutionalism, his political message is clear: a full embrace of the (Confucian) ethics of responsibility, predicated on the relational view of the world, will enable us to reconceive the very notion of constitutionalism from scratch (that is, without any philosophical implications with *liberal* constitutionalism) and this new mode of constitutionalism will be genuinely concerned with the wellbeing of the people because it is undergirded by care and responsibility for others. This is perhaps the most radical proposal for future "constitutionalism," if we can still use this term to describe what Jung has in mind. Of course, how to institute such constitutionalism in Korea and beyond is a wholly different matter, but certainly Jung's concluding chapter urges us to think more deeply about Confucian constitutionalism with full attention to Confucianism's philosophical potentials.

NOTES

1. Jin Y. Park, ed., *Comparative Political Theory and Cross-Cultural Philosophy* (Lanham, MD: Lexington Books, 2009); Hwa Yol Jung, *Transversal Rationality and Intercultural Texts: Essays in Phenomenology and Comparative Philosophy* (Athens: Ohio University Press, 2011).

2. Farah Godrej, *Cosmopolitan Political Thought: Method, Practice, Discipline* (New York: Oxford University Press, 2011).

3. Erin M. Cline, *Confucius, Rawls, and the Sense of Justice* (New York: Fordham University Press, 2013); Leigh Jenco, *Making the Political: Founding and Action in the Political Theory of Zhang Shizao* (Cambridge: Cambridge University Press, 2010).

4. Daniel A. Bell, *Beyond Liberal Democracy: Political Thinking for an East Asian Context* (Princeton, NJ: Princeton University Press, 2006); Joseph Chan, *Confucian Perfectionism: A Political Philosophy for Modern Times* (Princeton, NJ: Princeton University Press, 2014); Jiang Qing, *A Confucian Constitutional Order: How China's Ancient Past Can Shape Its Political Future*, eds. Daniel A. Bell and Ruiping Fan, trans. Edward Ryden (Princeton, NJ: Princeton University Press, 2012).

5. Martina Deuchler, *The Confucian Transformation of Korea: A Study of Society and Ideology* (Cambridge, MA: Harvard University Press, 1992).

6. By "rooted Confucian political and legal theory" I do mean that contributors in this volume are Confucian scholars or explicitly advocate a Confucian form of social, legal, or political life. As I note shortly, some of the contributors are gravely worried about the lingering influence of a certain negative version of Confucianism in Korea (and beyond) and they argue that such Confucianism should be overcome for the better protection of individual rights and freedoms and democratic consolidation. My point is that if we take all eight chapters in this volume *together* we will be able to appreciate how they are combined to contribute to a deeper understanding and socially relevant construction of Confucian political and legal theory that can avoid problems the critics of Confucianism in this volume attribute to Confucianism.

7. See Philip J. Ivanhoe and Sungmoon Kim, eds., *Confucianism—A Habit of the Heart* (Albany, NY: State University of New York Press, forthcoming).

8. Hahm's chapter, published originally in *Journal of Korean Law* in 2001, has been reprinted from its original form without any substantive changes or updates, but as discussed shortly, its core argument and the normative question it raises are still highly relevant in the current Korean context.

9. Unless noted otherwise, the romanization of the Chinese characters in this chapter is based on their Korean pronunciation.

I

In Search of Confucian Constitutionalism in the Korean Context

Chapter One

Conceptualizing Korean Constitutionalism

Foreign Transplant or Indigenous Tradition?

Chaihark Hahm

Most observers of Korea will agree that in recent years Korea has been moving steadily towards becoming a constitutional democracy. Beginning with the constitutional revision that took place in 1987 in response to the citizenry's overwhelming demand for more participation in the political process,[1] Korea started to move away from the authoritarian politics which characterized the better part of its recent past. In 1993, Korea brought into power its first civilian president in thirty years, and in 1998, Koreans experienced the first peaceful transfer of power to an opposition candidate. This period also saw the unprecedented prosecution and conviction of two former presidents who had come to power through a military coup d'etat. The special law enacted to allow this historic process listed "subverting the constitutional order" as one of the offenses committed by the ex-generals.[2] It appears that, along with democracy, constitutionalism is becoming one of the shared political ideals of Korean people.

For lawyers, one of the most interesting, and frankly unexpected, developments during this period has been the role played by the Korean Constitutional Court that was established under the constitution of 1987.[3] More a product of a political compromise than the result of any principled or reasoned deliberation, the Court not only has exceeded all expectations in carving out a secure role for itself in the legal and political life of the nation, but it also has contributed significantly to the process of democratization and the establishment of constitutionalism in Korea. Through many controversial decisions,[4] in a relatively short period of time, this Court has substantially cut back the power of the state to encroach upon the citizens' basic rights. Through such decisions, it has also been instrumental in changing the people's attitude toward law and the constitution.[5] It is transforming the Korean legal culture, as it were.

As a result, there is a growing perception that the constitution is a living norm that can actually be invoked to protect one's rights, a norm that is enforced through the Court's decisions. Frankly, this phenomenon is something new and unfamiliar to most Koreans. It may be fair to say that for decades since regaining their independence from the Japanese, Koreans have lived with a constitution that was more of an ornament than a document with binding force. A brief look at the record of the various constitutional organs that were entrusted with the role of enforcing the constitution is enough to confirm this. During the forty years up until the establishment of the present Constitutional Court, only a handful of legislation has been referred to such organs for adjudication, and even fewer have been held unconstitutional.[6] By contrast, as of February 2001, the Court has held a law or government action unconstitutional in 203 cases.[7] In addition, the Court has found in fifty-one cases that a particular legislative or government action was incompatible with the Constitution.[8]

There may be several explanations for this change in the way the constitution is perceived and utilized by the people. From an institutional point of view, one could attribute it to the establishment of the system of "constitutional petitions" which allows ordinary citizens to request the Constitutional Court for a remedy to a violation of their constitutional rights.[9] More generally, one could point to the scope of jurisdiction given to the Court as well as the appointment process of the Court's justices which allowed the opposition party to voice its demands.[10] For more political and sociological reasons, one could of course look to the fact that the current constitution was the outcome of the Korean people's growing desire for democratic politics.[11] Especially, given the fact that Koreans were trying to move away from a regime in which so much power was concentrated in the government, particularly the president, it is perhaps only to be expected that people would make use of the constitution which they revised in order to limit the power of the government.[12] Whatever the direct cause for this nascent constitutionalism in Korea, it is generally understood as a novel development in the political history of Korea.[13]

In this chapter, I would like to query the meaning of the statement that constitutionalism is a new phenomenon in Korea. I begin the next section by suggesting that that statement is problematic if we take a longer view of Korean political history. By redefining constitutionalism from a comparative perspective, I seek to establish in the third section the plausibility of understanding the political history of Korea as an instance of constitutionalism. Proceeding with such a revised definition of constitutionalism, I investigate in the fourth section the sources of constitutional norms in premodern Korea. I also argue that some conventional ideas concerning Korean legal history must be revised. In the fifth section, I attempt an interpretation of the terms and principles of the constitutional discourse of premodern Korea. [14] I shall close with some thoughts on the relevance of such constitutional history for the flourishing of constitutionalism in modern Korea.

The underlying premise of this chapter is that constitutionalism in any country must be supported by its cultural and political traditions. One anxiety that runs throughout this chapter is that in Korea, constitutional discourse is currently proceeding in a state of isolation from its cultural and political traditions. By providing a constitutional perspective on Korean political history, it is hoped that a small contribution might be made to remedy this situation.

HOW LONG HAS KOREA HAD CONSTITUTIONALISM?

As mentioned, with the enactment of the 1987 constitution, Korea is generally regarded as finally learning to practice constitutional politics. There is, however, an alternative way of looking at the burgeoning constitutionalism in Korea. It could be seen as the culmination of at least four or five decades of experimenting with constitutionalism. If we take a look at the popular Korean textbooks on constitutional law, most scholars begin the history of constitutionalism in Korea with the period following liberation, which saw the promulgation of the first constitution of the Republic of Korea in 1948. [15] Similarly, in 1998, Seoul National University held a conference to commemorate the fiftieth anniversary of Korean constitutionalism. According to this view, Koreans have been attempting to establish constitutionalism in Korea for at least a half-century. The recent "novel development" might be better seen as the fruition of a painful, decades-long process of trying to implement constitutionalism.

Perhaps a more "nationalistic" historical narrative would posit the Provisional Constitution of the Provisional Government of the Republic of Korea, which was established in 1919 right after the March First Independence Movement, as the starting point of Korea's constitutional history. This constitution, subsequently revised numerous times until the end of the Japanese occupation, proclaimed the first republican form of government of Korea and is sometimes seen as the first "modern" constitution of Korea. Apparently, the drafters of the current constitution took this position also, for in the preamble, the constitution lays claim to political legitimacy by declaring itself to be the successor of the Provisional Government's constitution. [16] If one wished to push back even further the origin of Korean constitutionalism, one might even look to the famous Kabo Reforms of 1894, with its fourteen-point *Hongbŏm* (Great Plan), which, among other things, proclaimed Korea's "independence" from China. This was followed in 1899 by the promulgation of *Tae Hanguk Kukje* (National Institutions of the Great Korea), according to which King Kojong was declared an "emperor," as the head of a state with equal status in the community of nations, according to public international law of the time. [17]

It is not my intention in this chapter to identify the "correct" starting point of constitutionalism in Korea. Instead, I am more interested in the concept of "constitutionalism" itself and how that term should be understood in the Korean context. I should note, of course, that even among Western scholars of constitutional law and political theorists, constitutionalism is not a well-defined term. As Louis Henkin says, "constitutionalism is nowhere defined." [18] Therefore, I do not pretend to have discovered a universal and uncontroversial definition of the term. My intent in the following pages is much more modest: I wish to offer some thoughts on how we might go about thinking about constitutionalism in relation to the entire span of Korean political history. My hope is to spur more reflection and discussion on the issue of how to conceptualize constitutionalism from a comparative perspective.

To return for a moment to the three possible starting points for the history of Korean constitutionalism mentioned above, it is obvious that each of them is supported by different historical narratives according to which a radical change took place at the respective dates. That is, to claim that Korean constitutional history began in 1919 rather than in 1894 or 1948 requires some evidence showing that that year marked a more significant break with the past than the other years. Similarly with the other positions. Participants of this imaginary historiographical debate [19] would therefore argue about and disagree on which set of events was more significant in terms of Korea's political and legal development.

For all their different interpretations and disagreements regarding the past, however, the three positions share one crucial assumption; namely, that constitutionalism was something unknown to Koreans prior to some identifiable point in time—however difficult it may be to identify that point. The very fact that one could debate about which year deserves to be marked as the inaugural year of Korean constitutionalism indicates that there was a time when constitutionalism did not exist in Korea. Yet, as soon as we start to unpack this assumption, a troubling situation emerges, which is in turn related to problematic assumptions underlying our conception of constitutionalism.

At the core of constitutionalism as a legal and political concept lies the idea of opposing arbitrary or absolute power. Despite the theoretical disagreements among theorists and historians of constitutionalism, they all agree that at bottom constitutionalism is an expression of the desire to limit or at least regulate political power. In short, to define it negatively, constitutionalism is the opposite of despotism or tyranny.[20] Now, if we combine this admittedly crude, negative definition of constitutionalism with the assumption that Korea did not have constitutionalism until the late nineteenth century, at the earliest, we are forced to conclude that Korean politics was defined by despotism or tyranny up to that point. That is, until constitutionalism was introduced (from the West), Koreans must have had nothing to restrain absolute power and nothing to protect people from the arbitrary exercise of such power.

Yet, it is unlikely that is a defensible conclusion. Indeed, one need not be a hot-headed Korean nationalist to see that there is something wrong with portraying the entire couple of millennia of Korean political history as one of domination and oppression under absolute power. To be sure, Korea had her share of despotic rulers, but the idea that Korea for centuries knew *only* such rulers runs counter to one of the few themes of Korean history on which most people agree. It is generally accepted that, aside from a couple of exceptions, rulers of traditional Korea were quite weak in their relation to their subjects. In comparison with the emperors of China or the shogun of Japan, the position of Korean kings generally was not the object of abject exaltation, and rarely commanded absolute power.[21] One of the salient features of the political history of the Chosŏn dynasty (1392–1910) is the prominence of the scholar-officials' position relative to the throne.[22] Moreover, it is highly unlikely that Korea would have led a continued existence for so long if its politics were pervasively arbitrary and authoritarian.[23]

What, then, does this imply for our understanding of constitutionalism and for the assumption that Koreans did not know constitutionalism until 1894, or 1919, or 1948? If Korean political history cannot be characterized as one of unmitigated despotism, then is it legitimate to use the term "constitutionalism" in describing it? If so, did Koreans practice constitutionalism without knowing it?[24] Surely, Koreans of the Chosŏn dynasty did not know of the term "constitution," although the current term *hŏnpŏp* does appear in some of the Chinese classics known to the scholar-officials of the time.[25] Did they then have a different term for their political system and ideal?

REDEFINING CONSTITUTIONALISM

Now, this of course is an age-old problem in the study of comparative law. That is, when we find a practice, institution, or concept in another legal tradition that is similar to but different from a well-known one in one's own tradition, is it legitimate to use one's familiar label to refer to the one found in the foreign setting? Especially when doing so will not only "enrich" one's own legal lexicon but also make it messier and more confusing? In other words, should we revise our understanding of constitutionalism to include political practices and institutions that do not have their roots in the familiar modern political experience of the West?[26]

Obviously, there are quite legitimate scholarly reasons for *not* doing so. For example, in order to preserve intellectual and theoretical consistency, it might be advisable to limit the use of "constitutionalism" to only Western or West-inspired political and legal arrangements. Also, describing something foreign with a label that refers to something functionally similar in one's own tradition may cause one to "read into" the foreign practice one's own values, assumptions, and beliefs which simply don't apply in the foreign case. In other words, it may contribute to "ethnocentric" distortions in representing the foreign political and legal practices.

Nevertheless, I think we should at least be equally mindful of the political import of such a decision. We should also be aware that restricting the use of a term to its original context may sometimes have the effect of implicitly casting negative judgment on the practice, institution, or concept found in other legal and political traditions. This is particularly the case with a term like "constitutionalism," which has now become a highly valued ideal for virtually all states. It is an "honorific term" nowadays which confers on a nation the status of being a member of the civilized world community.[27]

By insisting that we apply the term "constitutionalism" only to institutional arrangements having roots in, say, the Enlightenment context, we may be unintentionally perpetuating another kind of ethnocentrism; namely, an attitude of condescension and disdain toward non-Western countries. It is tantamount to refusing to regard the people of these countries as worthy of equal respect and dignity as Westerners. True, in some cases, their politics are in fact worthy of less respect. Nevertheless, that cannot justify a blanket dismissal of their entire political history.

Of course, another option might be to create a new category that is neither constitutionalism nor despotism, and use it to describe the political history or experience of non-Western countries. The goal would be to reject the binary opposition between constitutionalism and despotism and to use a third term which is at least as "respectable" as constitutionalism. Yet this option has its own difficulties. Creating an unfamiliar, *sui generis* category will more likely than not contribute to the needless mystification of non-Western politics that will only inhibit mutual understanding. Moreover, it may even provide occasions for new "orientalist" interpretations, which may end up demonizing the unfamiliar.[28]

I therefore believe that it is best to use the concept of constitutionalism to refer to non-despotic political arrangements in non-Western worlds as well. This means broadening the definition of constitutionalism beyond its usual referent of legal limitations on government powers through judicial review and other mechanisms codified in a written constitution. We must modify our understanding of constitutionalism to include political institutions, practices, and discourses that do not necessarily operate in terms of principles like the separation of powers, representative democracy, or even the rule of law.

Granted, this is an unusual way to define constitutionalism. Indeed, it might even appear to take away all the necessary elements that go into making constitutionalism work. Yet, for anyone who might be alarmed or skeptical about understanding constitutionalism this way, I would just point out that in fact historians of Western constitutionalism have also used the term in a similar fashion. That is, it is important to keep in mind that although the "modern" type of constitutionalism cannot do without those principles I just mentioned, historians have identified constitutional politics in premodern contexts where these principles were never invoked, such as Renaissance Venice, Ancient Greece and Rome, or even the Medieval Catholic church. [29]

Now, the problem is, even among Western scholars, there is little communication or exchange between the historians on the one hand and the constitutional lawyers on the other, such that we do not yet have a suitable definition of constitutionalism that can accommodate both the modern and the premodern species of constitutionalism. I therefore would like to propose a definition that would do justice to both, and which would also accentuate the distinctive features of constitutionalism vis-à-vis other related concepts.

My proposal is to define constitutionalism simply as the practice of disciplining political power. I'm loosely borrowing the term "discipline" from the works of Michel Foucault and I use it to refer to a set of institutional and discursive practices designed to control and regulate through a combination of both external incentive structure as well as internal, educative, processes of character formation. [30] The end-state, or goal, of discipline is self-surveillance through internalization of a variety of control mechanisms. When applied to political power, discipline means restraint and control of its exercise. Understood in this way, constitutionalism is still about opposing despotism, but it means opposing it in a disciplined manner.

Obviously, discipline of political power can be achieved in various ways. The more familiar way is to take a sort of mechanistic, or Newtonian, approach of checks and balances, or division of power. This approach in a way assumes a preexisting power that needs to be checked or balanced. Power is viewed as a physical entity which has a weight and a size, and therefore can be divided into smaller parts or balanced with another power of equal weight and size. Some historians describe American constitutionalism as the most representative of this approach. [31] In one of the *Federalist Papers*, James Madison famously wrote: "Ambition must be made to counteract ambition." [32]

Another approach might be to take a more constitutive, or formative, perspective and focus more on the control and restraint that results from molding both the power and the power-holder in a specific way. This approach would emphasize the continuous process of educating the power-holder by putting him or her under a constant state of surveillance and supervision. In my view, the ideal of Confucian political philosophy was to implement this second type of discipline. Contrary to the popular perception of Confucianism which views it as an authoritarian ideology, Confucian political philosophy was deeply concerned about disciplining the ruler.[33] At least as practiced by the scholar-officials of the Chosŏn dynasty, Confucianism provided the institutional and discursive resources that enabled them to discipline the monarch through constant surveillance and supervision.[34] This means that Koreans of the Chosŏn dynasty aspired to practice constitutionalism by taking this constitutive and formative approach. They may not have known or bothered to take the Newtonian approach, but they were aspiring to implement constitutionalism nonetheless.[35]

In order to evaluate the claim that traditional Korean politics can be understood as a form of constitutionalism, we need to know, among other things, what operated as the constitutional norms of that period.[36] In other words, what were the sources of Korea's premodern constitutional law? It might be thought that asking this very question is to prejudice the analysis, for this presumes that Korea had something called "constitutional law." If we were to adhere to a narrow, positivist definition of "law," as a type of norm that can be enforced through independent courts, we naturally will not find any such thing in Chosŏn-dynasty Korea. Yet, according to my definition of constitutionalism as the practice of disciplining political power, constitutional norms need not be enforced solely through the courts. To assume this would be to confuse constitutionalism with judicial review.

Granted, today some form of judicial review is considered an indispensable element of constitutionalism.[37] Yet I submit that to equate the two is both inaccurate and anachronistic. One must remember that judicial review was "created" through an imaginative legal maneuvering at the start of the nineteenth century by an American jurist named John Marshall.[38] He "read into" the American Constitution a power that was not even specified in the text.[39] By contrast, as is well known, American constitutional discourse itself was an outgrowth of centuries-old British constitutionalism.[40] To this day, the United Kingdom has maintained a constitutional polity without having adopted the principle of judicial review.[41] Thus, judicial review is a relative latecomer in the story of constitutionalism.[42] In fact, even in the United States, where judicial review is seen as the core of constitutionalism, there are constitutional norms that are not enforced through the courts. An example can be found in the congressional impeachment proceedings against the president and other civil officers prescribed in the American Constitution.[43] This is a system devised for enforcing constitutional norms in which the courts do not take part. The Constitution itself specifically entrusted that job to the House of Representatives and the Senate, that is, the legislative branch.[44]

The case of British constitutionalism is actually quite instructive in conceptualizing the political discourse of traditional Korea in constitutionalist terms. Even though Britain does not have a single written document called "the Constitution" that has the status of a higher law, and although its courts cannot strike down legislation for reasons of unconstitutionality, no one can reasonably deny there is something called the British constitution or that the United Kingdom is a constitutionalist state.[45] Similarly, I believe the lack of a single document labeled "the Constitution" or judicial review need not preclude an understanding of the Chosŏn political system as a constitutional regime.

It is often pointed out in many characterizations of the legal history of Korea and other East Asian countries that independent courts failed to develop which could annul or inhibit arbitrary acts by the government. The usual inference made from this fact is that those governments did not have the institutional arrangement necessary to practice constitutionalism.[46] Yet the British constitutional tradition calls into question the assumption that constitutionalism requires the courts' possession of the power of judicial review. Put differently, constitutional norms need not always take the form of law, in the strict, narrow sense of the word. Indeed, in most countries, constitutional norms comprise, in addition to judicially enforceable rules, a range of norms including political rules, precepts, conventions, and even tacit understandings about what is deemed proper in matters of government. It is in this broader sense that I am using the term "constitutional law."[47]

To identify the sources of constitutional law of traditional Korea, we must then look for not only strictly legal norms that may have been promulgated by the government, but also the seemingly vaguer and more ineffectual norms that informed the political discourse of the period. In this regard, again, comparison with the British system highlights, and facilitates our understanding of, another aspect of traditional Korean constitutionalism, namely, the importance of tradition as a source for constitutional norms. The British have developed a distinct terminology for this: "constitutional conventions." These refer to the unwritten rules of the constitution.[48] They are not enforceable in a court of law, but that does not diminish their importance or normative force. In fact, in Britain, the term "unconstitutional" means that something is contrary to constitutional convention, rather than simply illegal.[49] Although the fact that they are "non-legal" have led some commentators to characterize them as simply moral or ethical rules of governance,[50] many constitutional conventions do not derive their force from their moral persuasiveness.[51] Rather, their normative force derives from the fact that tradition has made them hallowed and sacrosanct. Violation of a constitutional convention therefore will occasion a major political controversy, in which the political legitimacy of the violator will be seriously impugned and compromised. In any such controversy, the point of reference will always be what has been done in the past, and arguments will turn on how much authority is to be conferred on tradition. Tradition, in other words, is an important source of constitutional norm. In Canada, the Supreme Court actually made it explicit that sources of Canadian constitutional norms consist of not only the constitutional documents (i.e., the Constitution Acts, and the Charter of Rights and Freedom), but also the constitutional traditions of Canada. [52]

Indeed, constitutional discourse in any country is pervasively a traditionalist discourse. This is so even in America, where constitutionalism is usually seen as part of the project of refuting tradition, for to the framers of the American Constitution, "tradition" represented hierarchy and oppression. This common image notwithstanding, it is undeniable that constitutional discourse in the United States is marked by an attitude of extraordinary deference to its tradition. For example, invoking the authority of the founding generation is a common way of arguing constitutional issues. Even when not focusing on the framers' "original intent," the discursive style of American constitutional discourse forces constitutional lawyers, both conservative and liberal, to rely on tradition to justify their arguments. [53]

That the normative force of many constitutional norms should depend on tradition is hardly surprising. Whereas the binding force of an ordinary law is ultimately dependent on the threat (real or potential) of coercive force of the state, a constitutional norm cannot rely on the coercive force of the state because, in this case, it is the state itself that is being subjected to the norm. It is the state itself that is being disciplined, and therefore the normal grounds of normative force do not apply here. As the wielder of the coercive force, the state, if it wanted to, could refuse to conform to constitutional norms. The fact that it does not and cannot so flout constitutional norms must be explained in other terms. Some explain it in terms of "persuasion" as another source of the binding force of laws in general. [54] Others seek to explain it by analogizing it to H. L. A. Hart's idea of the "rule of recognition," according to which people are able to identify what are to count as law in their society—a rule whose own source of normative force can only be located in the precarious fact of people's acceptance of it or their readiness to regard themselves as bound by this rule. [55] While these explanations are not wholly incorrect, they do not account for the temporal dimension of constitutional law. I submit that the power of tradition is in fact a dominant force in making people and the state accept the constitutional norms and arrangement that have been handed down by the preceding generation. Moreover, it is my contention that this is dramatically exemplified in the case of the constitutional discourse of traditional Korea.

SOURCES OF CONSTITUTIONAL NORMS
IN TRADITIONAL KOREA

Before turning to examine how the power of tradition was played out in the constitutional discourse of Chosŏn, it is important to have a clear understanding of what we mean by "constitutional law" in traditional Korea, or any other Confucian society.[56] The standard approach to Korean legal history has noted the existence of a national code, *Kyŏngguk Taejŏn* (Great Canon for Governance of the State), which was promulgated in the early part of the Chosŏn period.[57] Scholars generally tend to regard this code as "the constitution" of the Chosŏn dynasty. Koreans also tend to be proud of the fact that throughout the history of Chosŏn, the government was constantly involved in the project of codifications. The implication is that Koreans were from a very early period deeply concerned about governing in accordance with the law—that Koreans practiced their own kind of "rule of law."

Yet, if we examine the contents of *Kyŏngguk Taejŏn*, we find that the vast majority of the rules contained therein pertained to the administration of the government bureaucracy. The primary audience to whom they were directed was the officials who staffed the various ministries, bureaus, and offices. Very little of it is directly concerned with disciplining the power of the ruler. In modern terminology, most of the rules were "administrative" law rather than "constitutional" law.[58] Faced with this fact, it is all too easy to make either of two mistakes: On the one hand, this could be used as "evidence" that constitutionalism did not exist in traditional Korea, that Korea had no legal means of restraining the power of the ruler.[59] On the other hand, this fact could be "explained" by invoking the standard description of traditional Korea as an absolute monarchy, in which all power was concentrated at the center and which allowed no medium for restraining that power. In fact, the two moves tend to reinforce one another to form an essentially circular argument—since Chosŏn was an absolute monarchy, it was only natural that its so-called constitution would not provide for any mechanism for disciplining power, and the fact that its constitution did not include such mechanism was "further" evidence that Chosŏn was an absolute monarchy.

The critical element that undergirds this type of historiography is the assumption that the code *Kyŏngguk Taejŏn* was "the constitution" of Chosŏn. To test the soundness of this assumption, we need to have a clear understanding of what constituted the proper subject matter of codes under Confucian regimes. This may inevitably lead us to thorny debates about how to understand "law" in traditional East Asia. For decades, there have been debates as to whether the word *pŏp* (Chinese: *fa*) accurately translates the Western term "law." A related debate has been how to understand the conceptual relationship between the words *pŏp* (commonly translated "law") and *ye* (Chinese: *li*, commonly translated "ritual"). Rather than continuing these tired and interminable debates (which inevitably involves the philosophical question of what law is in the first place—something that is far from settled even among Western scholars), I believe we should take a less conceptual and more historical approach. That is, our understanding of Chosŏn constitutionalism will be better served by inquiring into this question: "What were the sources cited by political actors engaged in disputes which we would describe as constitutional?" Here I am again using the term "constitutional" to refer to matters relating to the disciplining and regulation of the ruler.

The conventional answer to this question is that, given the primacy of Confucian ideology, people cited from the classics to urge that the king become morally virtuous. According to the conventional image of Confucianism, moral virtue on the part of the ruler was all that was needed to bring peace, harmony, and justice in the state. While there are passages in the Confucian classics that could be read to support this,[60] I believe this is at best a partial and imperfect understanding of the Confucian political discourse as it was actually conducted in history. Indeed, if moral exhortation and admonition were all there was to Chosŏn political discourse, we would not be justified in regarding it as a form of constitutionalism. It is my contention that it was a far more structured discourse with its own discursive principles and institutional backdrop.

To get at the more concrete and institutional aspects of Confucian constitutionalism, then we need to examine the kinds of "codes" that the government compiled for various purposes. For, in actual political debates relating to constitutional issues, scholar-officials did not merely cite passages from the classics. They actually cited provisions from various "codes" compiled by the government. This means we need to query if the *Kyŏngguk Taejŏn* can really be regarded as Chosŏn's constitution, and whether other codes of similar authority and breadth might not have been compiled by its government.

In order to find out what other codification projects might have been undertaken by Chosŏn, we must first know what was considered proper subject matter for codification. In a study of the early codification projects of Ming-dynasty China, historian Edward Farmer has made the following comment, which I believe is equally relevant for Korea:

> Law in Ming China was really a combination of elements that included penal law but shaded off in one direction toward administrative regulations and in the other direction toward ritual. In fact one can draw no firm line between these elements. When we speak of Ming law we should keep the ritual elements in mind and not divorce them from our definition.[61]

He is using the term "law" to refer to legislation, or codified documents. In other words, the subject matters of early Ming codes included administrative rules, penal law, and ritual regulations. Indeed, in any given code we can probably locate materials of all three types of norms. It would be reasonable to expect that their compilers did not make a sharp distinction among them. The fact that administrative rules, penal law, and ritual regulations could all be legislated means that "law" to the Confucians encompassed these three types of norms. They represent different points on a continuum which make up the Confucian conception of "law."

On the other hand, we can also identify a certain correspondence between these three types, or categories, of law and the types of codes that were compiled by the government. It is a historical fact that ever since the Tang period in China (618–907 A.D.), each dynasty compiled three types of codes: ritual, penal, and administrative. Within a period of five or six years, the Tang government enacted in seriatim, *Da Tang Kaiyuan Li* (Ritual Code of the Kaiyuan Reign-period of the Great Tang) (732), *Tang Lü Shuyi* (Tang Penal Code with Commentaries and Subcommentaries) (737), and *Tang Liudian* (Six Canons of Tang) (738).[62] The first code specified the state ritual system to be observed by the government, the second was the penal law of the state, and the third was the administrative code modeled after a classic text, *Zhouli* (Rituals of Zhou).[63] Historically, the completion of these three codification projects represents the establishment and flowering of Tang political institutions.[64] They served as the model for later dynasties of China. For example, the Ming dynasty shortly after its founding commenced upon the codification of the three types of laws. These codification projects culminated in the enactments of *Da Ming Lü* (Penal Code of the Great Ming) (1397), *Da Ming Huidian* (Collected Canons of the Great Ming) (1503), and *Da Ming Jili* (Collected Rituals of the Great Ming) (1530).

We are now able to put the legislations of the Chosŏn period in perspective. We know that in compiling the *Kyŏngguk Taejŏn*, Chosŏn consciously took the *Zhouli* as the model. Thus, it is more appropriate to regard the *Kyŏngguk Taejŏn* as the administrative code of Chosŏn, which represents only one part of a tripartite code structure. For its penal code, as is well known, Chosŏn adopted the Ming dynasty's penal code (*Da Ming Lü*) as its own, instead of compiling a separate, independent code. Obviously, in order to implement it in an alien environment, it had to be modified and "localized" in various ways to fit the Korean context.[65] However, in principle, the Ming Penal Code was understood to be the general penal law of Chosŏn. In fact, the administrative code, *Kyŏngguk Taejŏn*, contains an explicit provision which incorporates the *Da Ming Lü* as the penal part of Chosŏn legal system.[66] As for its ritual code, Chosŏn did enact a separate code, which it began to compile very soon after its founding. In 1410 a special bureau for specification and determination of rites (*Ŭirye Sangjŏngso*) was established for this purpose, and a ritual code containing the state ritual program called *Kukcho Oryeŭi* (Five Rites and Ceremonies of Our Dynasty) was completed in 1474. And for this, too, there is a provision in the *Kyŏngguk Taejŏn* that specifies the use of this code in matters concerning ritual. [67]

As mentioned above, these three types of codes roughly correspond to the three types of norms that comprised the Confucian conception of law. There was not, however, a perfect match. For example, an administrative code might well contain provisions on ritual matters or on penal matters. Similarly, the penal code also contained regulations of an administrative nature. This perhaps was inevitable given the conception of law which was basically a continuum that ran from the administrative, to the penal, to the ritual. Thus, while each code would have a point of emphasis, corresponding to different points on the continuum, each unavoidably contained other types of norms as well.

With this conceptual framework in mind, we can now ask what types of provisions from which codes would have been invoked by Chosŏn scholar-officials in their constitutional disputations. Which type of norm and which type of code had the force of a constitutional norm—a norm that disciplined the ruler? The simple answer is: the ritual norms and the ritual codes. Of the three types of norms, it was only ritual regulations that could be directly applied to the ruler himself. Indeed, the ruler's observance of ritual regulations was of paramount importance in Confucian political theory, much like the duty of a modern-day president to uphold the constitution. In *Liji* (Record of Rituals), one of the ancient classics, it is written, "If he act [sic] otherwise [i.e., contrary to ritual], we have an instance of the son of Heaven perverting the laws, and throwing the regulations into confusion." [68] Ritual was a norm that even the king was expected to obey.

It should be clear that penal law could not be directly applied to the king for the purpose of restraining his power. Almost by definition, penal law was directed at the commoners, and sometimes at the scholar-officials, but never at the monarch. [69] As for the administrative code, its main audience was the bureaucrats. Indeed, the administrative code was in its origin a collation of previous edicts issued to the bureaucrats by the king, a collection of those edicts which were considered to have enduring validity. [70] It would have been therefore difficult to invoke the administrative code for purposes of disciplining the king, unless it was a ritual provision contained therein.

Of course, both penal and administrative norms could be involved in constitutional issues. Scholar-officials wishing to discipline the monarch might argue that these norms must be interpreted or applied in a certain way. By insisting on a specific manner of interpretation and application, scholar-officials might have been able to put a check on the discretionary power of the king, thereby achieving a certain constitutional effect. As we shall see in part 4, they might have argued that these codes must be understood in a way that is consistent with the relevant precedents. [71] Even so, those norms themselves were not directed at the monarch himself. The only part of Confucian law that applied directly to the ruler and his family were the ritual norms and ritual codes.

What then were these norms called "ritual" or, in Korean, *ye*? While we cannot explore all of the philosophical and cosmological aspects of this uniquely Confucian concept, it should suffice for our purposes to understand the "disciplinary" aspects of it. The first thing to understand about the idea of *ye* is that, according to Confucian political thought, observance of *ye* conferred legitimacy on the ruler. The Confucian classics were replete with remarks to the effect that no state that disregarded *ye* would endure long, or that the ruler himself must conform to the dictates of *ye* in order to govern properly.[72] Therefore, every political leader had an incentive to at least appear to be abiding by the precepts of ritual. That is why every regime deemed it necessary to engage in a codification project to specify the correct ritual regulations.[73]

The second thing to keep in mind in understanding *ye* is that its contents are not confined merely to the procedural rules of ceremony. To observe ritual norms is not merely to follow some fixed set of rules that explain how to perform sacrificial rites, although it is that too. To follow ritual means to subject oneself to the "restraining mold of minutely prescribed ceremonial behavior."[74] Ritual is a "formative" norm in the sense that it works by regulating the person's bodily movement and psychological temperament.[75] The idea is to make one's life a series of ritualized actions, so that one will know how to comport oneself in any given situation and be able to do what is expected of one without even thinking about it. In Foucaultian terms, it means to go through continuous training, observation, and surveillance so that one ends up internalizing the "normalizing gaze."[76] For the Confucian, this also meant the process of learning to become truly human, for according to Confucian philosophy, one's true humanity could only be attained through such a process of "ritualization."[77]

This should not, however, lead us to think that *ye* is basically about the cultivation of moral virtue. This can be seen in the sanctions prescribed for its violation. Violation of *ye* resulted in much more than mere moral condemnation or social censure. For example, the *Liji* warns: "Where any ceremony [ritual] had been altered, or any instrument of music changed, it was held to be an instance of disobedience, and the disobedient ruler was banished."[78] It was understood that "violations of ritual entail submission to punishment."[79] In another classical text, *Xunzi*, ritual is described as a legislative innovation by the ancient mythical sage-kings to deal with the social fact of scarcity of material goods in relation to human desires.[80] Ritual was an institutional form of norm that required formal legislation, rather than a moral norm whose enforcement depended on informal and social sanctions. Therefore, it should be recognized that ritual was as much a legal category as the other two types of norms.[81]

Next, it should be remembered that *ye* was not just a "personal" norm that regulated the conduct of the king; it pertained to the operation of the entire government.[82] In addition to defining the personal ritual responsibilities of the king and the royal family (e.g., weddings and coming-of-age ceremonies), Chosŏn's ritual code, *Kukcho Oryeŭi*, also prescribed ritual norms applicable to the more public aspects of the government. For example, it contained norms that regulated the conduct of the state's foreign relations with the neighboring states, as well as the conduct of its military forces.[83] This is also apparent in the nomenclature for government bureaus. The Ministry of Rites (*Yejo*) was the government department in charge of foreign affairs and legislation. It was the *Yejo* that was responsible for all the codification projects noted above. Yet *Yejo* was not the only government office in charge of ritual matters. The importance of ritual for the Chosŏn government went well beyond that. In a sense, the whole business of government was to ensure the proper observance of ritual norms.[84]

Lastly, in terms of our understanding of the constitutional function of ritual, it is extremely important to note the Confucian scholar-officials' relationship toward ritual. Historically, the word "Confucian" (*yu*; Chinese: *ru*) signified a person with expertise in ritual matters. Indeed, it is only a slight exaggeration to say that the whole Confucian tradition is a product of the intellectual and political triumph of a certain group of specialists on ritual who were able to transform their expertise into the dominant political discourse, the terms of which defined the regime's legitimacy as well as the values people should aspire to. Of course, even among Confucians, some were more adept at ritual matters than others. Yet, almost by definition, a Confucian scholar-official was assumed to be knowledgeable about ritual and the classics.

Given the fact that a regime's legitimacy depended on observance of ritual and the fact that Confucian scholar-officials were universally regarded as specialists on ritual, it was natural for them to consider themselves the custodians of political legitimacy. Since it was they who defined what was politically proper for the king to do, the king could not but be constrained by the Confucian scholar-officials. They were, in a sense, the "disciplinarians" of the ruler.[85] For example, codification projects were occasions to use their expertise to influence the exercise of political power according to their ideal. Of course, these were also occasions on which competing understandings of ritual vied for political power through royal recognition in the form of official legislation. When the process of codification was finished, Confucians continued to set the terms of political discourse through their interpretations of these codes, as well as their arguments based on classical texts. Although the ritual codes were intended to be permanent laws, they were also subject to frequent revision. And any debate concerning a perceived need for revising or amending the established ritual codes was thus necessarily a highly political activity with constitutional significance. [86] Discourse on *ye* was constitutional discourse. [87]

This allows us to understand the particular intensity and vehemence with which debates on ritual matters were conducted in the Chosŏn government. The famous Ritual Controversies of 1659 and 1670 were but the more conspicuous of such debates. [88] Correct observance of ritual rules being an issue of constitutional importance, it naturally evoked impassioned arguments in every scholar-official who had an opinion about ritual. Again, it is important to remember that these were not simply moral arguments urging the king to be virtuous. In putting forth their arguments, they would cite from the ritual provisions contained in the various codes. Therefore in order to appreciate the texture of Chosŏn constitutional discourse, we need to understand the various principles according to which disputants justified the correctness of their positions. It is to these discursive principles of Chosŏn constitutionalism that we now turn.

DISCURSIVE PRINCIPLES OF CHOSŎN CONSTITUTIONALISM

It might be objected that characterizing Confucian political philosophy as a constitutional theory is an exaggeration and/or misrepresentation. For, according to the conventional view, the Confucian position promoted a personalistic approach to politics, thereby neglecting the more stable and lasting institutional aspects of politics. In other words, Confucianism failed to distinguish between politics and morality. Being generally disdainful of law, Confucianism was, the story goes, naturally inimical to the "rule of law" and preferred to practice the "rule of man." [89]

However, in light of the foregoing interpretation of Confucian law, and of ritual in particular, I believe this conventional wisdom must be radically revised. To further support my claim that Confucian political ideals as they were theorized and practiced by Koreans of Chosŏn dynasty warrant their designation as a form of constitutionalism, I shall in this section examine the principles—constitutional discursive principles—that were invoked by Confucian politicians for the purpose of disciplining their ruler. In the eyes of someone conditioned to look for judicially enforceable norms, these may appear to be "mere" conventions or rhetorical devices, but as was seen above, constitutional norms often rest on grounds no firmer than the fact that they are accepted as normative by the force of tradition.

Particularly, when examining the politics of traditional Korea, it is exceedingly important to recognize the "traditionalist" element of its constitutional culture. In order to appreciate how constitutional issues were argued by Chosŏn scholar-officials whose political language was informed by Con-

fucianism, we need to understand that in the moral and political discourse of
Confucianism, tradition occupied a place of fundamental importance. More
importantly, we must understand that the authority of tradition could be, and
in fact was, invoked in various ways for the purpose of disciplining political
power. In other words, the vocabulary and arguments deployed in political
disputations derived their normative and justificatory force from tradition.

Indeed, in some ways, the whole Confucian outlook is one that is steeped
in a deep respect for tradition. For example, Confucius once described himself as a preserver and transmitter of tradition.[90] He idealized the cultural
traditions of the Zhou dynasty and lamented the decay and corruption of
those traditions.[91] For that, he is sometimes portrayed as a hopeless reaction-
ary or at best a conservative. Yet the reason that he wished to transmit the
Zhou cultural traditions was because, for him, they embodied the constitutional framework[92] required for civilized human existence. Therefore, for
later Confucians, it was natural to emulate their master in wishing to preserve
(and sometimes even revive) ancient traditions.

One powerful principle that informed their political discourse, and which
represented this strong disposition toward tradition, is the concept of the
"way of the former kings" (*sŏnwang ji do*; Chinese: *xianwang zhi dao*).
"Former kings" here refer to the ancient mythical sage-kings of China such
as Yao and Shun, who were said to have laid down the basic framework of
human civilization. Indeed, whatever they did (in matters of personal morality, friendship, family, politics, economics, criminal justice, etc.) was regarded as the perfection of human possibilities. As mythical figures, they
obviously predate Confucius, and Confucius himself talked about emulating
them. They were perennial models for later generations.[93]

The significance of the term "way of the former kings" for understanding
Confucian constitutionalism lies in the fact that scholar-officials of Chosŏn
were able to use this to discipline their king. They constantly urged the
monarch to discipline himself by taking the ancient sage-kings as his model.
They capitalized on the ancient past as the criterion by which to judge and
criticize the present.[94] If there was a disruption of peace and order in the
realm, it was attributed to the current king's deviation from the way of the
former kings. And it wasn't just because the former kings were perfections of
personal moral virtue. Matters of policy, such as tax, agriculture, and commerce, were also to be judged according to the models set by the former
kings, which were often referred to in the discourse as "ancient institutions"
(*koje*; Chinese: *guzhi*) or "ancient rituals" (*korye*; Chinese: *guli*). Invoking
such terms therefore had great rhetorical power because they represented the
normative force of tradition which the current king was required to follow.
They were the reference point to which later kings were expected to look for
guidance and enlightenment. In other words, the government and laws of the
former kings were to serve as a model for the present-day ruler.[95]

In order for the current king to follow the way of the former kings, he had to have access to records of the former kings. Since those records were to be found in the Confucian classics, this meant that the current ruler had to be educated in the classics. The government of Chosŏn therefore had specialized offices dedicated to the education of the ruler, starting from his days as the crown prince. These were specifically provided for in the administrative code.[96] While it is difficult to generalize or summarize the classics without great distortions, it is safe to say that an important aspect of them were the idealized representations of the ancient past in which sage-kings maintained peace and harmony through constant self-discipline.[97] And, although it may be difficult to regard them as constitutional documents in themselves,[98] the Confucian classics such as the Five Classics and the Four Books did function as sources for political norms whose meaning was to be re-presented and made relevant to the contemporary context. In other words, in order to ascertain the way of the former kings, one had to investigate and interpret the classics.

This points to another important aspect of Confucian constitutionalism; namely, the thoroughly "interpretive" nature of its constitutional discourse.[99] The classics had to be interpreted in order to be made relevant to one's own particular situation. Indeed, every Chosŏn scholar was aware of the enormous gap—temporal, spatial, social, cultural, and technological—that lay between themselves and the former kings. They recognized that in most cases the historical context had changed to such an extent that the laws of the ancient sage-kings could not be applied without modification or adaptation. Depending on one's estimation of this gap, a range of views were possible. At one end of the spectrum, one could think that just minimal adaptation was required to follow the laws of the former kings. At the other extreme, one could think that no amount of calibration would be sufficient to make them relevant to the present context. Of course, short of rejecting the entire Confucian outlook (and adopting a Legalist perspective), ignoring the dictate to follow tradition and creating outright new institutions or policies would not have been an option for Chosŏn scholar-officials. Nevertheless, disagreements on how to assess the gap (i.e., how to interpret the classics) were certainly a common feature of Chosŏn political history. They often fueled sharp contention among different political factions and sometimes even amounted to a major crisis in the constitutional order.[100]

Another principle that was based on the authority of tradition and repeatedly invoked within the constitutional discourse of Chosŏn was the concept of "ancestral precedents" or the "established laws of royal ancestors" (*chojong ji sŏnghŏn*; Chinese: *zuzong zhi chengxian*).[101] The idea was that whatever had been established by preceding kings had to be respected. Needless to say, the justificatory power of this idea stems from the core Confucian value of filial piety (*hyo*; Chinese: *xiao*). As a filial son, the ruler had the duty to honor and preserve his dynastic patrimony, and this meant that he could not make changes lightly to the laws, institutions, and policies of his forefathers. Any departure from ancestral precedents was severely criticized by remonstrating officials as a violation of the king's filial duty. In countless memorials to the king, Confucian scholar-officials urged him not to make new laws but to preserve and enforce the laws of his ancestors.

This principle was formally enunciated very early in the history of the Chosŏn dynasty. Ever since the third king, T'aejong (r. 1400–1414), ordered that provisions of a later code that altered the laws of the dynastic founder be struck out, ancestral precedents were treated with the utmost reverence. [102] When change in the law was unavoidable, it was ordered that the new law be appended as a footnote to the original law, which remained in the text even if it was no longer in force. [103] In the introduction to the *Kyŏngguk Taejŏn*, future monarchs are admonished to abide by the established laws contained in that code and never to alter or forget the code. [104]

Beyond the Confucian virtue of filial piety, however, there were more practical considerations behind this principle. Confucian scholar-officials were concerned about the effect that frequent changes in the law might have on the people's trust in the government. [105] Also, they were deeply worried about setting a precedent by making an exception to the ancestral laws. Consequently, they repeatedly reminded the king that departing from the ancestral laws in a given case will become a precedent, which less scrupulous future kings and officials could cite as justification for disregarding the entire "established laws of royal ancestors."

Obviously, the principle of unalterability and permanence of ancestral laws could not be observed to the letter. That is, even in a tradition-bound constitutional culture, changes in the law were inevitable and indeed necessary. One scholar of Korean legal history suggests that the principle of respecting the "established laws of royal ancestors" was actually more often honored in its breach. [106] As evidence, the fact is cited that throughout the dynasty, the government of Chosŏn was constantly engaged in the process of revising and updating its laws. Nevertheless, invocation of precedents was a permanent feature of the constitutional discourse of traditional Korea. In a way, it was due to this principle that Chosŏn had to constantly struggle with codification projects.

In this connection, we must revise another conventional view that is common among Western scholars of East Asian legal history; namely, the view that there was no doctrine of binding precedent like that of *stare decisis* in the Anglo-American tradition. [107] As we have seen so far, Korean law, or at least constitutional law, was pervaded by a sense of being bound by precedents. The two principles of "way of the former kings" and "ancestral precedents" are nothing if not a call to respect and follow precedents. What then is the source of the conventional view? I believe this is due to an assumption about what constitutes "law" in traditional East Asia, an assumption which effectively excludes from the scope of scholarly discussion anything that could be called traditional constitutional law. In other words, due to the assumption that there was no constitutional law, the discussion only focuses on either criminal proceedings or civil disputes among ordinary people. And in both cases, Confucianism is put forth as an explanation for the lack of *stare decisis*.

For example, one scholar attributes this to the Confucian preference for ritual over "law" (*pŏp*). Because *ye* was inherently a flexible norm, as opposed to the rigidity of *pŏp*, and because all disputes were to be resolved in accordance with *ye* rather than *pŏp*, Confucianism could not tolerate a doctrine that insisted on being bound by precedents. In other words, since *ye* required sensitivity to the specifics of each individual case, it had no need for a doctrine like *stare decisis*.[108] Although this view is right in emphasizing the importance of *ye* in Confucian legal and political thought, it fails to consider the fact that many dictates of *ye* were also incorporated into penal codes and hence became rigid rules themselves.[109] Moreover, as seen above, the governments of Confucian regimes compiled ritual codes in order to justify their mandate to rule. With the passage of time, the need also arose for handbooks and casebooks that could guide the administration of justice by the magistrates. Perhaps out of practical necessity, like cases were expected to be decided alike.[110] Of course, this is still different from a legal doctrine which requires the invalidation of a decision which failed to follow relevant precedents. Yet it does call into question the thesis that Confucianism had no need for a doctrine of binding precedents.

Another eminent scholar of Chinese law refers to the Confucian demand that all cases be decided according to the universally valid moral principles embodied in the classics as the reason why Confucianism was incompatible with *stare decisis*. That is, since those moral principles were accessible to anyone who studied the classics, there was no reason to look to previous cases for guidance.[111] While this view does take notice of the "power of the past" as manifested through the classics,[112] it neglects to consider the same power of the past that becomes visible in political discourse. That is, while it may be that in ordinary civil and criminal cases the judge could not really be faulted for not following precedents, in constitutional matters, failure to follow precedents (of either ancient sage-kings or royal ancestors) was deeply problematic, for that implied a disrespect for the Confucian tradition or an unfilial attitude toward the dynastic forefathers. As one historian of China has written, precedents "served to hold the Emperor's power within limits and to prohibit any decline into absolutism."[113] I believe there are sufficient grounds to say that the doctrine of binding precedents was a constitutional principle in a Confucian polity.

It was mentioned that the way of the former kings was accessible through interpretations of the classics. In the case of ancestral precedents also, the process of ascertaining the requirements of ancestral laws was similarly an interpretive task. In the first place, they were to be located in the codes that were promulgated by the royal ancestors. In addition, they were also found in individual edicts issued by previous kings, or historical records of the royal ancestors. These texts all needed to be interpreted in order to be understood, and in many cases, there were interpretations of intervening generations which also demanded attention as ancestral precedents. In some cases, there were multiple precedents which would not necessarily be consistent among themselves. Also, for later generations, the gap between themselves and the royal ancestors might have been too great to allow a literal application of the ancestral laws. As in the case of the way of the ancient sage-kings, adjustments and adaptations were necessary.

More significantly, there could be discrepancies between the dictates of the ancient sage-kings found in the classics and the ancestral laws found in the dynastic codes and historical records. Perhaps, in an ideal Confucian world, this would not happen. In the real world of less than sagely rulers, however, the precedents set by the royal ancestor might not always be worthy of compliance or respect. In such an instance, someone claiming to be more faithful to the classics, and therefore a "purer" Confucian, could invoke the principle of adhering to the way of the former kings to "override" the authority of the ancestral precedents. On the other hand, anyone wishing to preserve the institutions, policies, or practices handed down from the more recent past could always invoke the Confucian virtue of filial piety to argue for maintenance of the status quo. This does not mean that the principle of respecting ancestral precedents had an inherently "conservative" orientation, or that the principle of following the ancient sage-kings necessarily served a "radical" interest. What counts as conservative or radical would depend on which principle better justified the existing state of affairs. That is, depending on the baseline, either principle could be invoked to criticize the status quo and argue for a reform.

To a cynic, the fact that there was no "objective" way to adjudicate between the two principles of traditional authority might imply that these were "mere" rhetorical flourishes that could be utilized to justify any and all arguments. Yet, by the same logic, we would then have to conclude that the modern constitutional principles of, say, majority rule on the one hand and protection of the minority on the other are "mere" rhetorical flourishes employed on an ad hoc basis to justify whatever happens to fit one's interest. Likewise with the ideals of equality and liberty, or of individual freedom and the claims of community, which tend to pull in opposite directions, with no "objective" criterion for adjudicating or prioritizing the demands of the two. In the end, the answer to such issues depends on one's constitutional philosophy. A person with a liberal outlook will reach different resolutions than one who subscribes to socialism. In the field of comparative constitutional law, each state is said to reach its distinct resolutions to these and other issues, which in turn reflect their constitutional cultures. The crude, conventional view is that Americans have generally tended to give more priority to freedom and individual liberty than do people from other nations. Yet, even in America, these are ongoing issues and it is more realistic to expect that whatever resolution that obtains at the moment will likely change over time, with the change in the constitutional philosophy of the nation. [114]

The adjudication between the two constitutional principles of traditional Korea can be expected to be similarly dependent on the prevailing constitutional vision of the moment. No doubt, the constitutional vision of the era was Confucianism. And, unlike modern states, traditional Korea had an official state orthodoxy, in the form of the state-required curriculum for the civil service examination. Ever since the fourteenth century, governments in both China and Korea adopted the Song dynasty master Zhu Xi's commentaries on the classics (particularly the Four Books) as the authoritative and orthodox interpretation of the Confucian learning. [115] This certification of the school of thought represented by Zhu Xi—commonly known as Neo-Confucianism in English—as the official ideology of the state continued at least nominally until the end of the monarchy at the turn of the century.

This meant that for rulers and scholar-officials of the Chosŏn dynasty, Zhu Xi's doctrines operated as a third source of traditional authority, in addition to the former kings and ancestral precedents—a third constitutional principle, as it were. Everyone was expected to abide by Zhu Xi's interpretation of the classics and anyone who dared to disagree was criticized as a heretic. In constitutional discourse, the authority of Zhu Xi's thought could always be invoked to discipline the actions of the king. Historians generally agree that the authority of Master Zhu (as he was commonly called by his disciples) was even greater in Korea than in China. Whereas in China later political developments and intellectual trends seriously challenged the authority of Zhu Xi and his school, Koreans of Chosŏn continued to revere Master Zhu, even to the point of criticizing their Chinese contemporaries for failing to defend the orthodox teachings of Zhu Xi. In other words, the Zhu Xi orthodoxy in Korea was quite palpable to a degree never achieved in China. [116] Thus, to a certain extent, the issue of adjudicating between the principles of respecting the ancient sage-kings and adhering to ancestral precedents, and that of the potentially conflicting dictates of tradition generally, would have been resolved by relying on Zhu Xi's interpretations.

It must be added that even though Zhu Xi's interpretation was regarded as the definitive statement of the Confucian position on everything from politics and morality to metaphysics, that hardly meant that everyone had the same views. There were variations among the followers of Master Zhu, which soon developed into distinct schools of thought, and opposing political factions. [117] Moreover, even though hardly anyone dared to openly criticize Zhu Xi's interpretations of the classics, Korean scholar-officials, particularly of the later period, began to form their own independent opinions on the soundness of Master Zhu's commentaries. [118] While nominally professing to follow his interpretations, many achieved a level of scholarship that enabled them to view the commentaries critically, in light of their own understanding of the classics. [119]

Thus, in order to understand the constitutional discourse of Chosŏn, we must keep in mind that these three partially overlapping and partially distinct sources of authority were at work all at the same time. One's constitutional vision was necessarily the result of how one negotiated these three sources. Political and constitutional conflicts were the result of different people prioritizing them in different ways. Just as constitutional disputes can arise today through a clash among different people holding different answers to the problem of how to weigh the demands of equality and liberty, Chosŏn constitutional disputes arose from disagreements among people who assigned different weights to the dictates of ancient sage-kings, ancestral precedents, and Zhu Xi's orthodoxy.

For example, in the seventeenth-century Ritual Controversy alluded to earlier, one group based its arguments on the authority of ancestral precedent, or more precisely, ritual provisions found in the *Kyŏngguk Taejŏn*, and the orthodoxy of Zhu Xi. Its opponents tended to emphasize the authority of the former kings, whose teachings were found in the ancient classics. This, however, did not mean that the latter group was free to ignore the authority of Zhu Xi. In fact, its members claimed that they were the more faithful followers of Zhu Xi. Similarly, invoking the authority of ancestral precedents should not be seen as rejecting the way of the former kings, for ancestral laws themselves drew their authority from being modeled after the "ancient institutions." [120]

One way of understanding the relationship among the three sources of authority is to regard both ancestral precedents contained in the various codes and Zhu Xi's orthodoxy as different interpretations of the same former kings of antiquity. Zhu Xi was quite conscious about giving a contemporary and more relevant interpretation to the dictates of rituals found in the ancient classics. Faced with the realization that there were numerous gaps between the prescriptions of the former kings and the practices of his own time, he made numerous adjustments and compromises to fit the exigency of his day. [121] As seen above, the ancestral codes were based on the ritual prescriptions of the former kings, but were also the product of a similar process of adjustments and compromises necessitated by the gap between Zhou dynasty China and Chosŏn Korea. In sum, for Chosŏn Confucians, the way of the former kings was the primary source of authority, but they also had very pressing political and intellectual reasons for respecting Zhu Xi and the ancestral codes.

Sometimes the calculus became even more complicated because another source of authority had to be respected. For the government of Chosŏn, which regarded itself as a "kingdom" in relation to the "empire" that existed in China, the laws and institutions of the current Chinese court had to be accorded certain presumptive authority. Thus, the laws and institutions of the Ming dynasty, which was a rough contemporary of Chosŏn, were often referred to and cited in political debates. In fact, Korean scholar-officials began consulting Ming practice from the beginning of Chosŏn until even after the Ming had fallen in China and been replaced by the Manchu regime of Qing. In some constitutional disputes they were also held up as an authority, especially when domestic laws were unclear.

The rationale for according such respect to the Chinese practice was not simply related to considerations of international politics, such as the fact that China was the more powerful of the two nations. Confucian theory itself dictated a certain respect for the "institutions of the current king" (*siwang ji je*; Chinese: *shiwang zhi zhi*).[122] Although he might not be as worthy as the ancient sage-kings, there was a theoretical presumption (however unjustifiable in reality) that the current occupant of the throne would be the legitimate recipient of the Heaven's Mandate to rule,[123] and this in turn made his institutions presumptively worthy of some consideration. If we count this as another source of authority in Confucian political discourse, it might be regarded as the fourth principle of Chosŏn constitutionalism.

In practice, however, this demand for respecting the Ming practice was always tempered by the awareness that Korea was in important ways very different from China. Some Korean scholar-officials criticized some of the Ming practice for misunderstanding the way of the former kings. Others even claimed that some laws and institutions of the Ming were "corrupt" because they originated not from the ancient sage-kings but from degenerate tyrants of later generations.[124] Nevertheless, the Chosŏn government continued to accord presumptive weight to the institutions of Ming.

In sum, Chosŏn Confucians seeking to discipline the ruler could avail themselves of a number of discursive principles, which manifested different aspects of the authority of tradition. The fact that there were no guidelines as to how to prioritize them or which should take precedence in case their requirements were mutually inconsistent should not lead us to regard them as mere rhetorical formulae. They defined the terms of the Chosŏn constitutional discourse, and through their interaction they produced a political culture in which the authority of tradition had to be adduced in the form of some concrete provision or precedent.

CONCLUSION

The main argument of this chapter has been that constitutionalism is actually not a novel development in the history of Korea. To support that claim, I have described how Koreans of the Chosŏn dynasty tried to implement constitutionalism, and what resources and discursive principles were available to them. Yet despite this historical experience in conducting constitutional politics, Korea during the past century has undergone such a profound change that the modern constitutionalism that is being slowly implemented by the Korean Constitutional Court is quite different from the Chosŏn dynasty's Confucian constitutionalism. In a way, there *was* a radical break from the past, and it is hard to find traces of the Chosŏn constitutionalism in the present.

Without intending to belittle the profundity of the change that took place, however, I submit that it is still important to understand that Koreans have known and aspired to practice constitutionalism for many centuries. This is so because in order to practice the modern type of constitutionalism correctly and effectively, Koreans must be able to draw on their history and culture, for constitutionalism in the end depends on the existence of a certain culture, or shared symbols and strategies for action, which makes discipline of power possible. [125] Without a culture and a tradition to support it and hark back to, Korean constitutionalism will always remain a "derivative" practice, an epiphenomenon dependent on the constitutional experience of Germans or Americans. [126]

The importance of cultural support for a flourishing constitutionalism points to another aspect of constitutionalism as the practice of disciplining power; namely, that constitutionalism is very much an educative project. It is in fact educative in a double sense. First, it is educative in the sense that constitutionalism requires educating citizens about their constitutional tradition and culture. [127] It requires citizens who are socialized into a constitutional culture. This in turn calls for conscious efforts to highlight and interpret the national culture in constitutional terms. I submit that Korean tradition and culture has many elements which are conductive to the disciplining of political power. For example, the Confucian tradition of institutionalized remonstrance is something that is very familiar to every Korean. [128] More generally, as mentioned above, Chosŏn was a period in which the throne was constantly checked and even browbeaten by the ministers. In other words, contrary to the popular view which portrays Korean culture and tradition as having inhibited the growth of constitutionalism, I believe there are many historical and symbolic resources that can be mobilized to educate modern Koreans about their constitutionalist tradition.

Secondly, constitutionalism is educative in the sense that the experience of living under a constitutional regime will have a formative effect on the characters of the citizens.[129] As mentioned earlier, the activities of the Korean Constitutional Court are having a transformative effect on the citizens' outlook. Seeing that the discretionary power of the prosecutors is subject to constitutional limitations, or that the government cannot claim a privileged status in its relation to ordinary citizens, has contributed to educating the people about their rights and roles as citizens of a constitutional regime. In the United States, the famous constitutional law scholar Alexander Bickle has noted that the U.S. Supreme Court should play the role of a teacher in a "national seminar" on constitutionalism.[130]

I believe that, if constitutionalism is to take root and flourish in Korea, this doubly educative aspect of constitutionalism must be taken seriously. If Koreans are able to combine an understanding of constitutionalism as the disciplining of power with a proper understanding of the constitutionalist elements in their tradition and culture, they will have at their disposal a particularly rich cultural resource from which to draw.

One such resource is the concept of ritual (*ye*), which was described above as a constitutional norm of the Chosŏn dynasty. Although Korea is no longer an officially Confucian state, ritual is still a very important and familiar concept to modern Koreans. It still provides the means by which Koreans interpret and evaluate each other. People learn to relate to one another and define their place in family and society in terms of *ye*. A person who does not observe *ye* properly becomes a social outcast. Recently, even the Korean Constitutional Court had an occasion to note the important role played by *ye* in Korean society.

Given this centrality of ritual norms in Korea, it can help promote a constitutional culture among Koreans. This is because *ye* is essentially an educative norm. All Koreans understand that to be proficient in *ye* in interpersonal relationships, one must undergo a constant process of training and cultivation of a sense of what is proper to do in a given situation. *Ye* is about education and self-discipline. Unfortunately, it has become depoliticized today, so that its historical role of disciplining political rulers has been largely forgotten.

I believe constitutionalism in Korea today will be given a firmer cultural grounding when this aspect of *ye* is retrieved and translated into the modern context. The goal would be a cultural awareness that being adept at the requirements of *ye* means not only being courteous to others, but also having the ability to discipline political leaders. Korean constitutionalism will flourish when citizens of Korea are able to make an outcast of a political leader who fails to observe the requirements of *ye*, when a government that fails to be disciplined in the exercise of its power will automatically be regarded as illegitimate. When the Korean Constitutional Court is able to speak about *ye* in terms of its original constitutional role, and not just in terms of its ceremonial aspects, I believe constitutionalism in Korea will cease being a derivative practice.

NOTES

1. For an overview of the political events leading up to constitutional revision, see James M. West and Edward J. Baker, "The 1987 Constitutional Reforms in South Korea: Electoral Processes and Judicial Independence," *Harvard Human Rights Yearbook* 1 (1988), p. 135.

2. 5·18 Minjuhwa Undong e kwanhan T'ŭkpyŏlpŏp [Special Act Concerning the May 18th Democratization Movement], Law No. 5029, Dec. 21, 1995. This law itself became a center of controversy as many critics viewed it as a mere legal "cover" for carrying out political retribution. Legally, it also came under attack because it appeared to allow prosecution for offenses on which the statute of limitations had already run, and to violate the principle of double jeopardy. See generally David M. Waters, "Korean Constitutionalism and the 'Special Act' to Prosecute Former Presidents Chun Doo-hwan and Roh Tae-woo," *Columbia Journal of Asian Law* 10 (1996), p. 461.

3. The Constitutional Court itself began operation on September 1, 1988, after the National Assembly passed the Constitutional Court Act earlier that year. See generally James M. West and Dae-kyu Yoon, "The Constitutional Court of the Republic of Korea: Transforming the Jurisprudence of Vortex," *American Journal of Comparative Law* 40 (1992), p. 73; Dai-kwon Choi, "The Structure and Function of the Constitutional Court: The Korean Case," in *The Powers and Functions of Executive Government: Studies from the Asia Pacific Region*, ed. G. Hassall and C. Saunders (Melbourne: Centre for Comparative Constitutional Studies, University of Melbourne, 1994), p. 104; Dae-kyu Yoon, "New Developments in Korean Constitutionalism: Changes and Prospects," *Pacific Rim Law & Policy Journal* 4 (1995), p. 395; Kun Yang, "The Constitutional Court and Democratization," in *Recent Transformations in Korean Law and Society*, ed. Dae-Kyu Yoon (Seoul: Seoul National University Press, 2000), p. 33.

4. For discussions of major decisions of the Court, see Yoon, "New Developments in Korean Constitutionalism"; Yang, "Constitutional Court and Democratization." See also Gavin Healy, "Judicial Activism in the New Constitutional Court of Korea," *Columbia Journal of Asian Law* 14 (2000), p. 213.

5. But see Chan Jin Kim, "Korean Attitudes towards Law," *Pacific Rim Law & Policy Journal* 10 (2000), p. 1 (arguing that Korean attitudes toward law have not kept pace with economic development and are impeding transition to democracy).

6. For an account of the history of judicial review in Korea, see Dae-Kyu Yoon, *Law and Political Authority in South Korea* (Boulder, CO: Westview Press, 1990), pp. 150–70.

7. Statistics regarding the cases adjudicated by the Constitutional Court are available at the Court's website, www.ccourt.go.kr.

8. The Korean Constitutional Court has developed the practice of rendering decisions other than the black-and-white "constitutional" or "unconstitutional." One of these "altered judgments" (*pyŏnhyŏng kyŏlchŏng*) is to hold a law "incompatible with the Constitution" (*hŏnpŏp pulhapch'i*), which essentially is to recognize the unconstitutionality of the law in question but let it stand until a given deadline for the legislature to enact a new legislation compatible with the Constitution. If the legislature fails to take the necessary measures to correct the constitutional infirmity, the law will automatically lapse. Modeled after the practice of the German Federal Constitutional Court, this form of decision (*unvereinbar* in German) is based on the rationale that sometimes invalidating a law will bring about a vacuum and unnecessary confusion in the legal order, and that the principle of separation of powers requires the Court to respect the National Assembly's power and freedom to legislate.

9. Hŏnpŏp [Constitution] art. 111(1). In accordance with this provision, the Constitutional Court Act prescribes two types of constitutional petitions: one allows redress for unconstitutional state action or inaction which is not amenable to ordinary court proceedings (art. 68[1]), and the other permits citizens to request the Court to review the constitutionality of a law when an ordinary court has refused to refer the issue of the law's validity to the Court (art. 68[2]).

Though basically modeled on the German system of *Verfassungsbeschwerde*, the Korean system of constitutional petitions departs from that of Germany in providing for this second type of petition.

10. According to the constitution, a third of the justices must be appointed from candidates nominated by the National Assembly. Hŏnpŏp art. 111(3). At the time of the Court's inauguration, the opposition party held the majority in the National Assembly, and as a result it was able to influence the composition of the Court by nominating people who in their view would actively promote democracy and human rights.

11. West and Baker, "1987 Constitutional Reforms in South Korea," pp. 140–51.

12. For a view that regards the current constitution as still concentrating too much power on the president, see Jong-sup Chong, "Political Power and Constitutionalism," in *Recent Transformations in Korean Law and Society*, ed. Dae-Kyu Yoon (Seoul: Seoul National University Press, 2000), pp. 11, 16–20.

13. Yang, "Constitutional Court and Democratization," p. 45 ("This is quite a new phenomenon").

14. A fuller discussion of the claims I make in the fourth and fifth sections of this chapter require illustrations through copious historical examples. In the interest of economy of space, however, I have had to keep such historical cites to a minimum.

15. E.g., Young Huh, *Hanguk Hŏnpŏpnon* [Korean Constitutional Law] (Seoul: Pagyŏngsa, 2000), pp. 101–30; Young Sung Kwon, *Hŏnpŏphak Wŏllon* [Constitutional Law: A Textbook] (Seoul: Pŏmmunsa, 2000), pp. 91–102.

16. Hŏnpŏp [Constitution] preamble.

17. In his textbook, Professor Young Sung Kwon includes this 1899 code as the "prehistory" of Korean constitutionalism. Kwon, *Hŏnpŏphak Wŏllon*, p. 91. For English translation of the *Hongbŏm*, see *Sourcebook of Korean Civilization*, vol. 2, ed. Peter H. Lee (New York: Columbia University Press, 1996), pp. 384–85. For the Provisional Government's constitution, see Lee, *Sourcebook*, pp. 435–36. The Korean text of these early constitutions is available at the Constitutional Court's website, www.ccourt.go.kr.

18. Louis Henkin, "A New Birth of Constitutionalism," in *Constitutionalism, Identity, Difference, and Legitimacy*, ed. Michel Rosenfeld (Durham, NC: Duke University Press, 1994), pp. 39–40.

19. I do not mean to represent this as an actual debate among historians of Korea. To the best of my knowledge, this has not been the subject of any serious scholarly debate among Korean academics.

20. E.g., Charles McIlwain, *Constitutionalism: Ancient and Modern* (Ithaca, NY: Cornell University Press, 1947), p. 21 ("[constitutionalism] is the antithesis of arbitrary rule; its opposite is despotic government").

21. At least on two occasions, Chosŏn bureaucrats deposed their kings and installed substitutes who were more pliant and amenable to their bidding.

22. It is a well-known feature of Chosŏn history that a considerable number of the Confucian scholar-officials (*sadaebu*) regarded the throne as not much more than first among equals. According to one historian, traditional Korea was known in China as the land where the "king is weak and his ministers strong." Yi Sŏng-mu, "17 Segi ŭi Yeron kwa Tangjaeng" [Discourse on *li* and Factional Strife during 17th Century], in *Chosŏn Hugi Tangjaeng ŭi Chonghapchŏk Kŏmt'o* [A Comprehensive Review of Late Chosŏn Factionalism], eds. Sŏngmu Yi et al. (Sŏngnam: Han'guk chŏngsinmunhwa yŏn'guwŏn, 1992), pp. 74–75.

23. In the words of a noted Korean jurist:

It is difficult . . . for us to find a constitution as we know it today in the political life of our ancestors prior to the opening of the country in 1876. And yet, we would be making a grave mistake if we were to assert simply that our ancestors had no fundamental law. The fact that they had maintained a politically organized life for more than two thousand years belies such an assertion.

Pyong Choon Hahm, *The Korean Political Tradition and Law*, 2nd ed. (Seoul: Royal Asiatic Society, Korea Branch, 1971), p. 85.

24. The easy answer is that when we argue about the inaugural year of constitutionalism, we are talking about the history of "modern" constitutionalism in Korea. That is, even if traditional Korea did not necessarily have a despotic government, it did not operate in terms of a constitution in the sense of a written document that lays down the powers of the government and the rights of the individual. In this view, constitutionalism is an achievement of modernity, and as such, cannot be discussed in the pre-modern context. To be sure, constitutionalism as we know it derives most of its inspiration from the American constitutional "experiment," the spirit of the French Revolution, or the lessons of the Weimar Constitution. In that sense, it is hard to think about constitutionalism without invoking modernity. This, however, is problematic to the extent that how to understand "modernity" itself is the subject of serious debates nowadays. For a critique of the utility of "modernity" in understanding Korean law, see Chulwoo Lee, "Modernity, Legality, and Power in Korea under Japanese Rule," in *Colonial Modernity in Korea*, eds. Gi-Wook Shin and Michael Robinson (Cambridge, MA: Harvard East Asia Center, 1999), p. 21. Moreover, as will be argued below, the story of constitutionalism even in the West goes back much further than the period of so-called Enlightenment.

25. For example, the term (pronounced *xianfa* in Chinese) appears in such books as *Guoyu*, *Guanzi*, and *Huinanzi*, but its usual referent is either an abstract term like "the fundamentals of a state" or a more narrow idea of "regulation." The use of that term as the translation for the Western concept of constitution is said to have become fixed when the Japanese government sent emissaries to Europe in 1882 to study the constitutions of those countries. Chongko Choi, *Hanguk ŭi Sŏyangpŏp Suyongsa* [History of the Reception of Western Law in Korea] (Seoul: Pagyŏngsa, 1982), p. 294.

26. In view of the fact that Korean research on constitutional law is predominantly influenced by Western scholarship, I am here assuming that the perspective of the Western scholars will also be that of Koreans. That is, "we" and "our" in this context refer not only to Westerners but also to most Koreans who are similarly more familiar with the Western concept of constitutionalism than with the native political and legal traditions of Korea.

27. This explains why, in the imaginary historiographical debate above, the nationalist would wish to push back the starting point of Korean constitutionalism. It is grounded in the desire to represent Korea as a civilized country by bestowing upon it this honorific term. In order to portray Koreans as having entered the civilized world sooner, it becomes necessary to claim that Korean constitutionalism began at an earlier time.

28. As originally used by Edward Said, "orientalism" refers to the process by which Europeans of the early modern period essentially created the idea of the "Oriental" and filled its content with images and values opposite to their own (e.g., backward, immoral, and unenlightened). According to Said, the creation of this "Other" of Europeans' self-image in turn provided ideological justification for the imperialist policy of subjugating and exploiting the people of the Orient (i.e., the Middle East and India). Edward W. Said, *Orientalism* (New York: Vintage Books, 1978).

29. See, for example, Scott Gordon, *Controlling the State: Constitutionalism from Ancient Athens to Today* (Cambridge, MA: Harvard University Press, 1999); R. C. Van Caenegem, *An Historical Introduction to Western Constitutional Law* (Cambridge: Cambridge University Press, 1995); Brian Tierney, *Religion, Law and the Growth of Constitutional Thought 1150–1650* (Cambridge: Cambridge University Press, 1982). See also Harold J. Berman, *Law and Revolution: The Formation of the Western Legal Tradition* (Cambridge, MA: Harvard University Press, 1983) (arguing that the Papal Revolution of 1075 effectuated through the reforms of Pope Gregory VII introduced the first constitutional form of government in the West); Quentin Skinner, *The Foundations of Modern Political Thought*, vol. 2 (Cambridge: Cambridge University Press, 1978), pp. 113–85 (describing the Conciliarist Movement of the Catholic Church which sought to restrain the power of the pope through the council of bishops).

30. On Foucault's notion of "discipline," see generally Michel Foucault, *Discipline and Punish: The Birth of the Prison*, trans. Alan Sheridan (New York: Random House, 1979); Michel Foucault, "Two Lectures," in *Power/Knowledge*, ed. Colin Gordon (New York: Random House, 1980), p. 78; Michel Foucault, *History of Sexuality*, trans. Robert Hurley (New York: Vintage Books, 1980).

31. There is actually an ongoing historiographical debate about the extent of the influence of Newtonian thinking on the American founding generation and consequently on the American constitutional design itself. See generally, Michael Kammen, *A Machine That Would Go of Itself: The Constitution in American Culture*, 3rd ed. (New York: St. Martin's Press, 1994); Michael Foley, *Laws, Men, and Machines: Modern American Government and the Appeal of Newtonian Mechanics* (New York: Routledge, 1990).

32. James Madison, "Federalist # 51," in *The Federalist Papers*, ed. Clinton Rossiter (New York: A Mentor Book, 1961), p. 322.

33. By saying that Confucianism was not authoritarian, I am not thereby claiming that it was democratic. Confucian philosophy did not envision the people as their own masters, except in a very extenuated and rhetorical sense. That, however, should not lead one to think that it legitimated the use of absolute power or fostered "authoritarian personalities." One common mistake is to equate "anti-democratic" with authoritarian and despotic, and to assume that anything which predates the appearance of democracy was ipso facto supportive of authoritarian politics. Yet, as was alluded to above, historically constitutionalism was not necessarily predicated on the existence of democratic politics. Today, we are prone to regard the two as, if not identical, at least complementary, as is indicated by the expression "constitutional democracy." In fact, democracy and constitutionalism can be, and often are, in tension with each other. Constitutionalism is about disciplining and restricting the sovereign power, even if people are the sovereign, whereas democracy is about giving people what they want.

34. I am painfully aware of the danger in trying to generalize about Confucianism, for claiming that such and such was "the Confucian position" necessarily risks ignoring the remarkable diversity of positions within the Confucian tradition. An analogy would be trying to summarize Christianity in one sentence, disregarding the vast difference of outlook, tenor, and issues that characterized different people at different stages of its history (think of Aquinas, Luther, Kierkegaard, and Latin American liberation theology). Nevertheless, if it can plausibly be argued that these different Christians shared at least some common symbols, vocabulary, or rhetorical strategies, I think it is also plausible to assume the same with regard to Confucian thinkers. In this article, I intend only to describe certain terms which I believe were widely shared and used in political disputations among Chosŏn-dynasty Koreans.

35. In this regard, we should also be cautious about the simplistic dichotomy between "constitutional monarchy" and "absolute monarchy" and the use of the latter term to describe the Chosŏn dynasty. In common parlance, the former term refers only to those forms for government where the power of the throne is limited by or shared with some elected officials. As a corollary, all monarchies that lack this "democratic" element are assumed to have authorized the use of absolute power. According to my interpretation of the Chosŏn-dynasty Confucian politics, this is overly simplistic. In other words, although Chosŏn had no democratic government, there are many problems in calling it an "absolute monarchy."

36. Detailed examination of this issue is taken up in the fourth section of this chapter.

37. See generally, Mauro Cappelletti, *Judicial Review in the Contemporary World* (Indianapolis, IN: Bobbs-Merrill, 1971).

38. Marbury v. Madison, 5 U.S. (1 Cranch) 137 (1803).

39. Writing almost a century after the *Marbury* decision, Harvard law professor James Thayer noted that judicial review was still an anomaly among world constitutions. James B. Thayer, "The Origin and Scope of the American Doctrine of Constitutional Law," *Harvard Law Review* 7 (1893), pp. 129–30. To this day, American constitutional scholarship is plagued by whether judicial review was "really required" by the Constitution, and whether it can be justified on democratic grounds. The classic text on this issue is Alexander M. Bickel, *The Least Dangerous Branch*, 2nd ed. (New Haven, CT: Yale University Press, 1986).

40. Even in their fight for independence, American colonists used the terms of the British constitutional discourse to support their cause against the British. See Barbara A. Black, "The Constitution of Empire: The Case for the Colonists," *University of Pennsylvania Law Review* 124 (1976), p. 1157.

41. This is not to deny that there has been a steady growth in Britain of judicial review, in the sense of the court's review of administrative action, that is, checks on the executive by the courts. See Geoffrey Marshall, "Lions around the Throne: The Expansion of Judicial Review in

Britain," in *Constitutional Policy and Change in Europe*, eds. Joachim Jens Hesse and Nevil Johnson (Oxford: Clarendon Press, 1995), p. 178. Moreover, courts have recently been given further power to pass judgment on acts of the legislature as the Human Rights Act of 1998, which incorporates the European Convention on Human Rights into domestic law, finally entered into force October 2, 2000. Yet, this act still does not establish full judicial review, as the courts are only empowered to make a "declaration of incompatibility" with the ECHR, rather than strike down the offending legislation. Human Rights Act, 1998, § 4(2) (Eng.).

42. Of course, it is sometimes argued that the American "invention" of judicial review was also a development of certain elements in British constitutionalism. Some trace its genealogy to the famous *Doctor Bonham's Case* in which Edward Coke opined that whatever is contrary to common law is null and void. It is noteworthy, though, that in Britain the doctrine of parliamentary sovereignty has eclipsed any notion that the courts can override the will of the legislature.

43. U.S. Const. art. II, § 4.

44. U.S. Const. art. I, § 2, cl. 5 ("The House of Representatives shall have the sole Power of Impeachment."); U.S. Const. art. I, § 3, cl. 6 ("The Senate shall have the sole Power to try all Impeachments."). For an argument that there is nothing logically inconsistent with entrusting the legislature with the responsibility of enforcing constitutional norms, see Thomas C. Grey, "Constitutionalism: An Analytic Framework," in *Nomos XX: Constitutionalism*, eds. J. Roland Pennock and John W. Chapman (New York: New York University Press, 1979), p. 189 (describing judicial review as but one instance of "special enforcement" of constitutional norms).

45. The classic statement of British constitutionalism is of course A. V. Dicey, *The Law of the Constitution*, ed. John Allison (Oxford: Oxford University Press, 2013 [1885]). A work by a non-lawyer which is in some ways more informative is Walter Bagehot, *The English Constitution* (Cambridge: Cambridge University Press, 2001[1867]). For more recent works, see generally Geoffrey Marshall, *Constitutional Theory* (Oxford: Clarendon Press, 1971); T. R. S. Allan, *Law, Liberty, and Justice* (Oxford: Clarendon Press, 1993); Eric Barendt, *An Introduction to Constitutional Law* (Oxford: Oxford University Press, 1998).

46. See for example, Dai-Kwon Choi, "Development of Law and Legal Institutions in Korea," in *Traditional Korean Legal Attitudes*, eds. B. D. Chun et al. (Berkeley, CA: Institute of East Asian Studies, 1981), pp. 54, 65, 70–72 (noting the lack of differentiation in government functions and the absence of public law principles like judicial review). Professor Choi does state that "Confucian moral principals [sic] were the functional equivalents of public law," thereby suggesting that the Chosŏn monarch was subject to some form of restraint (72). For China, see Wm. Theodore de Bary, *Asian Values and Human Rights* (Cambridge, MA: Harvard University Press, 1998), pp. 94–97 (noting the absence in Chinese history of separate and independent courts to resolve "constitutional" issues).

47. I believe this is similar to the sense in which Professor Park Byung Ho understands the word "legal" when he discusses the "legal restrictions" (*pŏpchŏk cheyak*) on the royal power during the Chosŏn dynasty. Park Byung Ho, *Kŭnse ŭi Pŏp kwa Pŏpsasang* [The Law and Legal Thought of Modernity] (Seoul: Chinwŏn, 1996), pp. 444–52 (arguing that even though the king was considered the author of law, he was not at freedom to disregard it).

48. On British constitutional conventions, see generally Geoffrey Marshall, *Constitutional Conventions: The Rules and Forms of Political Accountability* (Oxford: Clarendon Press, 1984). See also Nevil Johnson, "Law, Convention, and Precedent in the British Constitution," in *The Law, Politics, and the Constitution*, ed. David Butler et al. (Oxford: Oxford University Press, 1999), p. 131 (noting the trend toward increased reliance on written rules in British constitutionalism).

49. Vernon Bogdanor, "Britain: The Political Constitution," in *Constitutions in Democratic Politics*, ed. Vernon Bogdanor (Aldershot: Gower, 1988), pp. 53, 56 (stating that in the British constitutional tradition, "unconstitutional" cannot mean contrary to law; "instead it means contrary to convention, contrary to some understanding of what it is appropriate to do").

50. For example, Marshall, *Constitutional Conventions*, p. 214.

51. In the words of the noted legal philosopher Jeremy Waldron:

They are not merely habits or regularities of behaviour. . . . But they are not merely subjective views about morality either. They have a social reality, inasmuch as they capture a way in which people interact, a way in which people make demands on one another, and form attitudes and expectations about a common practice with standards that they are all living up to. . . . Politicians refer to them when they are evaluating one another's behaviour. They are social facts, not mere abstract principles, because they bind people together into a common form of life.

Jeremy Waldron, *The Law* (London: Routledge, 1990), pp. 63–64.

52. In the Matter of § 6 of The Judicature Act, [1981] S.C.R. p. 753. Cited in Walter Murphy, "Civil Law, Common Law, and Constitutional Democracy," *Louisiana Law Review* 52 (1991), p. 114.

53. See Frank I. Michelman, "Super Liberal Romance, Community, and Tradition in William J. Brennan, Jr.'s Constitutional Thought," *Virginia Law Review* 77 (1991), pp. 1312–20 (differentiating between conservative and liberal uses of tradition in constitutional interpretation). Sanford Levinson distinguishes between the Protestant and the Catholic approaches to constitutional interpretation, wherein the former emphasizes the text and original intent, and the latter stresses the doctrines formulated through the Supreme Court's decisions. Sanford Levinson, *Constitutional Faith* (Princeton, NJ: Princeton University Press, 1988), pp. 27–53. In my view, the two approaches are but different species of traditionalist discourse, emphasizing different aspects of the constitutional tradition.

54. P. S. Atiyah, *Law and Modern Society* (Oxford: Oxford University Press, 1995), pp. 81–91 (noting that any law, especially constitutional law, must be supported by both compulsion and persuasion, if it is to be effective).

55. Waldron, *Law*, pp. 64–67: "It is the fragile readiness of those involved in political life to order their conduct by certain implicit standards that forms the basis of whatever claim Britain has to be a constitutional regime" (67).

56. For a more in-depth analysis of the issues discussed in this and the next parts of this article, readers are referred to Chaihark Hahm, "Confucian Constitutionalism," pp. 107–240 (unpublished S.J.D. dissertation, Harvard Law School, 2000).

57. Promulgated in 1485, this code was the culmination of a series of codification efforts that began with the founding of the dynasty in 1392. For a review of the codification process leading up to the enactment of this code, and its subsequent revisions, see Park, *Kŭnse ŭi Pŏp kwa Pŏpsasang*, pp. 81–87. See also William Shaw, "Social and Intellectual Aspects of Traditional Korean Law, 1392–1910," in *Traditional Korean Legal Attitudes*, eds. B. D. Chun et al., pp. 15, 29–32.

58. Of course, a code containing such rules might be called constitutional law in the sense that it lays out the duties, capacities, and composition of the various government offices. But that is not the sense that we are interested in when we speak of norms for disciplining the ruler. Moreover, it is hardly clear that the mere existence of such a code of government organization will have a disciplining effect on the ruler.

59. A notable exception is Park, *Kŭnse ŭi Pŏp kwa Pŏpsasang*, pp. 435–53.

60. For example, in the *Analects*, Confucius says: "To govern means to rectify. If you lead on the people with correctness, who will dare not to be correct?" James Legge, trans., *Confucius, Confucian Analects, The Great Learning & the Doctrine of the Mean* (New York: Dover, 1971), p. 258. Also: "When a prince's personal conduct is correct, his government is effective without the issuing of orders. If his personal conduct is not correct, he may issue orders, but they will not be followed" (266).

61. Edward L. Farmer, *Zhu Yuanzhang and Early Ming Legislation* (Leiden: Brill Academic Publisher, 1995), p. 13. See also Edward L. Farmer, "Social Order in Early Ming China," in *Law and State in Traditional East Asia*, ed. Brian E. McKnight (Honolulu: University of Hawaii Press, 1987), pp. 1, 6 (including within the definition of Confucian law such diverse items as "criminal law, rules governing the imperial clan, tables of organization for the bureaucracy, warnings to officials and commoners about improper conduct, rules applying to the management of local affairs, and on the proper way to conduct rituals").

All were compiled during the reign of emperor Xuanzong (r. 712–756 A.D.). Of these three, the *Tang Liudian* and the *Tang Lü Shuyi* were completed under the leadership of the same chief minister, Li Linfu, while the compilations of *Kaiyuan Li* and the *Tang Liudian* appear to have commenced during the regime of the same chief minister Zhang Yue. Denis Twitchett, ed., *Cambridge History of China*, vol. 3 (Cambridge: Cambridge University Press, 1979), pp. 390–91, 414–15.

62. The *Zhouli* was purportedly a description of the government structure of the ancient Zhou dynasty (1027–771 B.C.). According to Confucius and his followers, Zhou culture and society had attained a level of perfection that had never been surpassed by later generations. Its government institutions as laid out in the *Zhouli* were therefore idealized by most Confucian scholar-officials, including the compilers of *Kyŏngguk Taejŏn*. The introduction to this code specifically refers to the *Zhouli* as its model. Pŏpchech'ŏ [The Office of Legislation], ed. and trans., *Kyŏngguk Taejŏn*, vol. 1 (Seoul: Pŏpchech'ŏ, 1962), p. 3.

63. See Zhu Weizheng, *Coming Out of the Middle Ages: Comparative Reflections on China and the West*, trans. and ed. Ruth Hayhoe (New York: M.E. Sharpe, 1990), 3, 23 (referring to the trio of Tang legislations as having laid the framework for later state structure). Unfortunately, Zhu's discussion is impaired by the indiscriminate and inapposite use of terms like "feudal," "autocratic," and "Middle Ages" in reference to China.

64. For a detailed analysis of the adaptation of the Ming Code by Chosŏn, see Park Byung Ho, "Chosŏn Ch'ogi Pŏpchejŏng kwa Sahoesang" [Legislation and Social Conditions of Early Chosŏn], *Kuksagwan Nonch'ong* 80 (1998), pp. 1–36.

65. *Kyŏngguk Taejŏn*, vol. 2, p. 149.

66. *Kyŏngguk Taejŏn*, vol. 1, p. 250.

67. James Legge, trans., *Li Chi: Book of Rites*, vol. 1 (New York: University Books, 1967 [1885]), p. 375.

68. This does not mean that the penal code in its entirety was inapplicable to the ruler. To the extent that it contained ritual regulations, it could also be considered directly applicable to the ruler.

69. Bong Duck Chun, "Legal Principles and Values of the Late Yi Dynasty," in *Traditional Korean Legal Attitudes*, eds. B. D. Chun et al. (Berkeley, CA: Institute of East Asian Studies, 1981), pp. 7–8.

70. On the principle of respecting precedents, see the fourth section of this chapter.

71. For example, "Thus the sages made known these rules [ritual], and it became possible for the kingdom, with its states and clans, to reach its correct condition" (Legge, *Li Chi*, vol. 1, p. 367). The *Zuo Commentary* to the *Spring and Autumn Annals* provides: "It is ritual that governs the states and families, establishes the foundation of the country, secures order among people, and benefits one's future heirs" (My translation based on James Legge, trans., *The Ch'un Ts'ew with the Tso Chuen* in *The Chinese Classics*, vol. 5 [Taipei: SMC Publishing Inc., 1991], p. 33). Another passage states: "Ritual is the stem of a state; reverence is the vehicle of ritual. With no reverence, ritual will not observed; with no observance of ritual, status distinctions will be confused. How can such a state last many generations?" (My translation based on Legge, *Chinese Classics*, vol. 5, p. 158).

72. For example, in his coronation edict, the founder of Chosŏn, T'aejo (Yi Sŏnggye), declared that his government should rectify ritual practices and ordered the Ministry of Rites to research the classics and past practices and to establish the proper ritual institutions. *Sourcebook of Korean Civilization*, vol. 1, ed. Peter H. Lee (New York: Columbia University Press, 1993), pp. 481–82.

73. Noah E. Fehl, *Li: Rites and Propriety in Literature and Life* (Hong Kong: Chinese University Press, 1971), p. 183.

74. "When one disciplines himself to conform externally to the letter of the *li* [ritual] he will by its conditioning come to an inner sense of courtesy and propriety" (ibid.).

75. Foucault, *Discipline and Punish*, pp. 177–84.

76. Tu Wei-ming, "*Li* as Process of Humanization," *Philosophy East and West* 22 (1972). "In the Confucian context it is inconceivable that one can become truly human without going through the process of 'ritualization'" (198).

77. Legge, *Li Chi*, vol. 1, p. 217.

78. See generally Fan Zhongxin et al., *Qing, Li, Fa yu Zhongguoren* [Sentiments, Principle, Law and the Chinese People] (Beijing: Zhongguo Renmin Daxue Chubanshe, 1992).

79. John Knoblock, *Xunzi: A Translation and Study of the Complete Works*, vol. 3 (Stanford, CA: Stanford University Press, 1994), p. 55.

80. See Lee Seung-hwan, *Yuga Sasang ŭi Sahoe Ch'ŏlhakchŏk Chaejomyŏng* [A Reconsideration of Confucian Thought as a Social Philosophy] (Seoul: Korea University Press, 1998), pp. 169–77.

81. For example, "Therefore to govern a state without the rules of propriety [ritual] would be to plough a field without a share" (Legge, *Li Chi*, vol. 1, p. 390).

82. The ritual code of Chosŏn, like that of other Confucian regimes in China, was structured around the traditional system of Five Rituals (*Orye*; Chinese: *Wuli*) of the state. They were: (i) Rituals for Auspicious Occasions (*Killye*; Ch.: *Jili*), dealing with various sacrificial ceremonies offered to numerous "deities" of the state; (ii) Rituals of Ill Omen (*Hyungnye*; Ch.: *Xiongli*), concerned with illness and other sad occasions at court; (iii) Guest Rituals (*Pillye*; Ch.: *Binli*), regulating the ceremonies dealing with state visits by foreign emissaries; (iv) Military Rituals (*Kullye*; Ch.: *Junli*), regulating the conduct of military exercises and expeditions; and (v) Rituals for Felicitous Occasions (*Karye*; Ch.: *Jiali*), dealing with ceremonies such as weddings and comings of age within the ruling house.

83. The statement of historian Charles Hucker in relation to the Ming government is equally applicable to Chosŏn: "Performance of proper rituals was one of the most notable obligations of the government," such that "proper government in the Ming view was largely a matter of performing proper rituals." Charles O. Hucker, *The Traditional Chinese State in Ming Times (1368–1644)* (Tucson: University of Arizona Press, 1961), pp. 97–98.

84. Institutionally, they disciplined the king through such mechanisms as the censorate and the royal lectures. Unlike its Chinese counterparts, the Chosŏn censorate was more interested in disciplining and remonstrating against the king than in impeaching misconduct on the part of the officials. Some historians regard the censorate as a separate branch of the Chosŏn government which checked the powers of the throne and the "executive." JaHyun K. Haboush, "The Confucianization of Korean Society," in *The East Asian Region: Confucian Heritage and Its Modern Adaptation*, ed. Gilbert Rozman (Princeton, NJ: Princeton University Press, 1991), pp. 84–96. The royal lectures, which by definition were an educative and therefore disciplinary institution, also developed a highly constitutional function. Beyond the usual role of exposition of classical texts, it took on the role of a forum for policy deliberation. See generally Yon-ung Kwon, "The Royal Lecture of Early Yi Korea (1)," *Journal of Social Science and Humanities* 50 (1979); Yon-ung Kwon, "The Royal Lecture of Early Yi Korea (2)," *Journal of Social Science and Humanities* 51 (1980).

85. Patricia B. Ebrey, *Confucianism and Family Rituals in Imperial China* (Princeton, NJ: Princeton University Press, 1991), 34–37; Howard J. Weschler, *Offerings of Jade and Silk: Ritual and Symbol in the Legitimation of the T'ang Dynasty* (New Haven, CT: Yale University Press, 1985), p. 9 ("Confucians served as experts in the field of ritual, discoursing on its proper forms and manipulating it for political ends, both on behalf of and against monarchical power.").

86. For a similar interpretation of the ritual discourse in China during the Ming dynasty, see Ron Guey Chu, "Rites and Rights in Ming China," in *Confucianism and Human Rights*, eds. Wm. Theodore de Bary and Tu Weiming (New York: Columbia University Press, 1998), p. 169.

87. See generally JaHyun K. Haboush, "Constructing the Center: The Ritual Controversy and the Search for a New Identity in Seventeenth-Century Korea," in *Culture and the State in Late Choson Korea*, eds. JaHyun K. Haboush and Martina Deuchler (Cambridge, MA: Harvard University Asia Center, 1999). For an exposition of these ritual controversies from a constitutional perspective, see Hahm, "Confucian Constitutionalism," pp. 221–38.

88. The origins of these stereotypes are very old. In the West, one might even trace them as far back as to Montesquieu, who described the Chinese government as one committed to a rule by morality. Montesquieu, *The Spirit of the Laws*, translated and edited by Anne M. Cohler, Basia C. Miller, and Harold S. Stone (Cambridge: Cambridge University Press, 1989), pp. 317–21. East Asians too adopted this view in their self-descriptions. See, for example, Liang

Chi-Chao, *History of Chinese Political Thought during the Early Tsin Period*, trans. L. T. Chen (London: Kegan Paul, Trench, Trubner & Co., 1930) (contrasting Confucian "rule of man" with Legalist "rule of law").

89. Legge, *Confucius*, p. 195.

90. Ibid., p. 160 (proclaiming himself a follower of Zhou culture) and pp. 162–63 (lamenting the transgression of Zhou ritual regulations by usurpers).

91. The Confucian term for this is *ye-ak-hyŏng-jŏng* (Chinese: *li-yue-xing-zheng*), which literally means "rituals-music-punishments-regulations" and is often used as a shorthand for a state's entire social and political arrangements. See, for example, Legge, *Li Chi*, vol. 2, p. 93 ("The end to which ceremonies, music, punishments, and laws conduct is one; they are the instruments by which the minds of the people are assimilated, and good order in government is made to appear."); also see p. 97 ("When ceremonies, music, laws, and punishments had everywhere full course, without irregularity or collision, the method of kingly rule was complete.").

92. For example, Legge, *Li Chi*, vol. 1, p. 367 ("Confucius said, 'It was by those rules [ritual] that the ancient kings sought to represent the ways of Heaven, and to regulate the feelings of men.'"); *Mencius* 4A:1 ("There has never been anyone who has abided by the way of the former kings and fallen into error.").

93. What Professor William Alford has aptly described as the "power of the past" pervading all intellectual discourse of traditional China was also in operation in Korea. William P. Alford, *To Steal a Book Is an Elegant Offence: Intellectual Property Law in Chinese Civilization* (Stanford, CA: Stanford University Press, 1995), pp. 20–28.

94. Park, *Kŭnse ŭi Pŏp kwa Pŏpsasang*, pp. 401–4.

95. One of these was the *Kyŏngyŏn*, or Royal Lecture, mentioned above. Whereas this office was in charge of lectures to the king, another office, *Seja Sigangwŏn*, or princely lecture, was in charge of the crown prince's edification and enlightenment.

96. Obviously, not all classics purported to be records of the former kings' exemplary deeds. Some contained highly metaphysical discourses on human nature, while others were very mundane instructions on how to perform specific ritual ceremonies. Nevertheless, their authority as classics and as sources of constitutional norms was inextricably related to the claim that they all derived from antiquity and thus connected to the sage-kings. By the time of the Chosŏn dynasty, the scholar-officials were all familiar with the Five Classics (*Book of Poetry*, *Book of Documents*, *Book of Changes*, *Record of Rituals*, *Spring and Autumn Annals*) and Four Books (*The Great Learning*, *Analects*, *Mencius*, *Doctrine of the Mean*).

97. But see E. A. Kracke, Jr., *Civil Service in Early Sung China 960–1067* (Cambridge, MA: Harvard University Press, 1953). Describing the political outlook of the Song dynasty's ruling elite, Kracke wrote:

> The Confucian classics became a fundamental part of the state constitution, with a force which neither the Emperor nor his subjects could venture to deny. . . . This function of the classics was not formally stated in the legal codes; it was accepted as an assumption so basic that it required no statement. (21)

See also *Herrlee G. Creel, the Origins of Statecraft in China* (Chicago: University of Chicago Press, 1970), pp. 94–95 (describing some parts of the classics such as the *Book of Documents* as "a kind of constitution" that "defin[ed] both the duties of rulers and the grounds upon which . . . they might rightfully be deposed."). While it is certainly true that the classics were authoritative, to say that they themselves were the constitutions of a Confucian state is unhelpful. As mentioned above, they included many matters of non-political nature, which had nothing to do with disciplining the ruler. To regard them as the constitution would be like claiming that, since Americans were predominantly Christians at the time of the Revolution, the Bible should be viewed as their constitution.

98. For readers familiar with American constitutional theory, my use of the term "interpretive" might be confusing. As used by some American scholars, "interpretivist" refers to the position that denies the need to look anywhere other than the "four corners of the text," whereas "non-interpretivist" refers to the view that argues for the need to accommodate for the changed

circumstances that distinguishes us from the original drafters of the Constitution. See, for example, Thomas C. Grey, "Do We Have an Unwritten Constitution?" *Stanford Law Review* 27 (1975), p. 703; John Hart Ely, *Democracy and Distrust* (Cambridge, MA: Harvard University Press, 1980), pp. 1–2. Fortunately, in recent literature, scholars have largely abandoned this distinction, preferring instead to speak of "textualist vs. non-textualist" or "originalist vs. non-originalist" approaches. See Thomas C. Grey, "The Constitution as Scripture," *Stanford Law Review* 37 (1984), p. 1 (acknowledging the confusion caused by his earlier categorization). There seems to be a general recognition that law is an unavoidably interpretive exercise. On the significance of the "interpretive turn" in legal scholarship, see generally articles published in the "Interpretation Symposium" issue of *Southern California Law Review* 58 (1985).

99. Certain aspects of the famous Ritual Controversy of the seventeenth century can be understood in this light. One faction (Sŏin) favored the position that the ritual prescriptions found in the ancient classics, according to which the ordinary scholar-officials and royalty were to observe different rules, were not directly applicable to Chosŏn. The opposing faction (Namin) tried to argue that ignoring the class distinction prescribed in the ancient classics (i.e., "ancient institutions") was a grave mistake and that making the royal family observe ritual rules originally prescribed for the scholar-officials was tantamount to contempt of the throne. For more on this, see Hahm, "Confucian Constitutionalism," pp. 227–34.

100. Park, *Kŭnse ŭi Pŏp kwa Pŏpsasang*, pp. 51–52, 85–86, 404–6, 411–12; Chun, "Legal Principles and Values," p. 9.

101. Professor Park Byung Ho states that the establishment of this principle so early in the dynasty discouraged the practice of looking to foreign (i.e., Chinese) laws for either reforming or refining Korean laws. Park, *Kŭnse ŭi Pŏp kwa Pŏpsasang*, pp. 51–52, 85–86. From this, it might be tempting to infer that this principle of respecting ancestral precedents was somehow a Korean invention which contributed to Korean "nationalism." Such inference, however, would be unwarranted in light of Chinese imperial history. It is well-known that the founder of the Ming dynasty ordered his descendants and officials to honor his own laws and prescribed the death penalty to anyone who dared to suggest an alteration. See de Bary, *Asian Values and Human Rights*, pp. 94–97. De Bary writes that through "threats and imprecations Ming Taizu confirmed in blood the tradition of ancestral law as a 'constitutional order.'" (97).

102. In a way, this is similar to the amendment process of the American Constitution, in which older provisions that have been altered or even repealed by later amendments continue to stay on the text as part of the document. The most obvious example would be the amendment that enforced Prohibition (of alcoholic consumption) and the later amendment that repealed it. U.S. Const. amend. XVIII, *repealed by* U.S. Const. amend. XXI.

103. The writer of the introduction goes on to boast that observance of the ancestral laws will bring about enlightened government whose brilliance will even surpass that of Zhou, the dynasty which always served as the ideal for all Confucians.

104. Park, *Kŭnse ŭi Pŏp kwa Pŏpsasang*, pp. 412–15.

105. Shaw, "Social and Intellectual Aspects," p. 29. See also Park, *Kŭnse ŭi Pŏp kwa Pŏpsasang*, pp. 52, 86, 415.

106. The Western views described here deal with Chinese legal history, rather than that of Korea. I believe, however, they would be applied mutatis mutandis to the case of Korea if anyone were to theorize about its legal history.

107. R. P. Peerenboom, *Law and Morality in Ancient China* (Albany: State University of New York Press, 1993), pp. 125–32.

108. Often called the "Confucianization of law," this process refers to the utilization of rigid and coercive measures to enforce the requirements of ritual. T'ung-tsu Ch'ü, *Law and Society in Traditional China* (Paris: Mouton & Co., 1961), pp. 267–79. For an argument that the Chosŏn ruling class's outlook was at once thoroughly Confucian and harshly legalistic, see William Shaw, "The Neo-Confucian Revolution of Values in Early Yi Korea," in *Law and the State in Traditional East Asia*, ed. Brian E. McKnight (Berkeley, CA: Institute of East Asian Studies, 1987), p. 149.

109. For studies in English of such handbooks, see Derk Bodde and Clarence Morris, *Law in Imperial China* (Cambridge, MA: Harvard University Press, 1967) (analysis and translation of *Xingan Huilan* [Conspectus of Criminal Cases] of Qing dynasty); William Shaw, *Legal Norms*

in a Confucian State (Berkeley, CA: Institute of East Asian Studies, 1981) (examination of *Simnirok* [Records of *Simni* Hearings] of Chosŏn).

110. Alford, *To Steal a Book Is an Elegant Offence*, p. 22.

111. Ibid. (suggesting that the absences of binding precedents may be a reflection of "an even greater embracing of the past").

112. Karl Bünger, "Genesis and Change of Law in China," *Law and State* 24 (1981), pp. 66–80.

113. One recent example in American constitutional law is the issue of the proper line between the powers of the federal and state governments. After a period of steady expansion of the federal government, there has been a reversal in the direction of more autonomy for state governments.

114. Zhu Xi (1130–1200) lived during the Song dynasty, and although his views and interpretations of the classics were already quite influential during his lifetime, at the time of his death they were actually banned by the Song government as heterodox. In 1241, however, his teachings were given imperial sanction, and in 1313, his texts were adopted as expressions of official state doctrine by the Yuan (Mongol) dynasty. Hoyt C. Tillman, *Confucian Discourse and Chu Hsi's Ascendancy* (Honolulu: University of Hawaii Press, 1992). Korean scholars also had their first encounter with Zhu Xi's teachings during the Yuan period, and many scholar-officials who actively participated in the founding of Chosŏn in 1392 are said to have been motivated by a desire to reorganize the nation in accordance with Zhu Xi's interpretation.

115. See generally, *The Rise of Neo-Confucianism in Korea*, eds. Wm. Theodore de Bary and JaHyun K. Haboush (New York: Columbia University Press, 1985).

116. For a short genealogy of the political factions of Chosŏn and their different interpretations of the classics, see Mark Setton, *Chŏng Yagyong: Korea's Challenge to Orthodox Neo-Confucianism* (Albany: State University of New York Press, 1997), pp. 21–51.

117. For a study of the very few who in fact went against the orthodoxy of Zhu Xi, see Martina Deuchler, "Despoilers of the Way—Insulters of the Sages: Controversy over the Classics in Seventeenth-Century Korea," in *Culture and the State in Late Choson Korea*, eds. JaHyun K. Haboush and Martina Deuchler, p. 91.

118. See generally Setton, *Chŏng Yagyong*.

119. See Hahm, "Confucian Constitutionalism," pp. 236–37.

120. For a description of reinterpretations and modifications of the ancient rituals by Zhu Xi and his predecessors, see generally Patricia B. Ebrey, *Confucianism and Family Rituals in Imperial China* (Princeton, NJ: Princeton University Press, 1991).

121. According to Zhu Xi, Confucius chose to preserve and follow the practices of the Zhou dynasty because for Confucius they represented the "institutions of the current king" (*shiwang zhi zhi*). Zhu Xi, *Sishu Zhangju Jizhu* [Collected Commentaries on the Four Books in Chapters and Verses] (Beijing: Zhonghua Shuju, 1983), p. 36 (commentary on chapter 28 of *Zhongyong* [Doctrine of the Mean]).

122. According to the theory of the Mandate of Heaven, a political ruler had a right to rule only because Heaven had given him a mandate, the implication being that Heaven could always revoke the mandate and give it to someone else if the current ruler was not worthy of it. In the Confucian classic, the *Book of Documents*, this theory is invoked numerous times by the Duke of Zhou to justify Zhou's conquest of the Shang dynasty (1766–1122 B.C.). James Legge, trans., *The Shoo King [Shu Jing]* (Taipei: SMC Publishing, 1991), pp. 425–32, 453–63, 492–507. For discussions on the idea of the Mandate of Heaven, see Creel, *The Origins of Statecraft in China*, 81–100; Benjamin I. Schwartz, *The World of Thought in Ancient China* (Cambridge, MA: Harvard University Press, 1985), pp. 46–55. Though sometimes discussed as a Confucian analogue to the Western idea of natural law, and often mentioned for its potential for restraining the power of the ruler, it seems to have been used throughout history more often in a retrospective manner, to legitimize the rule of a new ruler or a newly founded dynasty, rather than as a constitutional argument for disciplining the ruler. For a summary of views that regard the Mandate of Heaven as a functional analogue of natural law, see William P. Alford, "The Inscrutable Occidental? Implications of Roberto Unger's Uses and Abuses of the Chinese Past," *Texas Law Review* 64 (1986), pp. 915, 935–37.

123. For example, during the Ritual Controversy of 1659, one side argued that the Ming regulation relied on by its opponents was unworthy of respect because it originated from the period of the evil usurper Empress Wu (Wu Zetian) (r. 690–705) of Tang-dynasty China.

124. Lawrence W. Beer, Introduction, *Constitutional Systems in Late Twentieth Century Asia*, ed. Lawrence W. Beer (Seattle: University of Washington Press, 1992), pp. 1, 16 (the constitution of a state must be connected with "the most important, most binding ideas at the heart of that culture"). See generally, *Political Culture and Constitutionalism*, eds. Daniel P. Franklin and Michael J. Baun (Armonk, NY: M.E. Sharpe, 1995).

125. Given that an overwhelming majority of Korea constitutional law scholars are German-trained, the German influence on Korean constitutional law scholarship needs no elaboration. For the relatively smaller, though by no means negligible, influence that American constitutionalism has had on modern Korea, see Kyong Whan Ahn, "The Influence of American Constitutionalism on South Korea," *Southern Illinois University Law Journal* 22 (1997), p. 71.

126. This need for educating citizens is not limited to what I have called the "formative" approach to constitutionalism. Even in the United States, where the Newtonian approach is said to be prevalent, this need has always been recognized. On the American experience with educating constitutional citizens, see Stephen Macedo, *Diversity and Distrust: Civic Education in a Multicultural Democracy* (Cambridge, MA: Harvard University Press, 1999).

127. By institutionalized remonstrance, I am referring to the role of the censorate in Chosŏn government alluded to above (see note 85). It is interesting to note that under the "modern" government structure instituted by the Kabo Reforms of 1894, the office of the censorate was abolished. The rationale seems to have been that the office of the censorate was contributing to factional strife within the government. Yet, it is still ironic that at the beginning of modern constitutionalism in Korea, one of the major organs responsible for disciplining power was eliminated.

128. Stephen L. Elkin, "Constitutionalism's Successor," in *A New Constitutionalism*, eds. Stephen L. Elkin and Karol E. Soltan (Chicago: University of Chicago Press, 1993), pp. 117, 122–24 (discussing the formative function of institutions).

129. Bickel, *The Least Dangerous Branch*, p. 26. In a similar vein, one historian of the Court has said that one of its important functions since the American founding has been that of a "Republican Schoolmaster." Ralph Lerner, "The Supreme Court as Republican Schoolmaster," in *The Thinking Revolutionary* (Ithaca, NY: Cornell University Press, 1987), p. 91.

130. 98 HŏnMa 168, 10–2 *Hŏnpŏpjaep'anso Pallyejip*, p. 586 (Oct. 15, 1998) (holding unconstitutional a provision in the Law of Family Ritual Standards which criminalized the practice of serving "unreasonable" amounts of food and drinks at weddings). The Court criticized the government for attempting to "legislate" morals and manners by imposing legal penalties. The Court also commented that traditional family rituals like weddings and funerals are part of the nation's cultural heritage, which the state has a duty to sustain and develop.

Chapter Two

Confucianism That Confounds

Constitutional Jurisprudence on Filial Piety in Korea

Marie Seong-Hak Kim

Is Confucianism compatible with modern constitutionalism? The question arises, in part, because Article 9 of the Constitution of South Korea declares that "the State shall strive to sustain and develop [Korea's] cultural heritage and enhance national culture." It does not identify Confucianism as a national cultural heritage, but there is little dispute that Confucianism, the state ideology of the Chosŏn dynasty (1392–1910), has deeply influenced Korean society and culture. The Chosŏn law codes were the embodiments of Confucian ideals and practices. Many law provisions, ranging from criminal punishments to civil matters, were imbued with the Confucian worldview. A number of them survived into modern laws, and today Korean law codes include various articles, both civil and penal, that were adopted from the traditional laws based on Confucian ideology. The hierarchical nature of Confucianism has caused some of these laws to be seen in conflict with modern constitutional principles. The past twenty years or so have witnessed a rising number of constitutional challenges that certain Confucian-based laws violate fundamental rights of individuals. Article 11 of the Constitution stipulates that "All citizens shall be equal before the law and there shall be no discrimination in political, economic, social or cultural life on account of sex, religion or social status."[1] In reviewing the validity of the laws that are identified with Korean culture and heritage but are suspected of infringing the principle of equality and other rights protected by the Constitution, the Constitutional Court of Korea has performed a delicate balancing act between the competing demands to preserve traditional culture on the one hand and to protect individual liberty on the other.[2]

Of particular interest among the modern laws that have been subject to constitutional review are the penal provisions that impose legal sanctions on the acts and behaviors deemed to contravene the Confucian ideal of filial piety. Notable examples include the laws in the Criminal Procedure that prohibit the filing of criminal complaint against one's lineal ascendants and the spouse's lineal ascendants, and also the laws in the Criminal Code that impose enhanced punishment for crimes committed against lineal ascendants such as murder and the infliction of bodily injury. Constitutional challenges to these penal laws have been much less successful than the challenges to the civil law provisions. It is well known that a number of laws in the Civil Code derived from Confucian family hierarchy were struck down by the Constitutional Court. In a landmark decision in 2005, the Constitutional Court ruled that the household headship system and the requirement that the child take the paternal surname were in violation of the constitution.[3] A few years earlier, in 1997, the Constitutional Court had found unconstitutional the prohibition of marriages between parties with surnames of common geographical origin.[4] These cases have received ample attention in scholarship because they attested to the willingness and determination of the Court to scrutinize the laws based on the Confucian lineage system that had been regarded as the backbone of the traditional family structure. But the constitutional review of the penal law provisions above illustrates the Court's continuing uneasiness about flaunting by judicial fiat the long-standing Confucian culture.[5] This chapter discusses the recent constitutional jurisprudence of the criminal laws that are grounded on the Confucian precept of filial piety. Criminal law provisions are potentially of greater significance than civil law provisions because they are the instruments by which the state prescribes and punishes certain conducts and behaviors for the purpose of promoting a just and sound public order.

In 2011, the Constitutional Court of Korea ruled that Articles 224 and 235 in the Criminal Procedure that prohibited descendants from filing a complaint against their lineal ascendants were constitutional.[6] In 2013, the Constitutional Court upheld Article 250(2) of the Criminal Code that imposed enhanced punishment for the murder of lineal ascendants.[7] This decision affirmed the Court's earlier decision in 2002 that Article 259(2) in the Criminal Code imposing enhanced punishment for assaults of lineal ascendants was constitutional.[8] The prevailing judicial reasoning in all these cases was that the challenged laws promoted the legitimate legislative purpose of filial piety. Constitutional blessings bestowed on them are proof of the powerful presence of the Confucian ideology in Korean law and society. Filial piety has consistently been viewed in Korea as the core value of traditional culture, morality, and national spirit. Respect for parents and grandparents is regarded as the essence of Korean identity, and its promotion receives broad support in society with little dissension.

Many of the filial-based statutes continue to withstand constitutional objections because, in part, they originated from old Korean laws. The Chosŏn dynasty criminalized the act of accusing one's lineal ascendants, and also punished crimes committed against them more harshly than the same crimes against strangers. *Kyŏngguk Taejŏn*, the Chosŏn state code, provided punishments for those who brought charges against their elder kins, and subjected those who injured or killed senior family members to aggravated penalties. Since these dynastic laws presumably embodied the traditional virtue of Confucian filial piety, their successors in modern law seemed to be endowed with certain historical legitimacy. It is likely that the consideration of their historical validity led the Constitutional Court to remain, at least in part, more reluctant to strike them down.

This chapter argues that the jurisprudence of Articles 224 and 235 in the Criminal Procedure (prohibition of criminal complaints against lineal ascendants) and Article 250 in the Criminal Code (enhanced punishment for crimes against lineal ascendants) needs to be revisited in light of a more accurate understanding of the Chosŏn laws of filial piety. The court opinions of the 2011 and 2013 cases were filled with historical analysis of the origins of the challenged laws. While the ancient laws were highlighted as the embodiment of filial piety and timeless symbols of morality and ethical behavior, the judicial analysis and reasoning did not always go in depth to investigate the historical meaning of those laws. Confucian filial piety was an ideology of loyalty and obedience. Scholars have pointed out that traditional law in Korea and East Asia was a means of controlling the political structure surrounding royal power and maintaining the social order grounded on the patriarchal family.[9] If the institutional rules of Chosŏn law had as their main purpose the preservation of hierarchy, a key notion in Confucianism, the current constitutional jurisprudence that construes them predominantly from the perspectives of ethical and moral virtue of filial piety and draws continuity between premodern and modern legal norms may prove to be the result of an ill-conceived undertaking.

The first section of this chapter reviews the 2011 decision concerning Articles 224 and 235 in the Criminal Procedure. Enhanced punishment for lineal descendants, the issue of the 2013 case, is a topic that requires a separate full treatment and remains beyond the scope of this chapter. Focusing on procedural matters may have an advantage, as it helps approach the constitutional questions from a legal perspective without being subsumed by the overarching issue of morality. The second section examines the historical origins of filial piety laws, and the third section discusses their modern adaptation. The value of filial piety is not disputed even by the critics of Articles 224 and 235, but its overriding weight as an ethical norm appears to have inhibited an objective assessment of the challenged laws. A more methodical, and candid, analysis of the notion of Confucian filial piety can shed light on the continuing debate on the evolving relationship between tradition and modernity.

It is interesting to note that Korea seems to preserve the traditional legal provisions based on filial piety more faithfully than other East Asian countries with a Confucian culture. Korea is the only country in East Asia that disallows offspring to lodge criminal complaints against their ascendants. [10] Japan previously had similar laws but abolished them almost a century ago. Taiwanese penal codes contain filial piety–based laws similar to those of Korea but Taiwan does not have a provision equivalent to Articles 224 and 235. It brings forth the question: Is Korea more Confucian than these countries that shared a Confucian tradition? A related question, with a broader ramification, is: Is Korea more prone to resorting to criminal law, through the use of state authority, in order to promote morality? Consideration of these questions can point to a potentially fruitful comparative inquiry of East Asian legal culture.

CONSTITUTIONAL REVIEW

The criminal justice system of Korea does not allow private prosecution. Under the Criminal Procedure, the state holds the exclusive right to prosecute (Article 246). Victims of crime can file a complaint against the alleged offenders and request the initiation of prosecution (Article 223). [11] A major limitation on this right is that a victim cannot file a complaint against his or her lineal ascendants as well as the lineal ascendants of their spouse. Article 224 states: "One cannot file a criminal accusation against his or her own or the spouse's lineal ascendants." Article 235 states that "the provision in Article 224 also applies to *kobal*." Article 224 concerns *koso*, that is, filing a complaint by the injured party or other person who has the right to complain as provided by law. Article 235 concerns *kobal*, filing of an accusation by someone other than the victim, providing information for investigation. Therefore, filing criminal complaints against the lineal ascendants, either by the victim or the third party, is comprehensively prohibited.

"Lineal ascendants" or "spouse" is a legally defined category. Under Articles 224 and 235, an individual is prohibited from filing criminal complaint against his or her parents, parents-in-law, maternal and paternal grandparents, and maternal and paternal grandparents-in-law. [12] In the case of a child born out of wedlock, the biological father does not become a lineal ascendant until the legal acknowledgement of the child has been completed. [13] The adopted child has two sets of parents as lineal ascendants, biological and adoptive, because adoption does not dissolve the birth family relationships. [14] The Supreme Court of Korea ruled in 1981 that the defendant was not subject to aggravated punishment for killing his mother as long as there was no satisfactory finding to show that the adoption process had been completed.[15] The fact that the classification of lineal ascendants is legally defined may appear odd, because it seemingly attenuates the main justification of the laws that they promote respect and obedience toward those in blood relationship, that is, toward those who deserve gratitude because they brought you into this world. But the legal definition certainly conforms to the notion of hierarchical and lineage-based Confucian family system in the dynastic era. In Chosŏn Korea, legal adoption took place in agnatic relations to continue the lineage rather than to promote the welfare of the child.[16]

The prohibition of criminal complaints by lineal descendants does not apply to sexual crimes and domestic violence crimes. Article 18 of the "Law on the Punishment of Sexual Assault and Protection of Victims," enacted in 1994, which in 2010 became Article 19 of the "Special Law on the Punishment and Related Matters of Sexual Crimes," and Article 6(2) of the "Special Law on the Punishment, etc. of Domestic Violence Crimes," enacted in 1997, allow the lineal descendants to file complaints against the lineal ascendants. Such exceptions were considered necessary because these types of crimes were often committed by persons in close family relationship with the victims.

In 2011 the Constitutional Court of Korea reviewed the constitutionality of Article 224 of the Criminal Procedure. The case involved a constitutional petition filed on June 12, 2008. The petitioner claimed that she suffered from abuse by her mother for over forty years. After one particular incident of physical altercation, the mother sued the daughter for assault. Under Article 257(2) and related provisions of the Criminal Code, causing bodily injury to lineal ascendants would entail enhanced punishment. The daughter was found not guilty by the court. The prosecutor appealed but it was dismissed. Subsequently, the daughter filed a criminal complaint against the mother for making false accusation and false witness during the preceding trial. The prosecutor refused to charge the mother on the grounds that the complaint was filed in violation of Article 224 of the Criminal Procedure. After her appeal against this decision was rejected by the Appellate Prosecutors' Office, the daughter filed a non-compliance petition with the Appeals Court pursuant to the Prosecutors' Office Act.[17] While the suit was pending, the daughter moved the court to certify for constitutional review of Articles 224 and 235 of the Criminal Procedure. The Appeals Court dismissed the non-compliance petition and also rejected the request for constitutional review for lack of judicable issue. The daughter filed a constitutional petition directly with the Constitutional Court.[18]

The Constitutional Court heard the parties' arguments on September 9, 2010, which were marked not so much by legal contentions as cultural and ideological clashes. The petitioner claimed that Articles 224 and 235 were grounded on feudal norms and were no longer applicable in modern family relationships. She disputed the claim that the prohibition of a complaint by the descendant would promote harmonious resolutions of conflicts among the family members. To the contrary, the petitioner argued, the denial of judicial recourse to the descendants risked relegating the matters to the realm of private justice outside the state authority. In rebutting her arguments, the Justice Ministry stressed the importance of the virtue of filial piety. Article 224 "originated from the criminal system of the Chosŏn period and has the values that deserve preservation in criminal law because the relationship between the descendants and ascendants concerns what is properly called heavenly morality." The law was a reflection of the ethical standards of Korean people and, contended the Justice Ministry, allowing the descendant to demand the punishment of his or her ascendant would jeopardize the fundamental moral order in society.[19]

The Constitutional Court's analysis focused on whether Article 224 violated the principle of equality by depriving lineal descendants of their rights to lodge a criminal complaint.[20] In constitutional review, if the challenged law contains a prohibited basis for classification, such as classification based on "sex, religion, or social status," it becomes a prima facie case of discrimination. Otherwise, the Court must decide what type of review standards is to be used. The Court takes into consideration the legitimacy of the legislative purposes and the necessity and suitability of the classification.[21] In the present case, whether the Court was to apply a strict scrutiny or a more relaxed reasonableness test depended on whether the prohibition of the right of the lineal descendants constituted an infringement of the right to make a statement in a trial. Article 27(5) of the constitution guarantees the victim's right to be heard in judicial proceedings: "A victim of a crime shall be entitled to make a statement during the proceedings of the trial of the case involved as under the conditions prescribed by law." Depending on whether Article 224 caused serious limitation in the exercise of the victim's right, the appropriate review standard would be different. This was the point over which the justices differed in their opinions.

The Court rendered its ruling on February 24, 2011. It was a sharply divided decision. Five justices found Article 224 to be unconstitutional and four justices found it constitutional. The first group argued that the proper review standard was strict scrutiny, whereas the second group argued that a reasonableness test was appropriate. In Korean law the declaration of unconstitutionality of a statute by the Constitutional Court requires a minimum of six votes.[22] Because only five justices held the law unconstitutional, the constitutional objection failed, despite the fact the votes for unconstitutionality formed a majority. The challenged law thus survived.[23]

THE CONSTITUTIONAL COURT DECISION

The four justices who formed the controlling opinion wrote that the victim's right to file a complaint was a right which could be legitimately limited by the legislature. According to them, there was no fundamental right infringed upon by the statute. They acknowledged that "under the current provision a victim who is a descendent of the accused cannot in theory exercise his or her right to be heard at the criminal proceedings." But, the justices pointed out, the law prohibiting lineal descendants' complaint had no effect on the prosecutor's ability to initiate prosecution. Filing a complaint was a cause for initiating an investigation but "prosecution can commence regardless of the filing of a complaint by the victim." Certain categories of crime require the victim's complaint. In these crimes, known as *ch'inkochoe (Antragsdelikt)*, the victim's complaint was an element prerequisite for litigation and the offender could not be prosecuted and criminally punished unless the victim had filed a complaint.[24] Even in these cases, the enactment of special laws on sexual crimes and domestic violence crimes allowed the victim to press charges against his or her lineal ascendant. Therefore the legal interest restricted by Article 224 was "relatively minor," affecting a limited number of crimes, and Article 224 "causes only indirect or formalistic restriction on the exercise of the victim's right to be heard at the criminal proceedings." From these considerations, the four justices concluded that Article 224 did not severely restrict the victim's right in criminal proceedings and that it was sufficient for the Court to apply the test against arbitrariness. They noted that the law "falls under a category where the legislature has a broad scope of power to legislate in order to pursue specific ethical or social purposes."[25]

When the justices proceeded to consider the law's purposes, they delved into a full-blown cultural analysis. They noted that Article 224 had its foundation in the Confucian tradition. They wrote:

> The current provision is based on our historical ideology of *"hyo,"* or the Confucian tradition of filial piety, which imposed on children a duty to take care of their parents or grandparents. According to this tradition, it is a good custom for a child to endure harm caused by his or her parents or grandparents; filing a criminal complaint against one's parents or grandparents is regarded as a behavior against morality.

The Court continued:

> Lineal ascendants work hard for the spiritual and physical upbringing and protection of their offspring, while descendants have the duty to share responsibility as family members and to appreciate and respect ascendants. The relationship between lineal ascendants and descendants involves values and ethics universal in any society, but the specific nature of such a relationship is to a

large degree influenced by a nation's distinct cultural and moral traditions, because the people of each nation and society create and preserve their traditions. Our country has accepted Confucianism and made it our own tradition. It remains an essential part of our identity, notwithstanding the introduction of modern Western ideals. . . . In particular, respect for one's parents is considered to be the highest moral virtue. It is natural that a statute regulating the relationship between lineal ascendant and descendant in our society reflects this tradition of filial piety.

Therefore, "prohibiting a descendant from filing a complaint against his or her lineal ascendant, for the purposes of deterring such an unethical behavior and of protecting our traditional norms, can be said to be a reasonable discrimination."[26] In conclusion, Article 224 did not violate the equality provision in the constitution.

The five justices who formed the non-controlling majority wrote in the dissenting opinion. Just like their four colleagues, they acknowledged that there was a legitimate legislative goal of promoting filial piety. They stated: "when the state takes up the protection of culture or morality as a legislative goal, it can promote its purpose to the fullest extent by providing material and systemic support."[27] In their opinion, however, Article 224 was not an appropriate means to achieve the proclaimed purpose. While the ascendant-descendant relationship could be a factor in determining the nature of the crime, its graveness, and the responsibility of the perpetrator, "it cannot be a reason for denying the state's exercise of its power to punish criminals." Article 224 restricted an important right of the descendants, that is, the right to be heard at criminal proceedings, and there was an absence of "reasonable balance between the aim and the means in providing differential treatment among the victims of criminal offences."[28] Lacking proportionality between the legislative purpose and the means to achieve that purpose, the dissenting opinion concluded, Article 224 violated the principle of equality.

The five justices roundly rejected the suitability of the Confucian-based hierarchical kinship order in modern Korea. "In modern society the family is not a patriarchal institution controlled by its head who required the obedience of other family members." The traditional family relations in premodern Korea based on the Confucian ideology were no longer appropriate in modern Korea. Article 224 was unconstitutional because it discriminated against the lineal descendants due to their status in the family.[29] Still, the dissenting justices no more disputed than their opposing colleagues that filial piety in traditional law was a timeless and sacrosanct virtue of morality. It is now necessary to examine the historical models of Article 224 in the Chosŏn law codes and revisit the meaning of filial piety in legal norms.

HISTORICAL ANALYSIS

In Korea, it is not uncommon that the courts conduct a historical survey of the backgrounds of the laws as a way of finding legislative intent. When the Constitutional Court or the Supreme Court had to deal with the contemporary laws based on traditional laws and customs, in particular Confucian kinship-based laws and practices, it was routine for them to undertake a lengthy historical inquiry, tracing the sources of the law back to the Chosŏn dynasty. In 1994, the Supreme Court did just that when it had to determine the validity of non-agnatic adoptions that took place under colonial law. [30] The Constitutional Court did the same when it reviewed the constitutionality of the household headship system and the prohibition of marriages between parties with surnames of common geographical origin. [31] In many cases, heated jurisprudential debate focused on whether the challenged law qualified as part of genuine Korean tradition. Whether the household headship system was a true Korean tradition or a Japanese tradition imposed on Korea during the colonial period, and whether the prohibition of marriages between parties with surnames of common geographical origin was an indigenous Korean practice or an alien Confucian tradition of Chinese provenance presented questions of vexing complexity, and they illustrated the daunting task of the judges to delineate the boundaries of Korean culture. [32] In the case of the prohibition of filing a complaint against the lineal ascendants, the Constitutional Court was relatively spared a similar difficulty, however, because the law at issue concerned filial piety, an uncontested human virtue, and there was no dispute that it formed a core Korean value. Among the law provisions that undoubtedly came from Confucian influences, some were more heartily accepted as Korean tradition than the others.

The Constitutional Court's task in 2011 also seemed simpler because the law under challenge was directly adapted from the provisions in the *Kyŏngguk Taejŏn* and *Sok Taejŏn*. The *Kyŏngguk taejŏn* (Great Code for Administering the Country), completed in 1471, was the central law code throughout the Chosŏn dynasty. It was revised and enlarged into *Sok taejŏn* (Supplementary Grand Code) in 1746. [33] The section of *"Kojonjang"* (告尊長 Accusing the Ascendants and Elders) in *Hyŏngjon* (Book on Punishment) in *Kyŏngguk Taejŏn* provided:

> The descendants, wives or concubines, or slaves who inform of the wrongdoings of the parents or the head of the household are subject to strangulation, except when the crimes involve treason or rebellion. The wife or the husband of a slave who informs of the wrongdoings of the head of the household is subject to the punishment of 100 blows of heavy bamboo and exile beyond 3000 *li*. [34]

The *Hyŏngjon* in *Soktaejŏn* retained a similar provision, stating:

> The descendants who file a complaint against their parents or grandparents are subject to criminal investigation and punishment in order to rectify human moral order, regardless of the accuracy or truthfulness of the complaint. [35]

These provisions came from Chinese law. The Chosŏn dynasty adopted the Ming Code (Tae Myŏng ryul; Da Ming lü) as the criminal law of the state. [36] The Ming Code included laws punishing the crime of "violating status and offending against righteousness" (干名犯義 *Kanmyŏng pŏmŭi* in Korean; *Ganming fanyi* in Chinese). Article 360 provided:

> In all cases where sons or sons' sons bring accusations against paternal grand-parents or parents, or where wives or concubines bring accusations against husbands or husbands' paternal grandparents or parents, they shall be punished by 100 strokes of beating with the heavy stick and penal servitude for three years. [37]

This provision is part of the so-called "Ten Abominations" (*sibak; shie*), ten categories of the most vicious crimes. In the beginning section of the Ming Code, the chapter on the "Ten Abominations" listed the most serious disruptions of the primary human relations. The lack of filial piety (*buxiao*) was the seventh abomination, which included the act of "accus[ing] to the court . . . paternal grandparents, parents, husband's paternal grandparents or parents." [38]

It is important to note that the veracity of accusation was only of secondary importance. The Chinese law cited above stated that "If they [i.e., the sons or grandsons] make false accusations, they shall be punished by strangulation." [39] But where accusation was lodged against the senior members of the second degree, the punishment remained the same regardless of the veracity of accusation: "For those who bring accusations against superior or older relatives of the second degree of mourning or against maternal grandparents, even if the accusations are true, they shall be punished by 100 strokes of beating with the heavy stick." [40] In Korean law, whether the accusation against the parents or grandparents was truthful was not a factor in determining the graveness of the punishment. *Kyŏngguk Taejŏn* subjected all the accusers in those cases to strangulation. [41] This provision continued in the later codes, such as *Sok Taejŏn, Taejŏn t'ongp'yŏn* (Great Code for Ruling the State, 1785) and *Taejŏn hoet'ong* (Grand Code for Ruling the State, 1865). [42] It is possible to infer from this difference between Chinese and Korean law that Korean law was more emphatic in categorically condemning the depraved act of denouncing one's own parents and grandparents.

In both China and Korea, the seriousness of a criminal offense and the severity of punishment depended on the relationship between the accuser and the accused as determined in the mourning grades: the closer the relationship between the two, the harsher the punishment. The mourning degrees were stipulated in ritual treaties in the Confucian classics. For example, the crime of accusing the relatives of the third degree of mourning called for ninety strokes, and the relatives of fifth degree seventy strokes.[43] This illustrated that crime and punishment were intrinsically related to the hierarchical relationship within the family.[44]

The regulations against accusation of the senior family members did not apply when treason or rebellion was involved. As seen above, the *Kojonjang* in *Kyŏngguk Taejŏn* explicitly excluded the crimes of treason or rebellion from coverage. Likewise, the Ming Code provided: "For those who accuse others of plotting rebellion or great sedition [Art. 277], plotting treason [Art. 278], . . . the accusations shall be permitted. The provision of violating status and offending against righteousness is not applicable."[45] The exclusion of reporting political crimes against the state from the prohibited acts shows that the laws based on filial piety had a clear political dimension. This is an aspect that has been commonly overlooked when contemporary commentators commended the traditional law for extolling filial piety. Without the consideration of political implications, the precise nature of the traditional law provision may become distorted, rendering an effort to draw continuity with a modern law like Article 224 in the Civil Procedure problematic.

THE MEANING OF FILIAL PIETY

The broadest meaning of filial piety approximates the notion of *chonbi sangha* (尊卑上下 the noble and the servile, and the high and the low) in traditional ritual rules, which formed the most basic characteristics of orderly relations.[46] Confucian ideology presupposed the existence of a chain of subordination in the elder-younger relationship, and subordination to the authority conformed to morality. Filial piety was crucial for preserving the hierarchical order within the family, which was equated with preserving the natural order. Accusing the lineal ascendants of crime was a serious matter because it caused a disruption of family hierarchy, a disorder in morality, and a revolt against the natural order.

The view that the prohibition of accusations against the lineal ascendants was necessary to promote love and harmony among the close blood relations becomes questionable when we examine the language in the *Kojonjang* in *Kyŏngguk Taejŏn* closely. In this provision, the crime of accusing the lineal ascendant by the descendant was lumped together with the crime of accusing the master by the slave ("The descendants, wives or concubines, or slaves who inform of the wrongdoings of the parents or the head of the household are subject to strangulation"). The law treated the son who accused the father the same as the slave who accused the master. Here it becomes clear that the prohibition of challenging the seniors was predicated on the preservation of the authority and the existing hierarchy. The equivalent provisions in the Ming Code stated:

> If slaves accuse household heads or household heads' relatives of the fifth degree of mourning or above, they shall be punished the same as sons or sons' sons or other inferior or younger relatives. If hired laborers accuse household heads or household heads' relatives, their penalty shall be reduced one degree from that for slaves. If the accusations are false, the penalty shall not be reduced.[47]

In the Korean case, even the wife or husband of the slave, who apparently was not in formal master-slave relations, was subject to a heavy punishment. In fact the punishment for them was heavier than the kind meted out in the Ming Code for the slave currently owned by the master.

The second part of the *Kojonjang* provision stated:

> Where an official lower in rank insults an official who is superior in rank by one degree, he is punished one degree harsher than the ordinary punishment for the crime of insult; if he insults an official who is superior in rank by two degrees, another degree of punishment is added, up to 100 strokes. If a slave owned by the Ministry of Public Works insults someone, he is punished by one degree higher no matter whether the insulted party is an official.[48]

This provision highlights the fact that the law was concerned about maintaining the hierarchy, not just within the family but in society at large. The relationships between the son and the father, between the slave and the master, and between the low-rank official and the high-rank official were all placed in the same realm and on the same horizon.

Neither the Korean nor the Chinese codes punished the ascendants for accusing the descendants, even if it involved false accusation. According to *Kyŏngguk Taejŏn*, "if paternal grandparents or parents falsely accuse sons, sons' sons, daughters' sons, wives or concubines of sons or sons' sons, or their own concubines, slaves, or hired laborers, in each case they shall not be punished."[49] These provisions further indicate that the goal of promoting love and ensuring family harmony was of limited importance. Not all quarrels and disputes among the family members were frowned upon; only the act of insubordination by the younger members was denounced and punished. The family could be a dangerous place for younger members.[50] When the descendant accused the ascendant, the accused elder, even when proved guilty, was punished lightly: that person was treated as though he or she had voluntarily surrendered, and the punishment was commuted three degrees from the regular punishment of the crime. Sometimes the guilty senior was exempted from punishment altogether.

In the Confucian ideology of *samgang oryun* (三綱五倫 three fundamental principles and five moral relationships), there was no division between loyalty and filial piety. Together they underpinned the relationships between the father and the son, the elder and the younger, the husband and the wife, and the ruler and the subject. The parallel, and at the same time intertwined, concepts of filial piety and loyalty formed a core foundation of East Asian society and the state system. The exclusion of treason and rebellion from the *Kojonjang* provision exemplifies this point. Recently the Chinese legal historian Jérôme Bourgon has argued that parricide in traditional China was not a crime against paternal authority but a crime against the rule of subordination which covered all the relatives of the lineage.[51] Normally the father was regarded as a delegate of heaven. But, according to Bourgon, this emphasis on the father-figure in premodern China did not concern the father himself as an individual; rather, the father was merely a link in the chain of subordination in the family, just one of the many senior members of the family who were protected by the law.[52]

Here one can argue that the virtue of obedience and respect prescribed in the law in traditional East Asia was not about privileging the relationship between the parents and the children. It was not the kind that embodied the relationship between the parents and the children (in the sense of "honor your father and your mother" in the Judeo-Christian tradition) but the kind that was expected to play an important role in a stratified order in the family and in the state. In the Confucian legal order, as Bourgon argued, the political order was replicated in the family order, and vice versa. The protection of the political authority was systematically expanded to the sphere of the family. The emphasis on the hierarchy on the family level could be directly applied to the hierarchy on the social and the state levels. Law represented instruments of the state in controlling the existing political and social order through the imposition of approved values and practices. Filial piety and loyalty became a twin concept that transcended ordinary law through Confucian rites. According to Bourgon, "the family was in many respects a blind spot of the legislation, a source of inequalities and of derogations, which compromised the coherence of the whole. A privileged site for the rite and for 'human feelings,' the family hierarchy was a kind of sanctuary sheltered from the common law."[53] In short, it was a sort of extralegal realm.

What are the implications of this observation in modern law? The proponents of Article 224 in the Korean Criminal Procedure stressed that the law was geared to prevent unethical behaviors by the lineal descendants. The Constitutional Court echoed this sentiment when it expounded: "law inevitably shares a certain common ground with morality and, at the bottom of our legal consciousness, individualism derived from modern Western ideals exists side by side with Confucian ethics centered on community and blood relations."[54] But the Chosŏn laws of filial piety were part of the state effort to preserve the hierarchical order in society.[55] Filial piety toward parents (*hyo*) in traditional Korean law was tied in essence with loyalty toward the ruler (*ch'ung*). Once intrinsically connected, however, these two concepts can rarely exist in tandem in modern law. No law today demanding subordination of the people to the ruler would have a chance to survive constitutional review.

MODERN ADAPTATION

The provision in the Chosŏn code punishing those who accused their lineal ascendants continued to exist through the end of the dynasty. The *Hyŏngpŏp taejŏn*, the last Chosŏn law code promulgated in 1905, retained the provisions in *Kyŏngguk Taejŏn* and *Sok Taejŏn*. In 1908, in the wake of the modernization of traditional laws and the legal system under Japanese influence, a number of laws criminalizing acts against filial piety were abolished.[56] After Korea's annexation to Japan in 1910, the Japanese Criminal law and Criminal Procedure were imposed on Korea. The Japanese Criminal Procedure, promulgated in 1922, contained provisions disallowing the filing of complaints against lineal ascendants: Article 259 prohibited filing a complaint by the victim of a crime against his or her parents and grandparents; Article 270 prohibited filing a complaint by someone other than the victim against his lineal ascendants.[57] These two articles were the direct models of the modern Korean laws. After Korea obtained independence in 1945, colonial laws continued to have legal force until Korean codes were enacted. In Japan, Articles 259 and 279 were repealed in the new Criminal Procedure issued in 1948, but in Korea the two colonial law articles continued to be enforced up to 1954. When the first modern Korean Criminal Procedure was written in 1954, the prohibition of the descendants' filing a criminal complaint against the lineal ascendants was securely retained.

It is noteworthy that the Korean laws not only retained the provisions in the old Japanese Criminal Procedure of 1922 but expanded their scope. The Japanese laws prohibited filing complaints against "parents and grandparents." The Korean laws prohibited filing complaints against the same and, in addition, against the parents and the grandparents of the spouse. Where did this idea of adding the spouse's ascendants to the protected group derive from? There is no concrete evidence from which we can gather the legislative intent. A rare example in the traditional codes of the protection of wives' parents is found in Article 360 of the Ming Code, which stated: "The accused superior or older relatives of the third or second degree of mourning, maternal grandparents, or wives' parents shall be exempted from punishment as if they themselves had voluntarily confessed."[58] It is not certain whether the Korean legislators in 1954 took account of this obscure provision, but at least it is clear that the legislature believed that harmony among the family members needed to extend to the in-laws. Perhaps the inclusion of spousal ascendants under Article 224 reflected the effort of the new republic to demonstrate its willingness to overcome the patriarchal and virilocal presumptions of Confucianism. Or, more likely, it was the result of the nationalistic legislative effort to differentiate the Korean provisions from the Japanese models that had governed Korea as laws of the land.

At any rate, Korea is the only country in East Asia today that comprehensively prohibits the lineal descendant from bringing a criminal suit against the lineal ascendant. The current Japanese Criminal Procedure does not have equivalent provisions.[59] The case of Taiwan requires discussion in detail. The Chinese Criminal Procedure promulgated by the Nationalist government in 1928 provided that private prosecution was not allowed against "lineal relatives, spouse, and relatives living together and sharing the same property" (Article 339). The code was amended in 1935 to state that private prosecution was prohibited against "lineal ascendants and spouse." Article 321 of the current Taiwanese Criminal Procedure stipulates: "A private prosecution shall not be initiated against a lineal ascendant or spouse." Unlike Korea, however, Taiwan allows private prosecution (*sisu*).[60] This difference sets the meaning of Article 321 in Taiwanese law apart from that of Article 224 in Korean law.

The Korean law of Article 224 does not prohibit filing a criminal complaint against the spouse; prohibition applies only to accusing the spouse's lineal ascendants. In contrast, the Taiwanese law of Article 321 treats the spouse and the lineal ascendants on the same level. Here one can refer to a famous case decided in 2003 by the Council of Justices in the Judicial Chamber (*Sifa Yuan*) of Taiwan (equivalent to the Supreme Court and the Constitutional Court combined in Korea). In this case, the Council observed that Article 321 was intended to prevent antagonistic fights between husband and wife from taking place, face-to-face, in the courtroom during the private prosecution proceedings.[61] Because Taiwan allows private prosecution, highly awkward and scandalous scenes could take place in public, where the children denounced their parents and the spouses accused each other in adversarial setting (*"duibu gong tang"*). Article 321 intended to avoid this problem. Harmonious family life and filial piety might certainly have been taken into account, but the main focus of the Taiwanese law was different from that of the Korean law.

In Taiwan, as explained by the Judicial Council, while one is not allowed to institute private prosecution against the spouse, he or she is free to "initiate a criminal complaint" against the spouse, that is, to seek public prosecution under the law by filing a complaint with the prosecutor.[62] One can infer that in Taiwan the lineal descendant is prohibited from launching private prosecution against the lineal ascendant but he or she can file a criminal complaint with the prosecutor. It indicates that, unlike in the 2011 case in Korea, the Taiwanese prosecutor would not reject the lineal descendant's filing of a criminal complaint against the lineal ascendant on the grounds of Article 321, and that the Taiwanese court would not dismiss the lineal descendant's petition for non-compliance.

In Korea, too, Article 224 does not prevent the prosecutor from charging the ascendants for crimes committed against their descendants. This was one of the main arguments of the justices of the Constitutional Court who found the law constitutional in the 2011 case. Here, one may take note of an interesting case decided in 2012. [63] The husband was charged and found guilty for fraud, forgery of private documents, and other crimes. The wife had filed a complaint against him. The husband filed a constitutional petition with the Constitutional Court, challenging the validity of Articles 224 and 235 of the Criminal Procedure. He claimed that, as long as the legislative purpose of these provisions was to promote and enhance the basic values of Korea's social ethics and the Confucian cultural tradition, excluding the spouse from the protected persons from prosecution violated the principle of equality under Article 11 and also Article 36(1) that guaranteed the freedom of marriage and family life.

This creative argument was rejected by the Constitutional Court. The Court noted that the crimes that the petitioner was charged with did not require complaint by the victim. In the case of crimes other than *antragsverbrechen*, "*koso* and *kobal* are elements-in-fact of investigation, and prosecution can be initiated" by the state regardless of Articles 224 and 235. [64] Therefore, the question of which groups of people were prohibited from filing complaint under those provisions did not become an issue for constitutional adjudication. For example, whether only the son was prohibited from filing complaint or whether both the son and the spouse were prohibited from doing so did not make a difference.

The pertinence of this case for our purposes is that the Constitutional Court grounded its argument on the fact that the prosecutor could charge the criminal offender no matter whether he or she was a lineal ascendant or the spouse of the victim. In other words, the Court downplayed the practical effects of Articles 224 and 235. In reality, however, once the prosecutor has decided not to prosecute under those provisions, the chances for the victim to challenge that decision successfully become slim. The daughter in the 2011 case experienced this difficulty. Sometimes it was the state itself that was deterred from prosecuting the offender because of Articles 224 and 235. An interesting case from the 1970s illustrates this point. [65] The wife had an affair. When it was discovered by the husband, she poisoned him to death. Because the crime of adultery required the complaint by the victim (in this case the deceased husband), the prosecutor designated, under Article 225 of the Criminal Procedure, the son of the couple as the party to file a complaint against his mother and her lover for adultery.[66] In 1979 the Supreme Court dismissed the charge of adultery because under Article 224 the son was not allowed to file a complaint against his mother. The situation was different from the one in which the surviving siblings of the victim could file a complaint for adultery.[67] This case reveals that the legal effect of the prohibition of complaints by lineal descendants may not be as limited as has been contended in the controlling opinion of the Constitutional Court in 2011.

One of the main arguments of the justices in 2011 who found Article 224 constitutional was that the potential harm from limiting the rights of the descendants was significantly reduced because of the enactment of the special laws on sexual crimes and domestic violence. These laws created a new classification among the victims of crimes committed by the ascendants: one group of victims who were allowed to file complaints and the other group of victims who were not. Article 224, when enacted in 1954, had used a different classification: it distinguished the victims of a crime who were lineal descendants of the alleged perpetrators from the victims of the same crime who were not lineal descendants of the alleged perpetrators. As the state started punishing sexual crimes and domestic violence crimes committed by lineal ascendants, the operating classification scheme of Article 224 changed. The original classification, separating the lineal descendants from the ordinary victims, was replaced by a new classification, separating the victims of sexual and domestic violence crimes from the victims of other crimes.[68] This means that the current classification no longer has direct relevance to achieving the original legislative purpose of promoting filial piety. The enactment of the special laws evinced the state's acknowledgment that the necessity to punish the perpetrators of sexual crimes and domestic violence crimes outweighed the significance of the ideal of filial piety.[69] The controlling opinion of the 2011 case may have paid insufficient attention to this changing legal consciousness.

The reasoning in the controlling opinion amounted to the following: in the case of the victim of sexual crimes and domestic violence filial piety has to give in; in the case of the victim of other crimes, like false testimony as in the case before the Court, the victim should endure the injury for the sake of filial piety. Filial piety has now become a relative, situational virtue. Or, differently put, while the ideal of filial piety remains intact, the relationship between the legislative purpose based on that universal ideal and the means to achieve that legislative goal became tenuous.[70] When there are several means to achieve the same legislative purpose, the state must choose the means that limits basic rights the least. The most serious form of restricting basic rights is to deprive one of the very opportunities to test the boundaries of those rights.

In Korea, as reiterated above, the prosecutor always has the right to press charges. Article 224 notwithstanding, the state can still conduct investigations and prosecute the offender. Only in crimes that require the victim's complaint, the prosecutor cannot launch judicial proceedings.[71] Then what is the practical consequence of not allowing the lineal descendant to file a complaint? When a complaint is filed and the state decides not to indict the alleged offender, the prosecutor notifies the complainant of that decision in accordance with the Prosecutorial Regulations of Cases Management.[72] In case of crimes allegedly committed by lineal ascendants, the prosecutor's office refers to the regulation Article 69(3)(5), which states: "complaints in contravention of Article 224 and Article 235 of Criminal Procedure . . . are dismissed." This regulation has been routinely interpreted that the prosecutor should not prosecute the lineal ascendants when the victims are the lineal descendants, but for exceptional circumstances. One notes here that what is at issue is the prosecutor's refusal to investigate the evidence citing this internal regulation.

If the prosecutor makes an independent determination whether to prose-cute on the basis of the substantive merit of the case, instead of pro forma reference to Article 224, there seems to be little practical effect for Article 224 in the Criminal Procedure, other than its underlying purpose for uphold-ing filial piety. When the Constitutional Court in 2011 defended restriction of the descendants' rights by resorting to the authority of the traditional laws of filial piety, they seemed to obscure the nature of the old laws and as a result skewed the constitutional evaluation of the modern laws.

If the Chosŏn law punishing the act of accusing the senior members in the family did not really center on the goal of extolling love and respect toward the senior family members, one may ask whether there were any other laws that possibly better reflected that ideal. One can point out the laws in the Chosŏn codes that allowed the hiding of the crime of the family members. Under this system, called the system of "family relations for mutual tolera-tion and concealment" (*ch'injok sangyongŭn che*), one was not required to report to the authorities the crimes of his family members, with the exception of treason or rebellion. The son who accused his parents was considered a most depraved creature and severely punished, but the son who concealed the crime of his parents and relatives was praised.[73] Unlike the *kojonjang* provi-sion, the laws concerning providing asylum to criminal family members covered all the family members regardless of the senior-junior status. This system of mutual hiding of the offenses within the family seems to be closer to the ideal of filial piety or familial piety. Still, one notes that the cases of rebellion or treason were clearly excluded from these laws. When the result of an offense affected the stability of society or the state, there was no room for the virtue of shielding the loved ones from the wrath of the state.

Another tradition that emphasized tight relationships among the family members concerned theft within the family. In Chosŏn, theft between family members was treated with more leniency than theft between strangers. Under the Confucian moral viewpoint, stealing a relative's property was regarded as less blamable than stealing someone else's property.[74] These regulations illustrated that the nature of blood relations was integral in determining the seriousness of the crime and the punishment.[75] These sentiments survived in modern law. In modern Korean law, a person who commits theft against his or her lineal relations, spouse, co-habiting relatives, or co-habiting family members and their spouses is exempt from punishment.[76] Theft against the relatives other than the above can be prosecuted only upon the complaint of the victim.[77] These special treatments are applied to almost every crime relating to property, such as larceny, fraud, extortion, embezzlement, and the crime of receiving stolen property.[78]

The Constitutional Court in 2013 upheld enhanced punishment for the crimes committed against lineal ascendants. In modern Korean law, enhanced punishment is prescribed to murder, assault, inflicting bodily injury, abandonment, abuse, false arrest, false imprisonment, and intimidation by the lineal descendants of the lineal ascendants. Altogether there are thirteen law provisions that impose enhanced punishment for crimes against lineal ascendants. These are the laws that were also adopted from traditional law codes based on Confucian ideology. Japan previously had the aggravated punishment laws but in 1973 the Japanese Supreme Court struck down the parricide law.[79] Subsequently the Japanese Diet comprehensively abolished in 1995 all the provisions that imposed aggravated punishment on the crimes against lineal ascendants. The same year, the Korean National Assembly reviewed the parricide provision, but refused to abolish it and only reduced the penalty.[80] Taiwan maintains aggravated penalty provisions similar to those in Korea. Normally the punishment for a lineal descendant for a crime against the ascendant is increased up to one half of the punishment for the same offense against a stranger.[81]

There is a measure of truth in the assertion that the continued existence of the aggravated penalty provisions in Korea and Taiwan is a reflection of each country's professed Confucian culture, especially the postulation of filial piety as the essence of the national identity. As seen above, the prohibition of accusation of lineal ascendants still sets Korea apart from Taiwan. A country's criminal law is an expression of its cultural and social consciousness. For Korea, perhaps more so than Taiwan, these provisions formed a part of its nationalistic agenda, persisting in the efforts to separate its laws from those of Japan and resisting reforms that took place in Japan.[82]

Whatever the consideration, the existence of the laws against lineal descendants in Korea has become increasingly difficult to justify. The Chosŏn models of Articles 224 and 235 were grounded on the double notions of subordination to the political order and the perpetuation of the family order. In these laws, there was no conceptual distinction between subjection and loyalty to the ruler and submission and obedience to the senior members in the family. Today few would contend with a straight face that laws demanding unconditional subordination to the ruler are consistent with a liberal and democratic constitution based on popular sovereignty. The Constitutional Court was understandably less than willing to invalidate as unconstitutional the law provisions that had been enshrined in the traditional codes, but seeking justification from historical examples may have its limits.

CONCLUSION

This article has suggested that certain filial piety–based criminal laws in modern Korea, when stripped of historical trappings, prove lacking in justification. Confucian filial piety represents a particular vision of morality. It seems important to recall that Confucianism is an ideology premised on inequality between male and female and between the senior and the junior. This precept is bound to conflict with the principle of equality in modern liberal constitutions. It is little disputed that hereditary elites in the Chosŏn dynasty paid scrupulous attention to order and hierarchy and that Confucian rituals and concepts played an important role in consolidating and perpetuating the hereditary status. When this historical background is taken into consideration, the overwhelming weight of the seemingly obligatory consideration of morality in filial piety–based law subsides. The burden of tradition should not obscure an objective ascertainment of the nation's laws.

A related and potentially broader issue is the relationship between criminal law and the sphere of morality and ethics. Is it the proper role of criminal law and the legitimate exercise of the state power to impose morality through legal sanctions? The legal disadvantages imposed on the lineal descendants result from their status in family, solely determined by birth. Could inequality born of status in the family be seen as part of inequality caused by social status as listed in Article 11 of the constitution?

Legal consciousness in society evolves, and so does—should—the state's criminal justice policy. The direction of changing legal perception is not always predictable. In the past, sexual crimes and domestic violence had not been given serious consideration, partly under the shadow of the state's conventional non-intervention policy in family matters. But the enactment of the special laws in the last couple of decades clearly exhibited the changes in society's attitude to the issues. In 2002, the Constitutional Court upheld Article 304 of the criminal law which criminalized obtaining sexual intercourse under the pretense of marriage. Seven years later in 2009, however, the Court reversed its position and declared it unconstitutional—an excessive interference in the private sphere by the state. [83] The line between public and private realms constantly shifts. Meanwhile, the long debate over the constitutionality of the adultery law under Article 241 of the Criminal Code still draws out.[84]

The jurisprudence of the prohibition of filing criminal complaints against lineal ascendants illustrates the unfolding uncertainty of the filial piety laws in Korea. Not many people in Korea would disagree with the view that accusing one's own father or mother with a crime contravenes the ordinary sense of morality and propriety. Still, there is a growing opinion that it is a weak justification for denying the descendant victim's exercise of right. Even if the current law were constitutionally struck down and the descendant were allowed to file a complaint against his or her parent, it would not be an easy exercise of right because that person would face serious ethical criticisms from society.

The boundaries between legal and moral issues are not always clear-cut. At least, it may as well be good to remember that preserving the value of genuine love and respect for parents need not be in conflict with promoting liberal-democratic constitutional ideals. A candid consideration of the interplay of Confucianism and constitutionalism in modern Korea can help a more accurate understanding of Korean law and legal history.

NOTES

* The writing of this chapter was undertaken during my fellowship at the Netherlands Institute for Advanced Study (2013–2014).

1. Article 11, section 1.

2. The constitutional debate has focused on whether the statutes grounded on the ancient law codes and practices permeated with Confucian ideology encroached upon the principles of equality (Article 11), property rights (Article 23), and gender equality (Article 36). The right to pursue happiness (Article 10) has also been frequently invoked: "All citizens shall be assured of human dignity and worth and have the right to pursue happiness. It shall be the duty of the State to confirm and guarantee the fundamental and inviolable human rights of individuals." See Marie Seong-Hak Kim, *Law and Custom in Korea: Comparative Legal History* (Cambridge: Cambridge University Press, 2012), pp. 285, 288–92.

3. Constitutional Court [Const. Ct], 2001Hŏn-Ga9 to 15 (consolidated); 2004Hŏn-Ga5, Feb. 3, 2005. The Civil Code was revised in March 2005 and the *hoju* system was abolished effective January 1, 2008.

4. Constitutional Court [Const. Ct], 1997Hŏn-Ga6 to 13 (consolidated), July 16, 1997.

5. The recent cases upholding the ritual property succession provision in the Civil Code illustrated a cautious jurisprudential approach to tradition-based laws. Marie Seong-Hak Kim, "In the Name of Custom, Culture, and the Constitution: Korean Customary Law in Flux," *Texas International Law Journal* 48 (2013), pp. 357–91.

6. Constitutional Court [Const. Ct], 2008Hŏn-Ba56, Feb. 24, 2011.

7. Constitutional Court [Const. Ct], 2011Hŏn-Ba267, July 25, 2013.

8. Constitutional Court [Const. Ct], 2000Hŏn-Ba53, Mar. 28, 2002.

9. Pak Pyŏng-Ho, "Hyo yulli wa pŏp kyubŏmhwa wa kŭ sŭnggye," *Kŭnse ŭi pŏp kwa pŏp sasang* (Seoul: Chinwŏn, 1996), p. 508.

10. Ibid., p. 518.

11. For a survey of the Korean criminal procedure, see Kyoon Seok Cho, "The Current Situation and Challenges of Measures for Victims of Crime in the Korean Criminal Justice System," Resource Material Series No. 81 (2010), The 144th International Senior Seminar

Visiting Experts' Papers, pp. 76–96, available at www.unafei.or.jp/english/pdf/RS_No81/No81_10VE_Seok.pdf.

12. Yu Ki Ch'ŏn, *Hyŏngpŏphak (Kangnonkangŭi* I) (Seoul, 1980), pp. 30–31. The spouse refers to the legal spouse only, not the common-law marriage spouse. Most scholars agree that the lineal ascendants of the deceased or former spouse are not covered either under Articles 224 and 235 or under the aggravated punishment provisions.

13. The biological mother automatically becomes a lineal ascendant of her extramarital child. Supreme Court of Korea [S.Ct.], 86 To 1982, Nov. 11, 1986.

14. Supreme Court of Korea [S.Ct.], 66 To1483, Jan. 31, 1967.

15. Supreme Court of Korea [S.Ct.], 81 To 2466, Oct. 13, 1981.

16. Kim, *Law and Custom in Korea*, pp. 228–29.

17. Article 260 of the Criminal Procedure provides that the one who lawfully filed a complaint and received a notice from the prosecutor of non-prosecution can apply for a review of the prosecutor's decision by the Appeals Court of that jurisdiction.

18. Article 68(2) of the Constitutional Court Law.

19. For analysis of the 2011 case, see Nam Pok-Hyŏn, "Chikkye pisok ŭi chikkye chonsok e taehan koso kwŏn pakt'al ŭi wihŏnsŏng," *Hŏnpŏp hak yŏngu* 18 (2012), pp. 147–80; Pak Yong-Ch'ŏl, "Hyŏngsa pŏp sang chonsok kwa pisok ŭi ch'abyŏl chŏk ch'wigŭp e kwanhan yŏngu," *P'ihaeja hak yŏngu* 20 (2012), pp. 535–58; Chang Chin-Suk, "Chikkye chonsok koso kŭmji chohang kwa hyo sasang," *Hŏnpŏp hak yŏngu* 18 (2012), pp. 203–43; Son Tong-Kwŏn, "Hyŏngsa sosongpŏp sang chikkye chonsok e taehan koso (kobal) kŭmji kyujŏng ŭi wihŏnsŏng yŏbu," *Ilgam pŏphak* 22 (2012), pp. 272–97.

20. The Constitutional Court limited its review to Article 224 because the case concerned the restriction of *koso*, not *kobal* under Article 235.

21. "In general, for purposes of ascertaining violation of equality, the principle against arbitrariness is employed, but in those cases where the Constitution specially demands equality or where differential treatment causes a significant burden on the related fundamental rights of other individuals, the constitutional review shall be conducted using a strict standard of the principle of proportionality." [Const. Ct], 2008Hŏn-Ba56, Feb. 24, 2011, citing the following precedents: 98 Hŏn-Ma363, Dec. 23, 1999; 98 Hŏn-Ba33, Dec. 23, 1999; 97 Hŏn-Ga12, Aug. 31, 2000.

22. Under Article 113(1) of the Constitution and Article 23(2) of the Constitutional Court Law, a decision of the unconstitutionality of a law requires the concurrence of six justices or more.

23. The decisions upholding enhanced punishment for lineal descendants were less contentious: the 2002 ruling was unanimous; the 2013 case was a 7-2 decision. On the other hand, in 2010 the Constitutional Court found, in an 8-1 decision, that Article 818 of the Civil Code was incompatible with the constitution. This law excluded lineal descendants from the list of people who could file a claim for the annulment of bigamy. Constitutional Court [Const. Ct], 2009Hŏn-Ga8, July 29, 2010. The law was revised in 2012 to grant lineal descendants the same right as had been allowed the party, the spouse, the lineal ascendants, and certain blood relatives.

24. Examples of *ch'inkochoe* include rape and slander.

25. [Const. Ct.], 2008Hŏn-Ba56, Feb. 24, 2011.

26. Ibid.

27. Ibid.

28. Ibid.

29. Ibid.

30. Supreme Court [S. Ct.], 93Mŭ119, May 24, 1994. See Kim, *Law and Custom in Korea*, pp. 278–79.

31. See notes 3 and 4.

32. Kim, *Law and Custom in Korea*, pp. 289–92.

33. Ibid., pp. 21–22.

34. *Yŏkchu Kyŏngguk Taejŏn*, trans. Han U-Kŭn et al. (Seoul: Hanguk Chŏngsin Munhwa Yŏnguwŏn, 1985), p. 437.

35. Cited from Pak, "Hyo yulli wa pŏp kyubŏmhwa wa kŭ sŭnggye," p. 516.

36. *Tae Myŏng Yul Chikhae* [The Korean Great Ming Code Directly Explicated] was promulgated in 1395.

37. *The Great Ming Code / Da Ming lü*, translated and introduced by Jiang Yong-lin (Seattle: University of Washington Press, 2005), p. 198.

38. *The Great Ming Code / Da Ming lü*, p. 18.

39. Ibid., p. 198.

40. Ibid.

41. Pak, "Hyo yulli wa pŏp kyubŏmhwa wa kŭ sŭnggye," pp. 510–11.

42. *Sok Taejŏn* (Seoul: Pŏpchech'ŏ, 1965), p. 286; *Taejŏn t'ongp'yŏn* (Seoul: Pŏpchech'ŏ, 1963), p. 613; *Taejŏn hoet'ong* (Seoul: Hanguk Kojŏn Kuggyŏk Wiwŏnhoe, 1960), pp. 558–59. Cited from Tae Hee Lee, "The Impact of the Family on Criminal Law in the Yi Dynasty," in *Introduction to the Law and Legal System of Korea*, ed. Sang-Hyun Song (Seoul: Kyung Mun Sa Pub. Co., 1983), p. 1060.

43. *The Great Ming Code / Da Ming lü*, p. 198.

44. Françoise Lauwaert, "Framing the Family in Late Imperial China: An Anthropological Glance at Some Family Cases in the Conspectus of Penal Cases (*Xing'an huilan*)," in *Law and Anthropology: Current Legal Issues*, eds. Michael Freeman and David Napier (Oxford: Oxford University Press, 2009), p. 526.

45. *The Great Ming Code / Da Ming lü*, p. 200.

46. Pak, "Hyo yulli wa pŏp kyubŏmhwa wa kŭ sŭnggye," p. 509.

47. *The Great Ming Code / Da Ming lü*, p. 200.

48. *Yŏkchu Kyŏngguk Taejŏn*, p. 437.

49. Ibid.

50. Lauwaert, "Framing the Family in Late Imperial China," p. 530.

51. Jérôme Bourgon, "Lapsus de Laïus: Entre régicide et parricide, l'introuvable meurtre du père," Extrême-Orient Extrême-Occident, hors-série (2012), pp. 313–39, available at extremeorient.revues.org/229.

52. Ibid., p. 320, p. 330.

53. Jérôme Bourgon, "Un juriste nommé Yuan Mei. Son influence sur l'évolution du droit à la fin des Qing," *Etudes chinoises* 14, no. 2 (1995), p. 136.

54. [Const. Ct], 2008 Hŏn-Ba 56, Feb. 24, 2011.

55. Cho Chi-Man, "*Kyŏngguk Taejŏn Hyŏngjŏn kwa Tae Myŏng Yul*," 26, n81; Sin Tong-Un, *Hyŏngsa Sosong Pŏp*, 3rd ed. (Seoul: Pŏmmunsa, 2005), p. 87.

56. Pak, "Hyo yulli wa pŏp kyubŏmhwa wa kŭ sŭnggye," p. 517.

57. Taishō Criminal Procedure Law (Taishō Kenji sosyōhō), also known as the Old Criminal Procedure Law, available at www.geocities.jp/lucius_aquarius_magister/T11HO075.html.

58. *The Great Ming Code / Da Ming lü*, p. 198.

59. Article 230 of the current Japanese Criminal Procedure, equivalent to Article 223 of the Korean Criminal Procedure, states that the victim of a crime can file a complaint. There are no limitations due to family status.

60. Chapter 2 of the Taiwanese Criminal Procedure deals with private prosecution. Article 319 states, in part: "The victim of a crime may file a private prosecution."

61. See the decision of the Council of Justices in the Judicial Chamber of Taiwan, J.Y. No. 569, rendered on Dec. 12, 2003. The issue was whether under Article 321 of the Criminal Procedure an individual was prohibited from instituting private prosecution against the person who had allegedly committed adultery with his or her spouse. The Council held that Article 321 "represents a reasonable restriction imposed to maintain the personal and ethical relationship between husband and wife and does not go beyond the scope defined by the Legislature at its discretion," but ruled that one could initiate private prosecution against the partner of the adulterous spouse, even if one could not initiate private prosecution against the adulterous spouse. The text is available at www.judicial.gov.tw/constitutionalcourt/p03_02_printpage.asp?expno=569; English translation at www.judicial.gov.tw/constitutionalcourt/en/p03_01_printpage.asp?expno=569.

62. Ibid.

63. [Const. Ct], 2011Hŏn-Ba121, July 26, 2012.

64. Ibid.

65. See *Kyŏnghyang Sinmun*, June 19, 1979, p. 7 ("The son cannot be assigned the right to file a complaint against the mother who committed adultery").

66. On the death of the victim, the victim's legal representative, surviving spouse, lineal relatives, or siblings may file a complaint, if such complaint is not against the expressed intent of the demised victim (Article 225 of Criminal Procedure).

67. See [S. Ct], 67To878, Aug. 29, 1967.

68. Nam Pok-Hyŏn, "Chikkye pisok ŭi chikkye chonsok e taehan koso kwŏn pakt'al," p. 170.

69. Ibid.

70. Ibid., p. 173.

71. See note 24 and the accompanying text.

72. Kŏmch'al Sakŏn Samu Kyuch'ik.

73. Pak, "Hyo yulli wa pŏp kyubŏmhwa wa kŭ sŭnggye," pp. 518–20; Lee, "The Impact of the Family," p. 1068.

74. Sŏ Il-Kyo, *Chosŏn wangcho hyŏngsa chedo ŭi yŏngu* (Seoul: Pakyŏngsa, 1968), p. 99.

75. Ibid., p. 228.

76. Article 328(1). See Lee, "The Impact of the Family," p. 1066.

77. Article 328(2).

78. Articles 344, 354, and 361 of the Criminal Code.

79. Supreme Court of Japan Decision of April 4, 1973, Shōwa 45(A) 1310. See Charles Qu, "Parricide, Equality and Proportionality: Japanese Courts' Attitudes towards the Equality Principle as Reflected in *Aizawa v. Japan*," *Murdoch University Electronic Journal of Law* 8 (2001), available at www.austlii.edu.au/au/journals/MurUEJL/2001/13.html.

80. See Yu, *Hyŏngpŏphak*, pp. 33–34, note 896a, citing the doctrinal debate that took place in postwar Japan before Japan abolished the penal law provisions imposing enhanced punishment for crimes by lineal descendants. Much of the same argument is voiced in contemporary discussions in Korea.

81. For example, see Criminal Code of the Republic of China, Articles 271–72, 277–78, 280–81, 294–95, 302–3.

82. See Kim, *Law and Custom in Korea*, chapter 8.

83. [Const. Ct], 99Hŏn-Ba40, Oct. 31, 2002 (finding Article 304 constitutional); [Const. Ct], 2008Hŏn-Ba58, Nov. 26, 2009 (finding the same law unconstitutional).

84. See the following cases: [Const. Ct], 89Hŏn-Ma82, Sept. 10, 1990; 90Hŏn-Ga70, Mar. 11, 1993; 2000Hŏn-Ba60, Oct. 25, 2001; 2007Hŏn-Ga17, Oct. 30, 2008.

Chapter Three

Locating Feminism beyond Gender and Culture

A Case of the Family-Head System in South Korea

Hee-Kang Kim

On February 3, 2005, the Constitutional Court in South Korea ruled that Article 778, Article 781(1), and Article 826(3) of the Civil Code, which constitute the core of the family registry, or the family-head (*hoju*) system, were incompatible with the constitution.[1] Under the system, all citizens of South Korea belong to the family (*ka*), wherein a child belongs to a father's family, a wife belongs to a husband's family, a family-head represents the family, and the eldest son has priority to succeed to the family-headship. South Korean feminists had criticized the family-head system, arguing that it represented a typical patriarchy under which women were discriminated against in family relationships. In contrast, Confucians, or the advocates of traditional Korean culture, had contended that the family-head system as a Korean cultural practice and custom should be preserved regardless of its patriarchal nature. In the decision, the Constitutional Court held that the family-head system violated the constitutional provisions concerning gender equality and human dignity in marital and family life because the system supposedly "discriminated against women on the basis of the gender-role ideology that it presupposed."[2] Upon the decision, feminist groups issued a statement to welcome the ruling as a breakthrough in the history of South Korean feminist movements, while Confucian groups issued a statement against the ruling, arguing that the abolishment of the current system might lead to the collapse of the family system itself.[3] On March 2, 2005, the National Assembly passed the amendment of the Civil Code, which eliminated the provisions of the family-head system. The amendment was effective on January 1, 2008.

This court decision on the family-head system in South Korea provides an important insight into the topic to which current feminist scholarship has paid special attention: a dilemma between gender universalism and cultural relativism. Defenders of gender universalism claim that gender equality is a universal norm applicable to diverse cultures. If indigenous cultural practices and customs fail to meet the universal norm of gender equality, they should be either recast or eliminated. In contrast, proponents of cultural relativism contend that there is no universal norm of gender equality across different cultures. Because the norms of gender equality are fundamentally rooted in particular cultures, each culture is a unique designator of its norm of gender. Interestingly, the controversy between the feminists and the Confucians in the above case of the family-head system resembles much the gender-culture dilemma.

In this paper, however, I will argue that the binary understanding of gender and culture, which is a source of the dilemma, inadequately accounts for the case of the Korean family-head system. By analyzing the feminist family-law reform movement and by focusing on the feminist logic and the feminist rhetoric developed in the movement, I will show how the relation-ship between gender and culture is not simply oppositional. Although my aim here is not to disregard tensions and conflicts arising from views on gender and culture, whether these views belong to the feminists or to the Confucians, I will argue that any rigorous comprehensive analysis of the case must account for contextual mechanisms moving beyond the gender-culture binary. If then, the demand of gender equality and the quest of preserving culture can be compatible with each other.

For this purpose, first I will examine a gender-culture dilemma in contem-porary feminist scholarship. Second, I will outline the debate over the abol-ishment of the family law's family-head system in South Korea, primarily in regard to the confrontation between the feminists and the Confucians. Third, by analyzing feminist logic and feminist rhetoric in three contexts (post-colonial, post-Confucian, and neo-colonial contexts), I will show how the binary framework of gender and culture is improper for a rigorous treatment of the feminist movement and thus why such a treatment must make room for contextual examination. Dialoguing with the history and the reality of the context, finally, I will articulate some significant features of South Korean feminism.

POSING A DILEMMA: GENDER VS. CULTURE

In contemporary feminist scholarship, scholars have addressed the apparent inconsistency between the demand for gender equality as a universal norm and the demand for cultural difference as a relativist conviction. In this section, I will examine each position's arguments and their contribution to the creation of a gender-culture dilemma. This framework of gender universalism and cultural relativism will be a theoretical basis for analyzing the debate over the family-head system in the next section.

Some people (often Western feminists, although not exclusively) argue that women's issues have important cross-cultural similarities and that generalized cross-cultural standards must precede the realization of gender equality.[4] In making her "defense of [gender] essentialism," Susan Okin claims that the situations of women in different cultures are "not qualitatively *different*."[5] She goes on to state that because many features of gender inequality can be generalized, theories developed in Western contexts can apply to women situated in different cultural contexts. There are "similarities in specifics of these inequalities, in their cases and their effects, although often not in their extent or severity."[6] That is, women's issues are cross-culturally similar, and the differences are only of degree. Okin argues that, compared to women in Western culture, women in non-Western culture suffer gender injustice that is similar in form but more pronounced.

Nonetheless, it should be mentioned that these scholars do not dismiss cultural difference. Their argument is not that all women's questions generated from different cultures are merely identical. They contend that the ideas of women's freedom and equality, rather than being uniquely Western, are universal values—that these ideas are applicable to diverse issues sensitive to cultural differences.[7] Along this line, consider Martha Nussbaum's proposal of the capabilities approach. Nussbaum introduces the concept of capability as a universal value applicable to all women (and all human beings) in different nations and cultures for the purpose of challenging gender inequality and ultimately guaranteeing a basic quality of life for all human beings.[8] On her account, there exists the possibility of "a reasonable pluralism in specification." "The capabilities approach urges us to see common needs, problems, and capacities, but it also reminds us that each person and group faces these problems in a highly concrete context."[9]

Indeed, the issue of greatest concern to these scholars is the violation of women's equality under the name of culture. They warn that "cultural justification" could help violate the universal norms of gender equality and of women's human rights.[10] They point to cases where respect for cultural difference has served to justify a denial of women's rights. For example, although many countries—in support of women's rights—officially signed onto and ratified the Universal Declaration of Women's Rights (1967) and the Convention on Elimination of All Forms of Discrimination against Women (1979), some of these states in fact restricted women's rights and justified these restrictions on the basis of the states' long-standing cultural or religious gender inequality. Worried about the possible untoward effects of cultural justification on women's rights, universal-norm feminists claim that human rights—not women's rights—should be the basis of gender equality.[11] This agenda characterizes the Program for Action proposed in the Fourth World Conference on Women, held in Beijing (1995). The program stipulates that human rights and fundamental freedoms should be promoted and protected by states in spite of their different political, economic, and cultural systems (Covenant for the New Millennium).[12]

In contrast to universal-norm feminists, some people (often non-Western feminists, although not exclusively) reject the gender essentialist view and support the culture-specific perspective. They criticize the gender essentialist idea because it totalizes the category of women as an ahistorical and homogeneous unity: women are often depicted as Western, white, and middle-class. According to cultural-relativist feminists, the gender essentialist concept regards non-Western culture as stagnant, backward, and oppressive and people in those cultures as childlike, gullible, and lacking in agency: women in non-Western cultures are usually read as being "ignorant, poor, uneducated, tradition-bound, domestic, family-oriented, victimized," whereas women in Western cultures are usually portrayed "as educated, as modern, as having control over their own bodies and sexualities and the freedom to make their own decisions."[13] Again, according to cultural-relativist feminists, gender essentialism is the product of chiefly Western scholars and amounts to cultural imperialism under which people misjudge and underestimate non-Western culture on the basis of Western cultural standards.[14]

Cultural-relativist feminists subscribe to the principle of cross-cultural incommensurability.[15] These feminists argue that our knowledge of gender equality and women's equality is not "culture-free" but inevitably conditioned by dominant cultures; therefore, cultural difference merits serious consideration.[16] In this school of thought, cultural relativism is considered to be "a weapon against intellectual tyranny" of gender essentialism and cultural imperialism.[17] The declaration goes something like this: my culture is different from yours, and my culture's ideas deserve your respect. Further, cultural relativists emphasize the possibility of developing culturally rooted authentic brands of feminism. Non-Western patriarchal culture itself has contained sources of feminism that were uninfluenced by Western missionaries or by imported foreign values. Women in non-Western culture are not all simply subjugated by patriarchal cultural traditions; these women are also empowered within their culture.[18]

So far I have examined the basic arguments of gender universalism and cultural relativism. I will discuss South Korea's family-head system at the crux of this gender-culture quandary. In addition to the family-head system, such non-Western cultural practices as female circumcision, polygamy, female infanticide, arranged and child marriage, and bride burning are also frequently discussed at the center of the quandary. Consider the case of female circumcision. For gender essentialists, it is viewed as one of the "cruelest" and "most oppressive" practices that "brand" women, and thus its abolishment is an urgent objective.[19] In contrast, cultural relativists point to the harm done by Western feminists who oppose the practice, rather than the harm done to non-Western women who perform it.[20] Given the situation that the "bizarre" practice of Jews' male circumcision has been normalized in Anglo-American culture, for example, Sander Gilman claims that not the abolition but the accommodation of it through its medicalization is a solution.[21]

In short, as Kathy Rudy points out, the binary view of gender and culture creates a dilemma under which cultural sensitivity leads to moral indifference, while cultural insensitivity leads to universalizing essentialism.[22] Indeed, there have been some feminist efforts to resolve this dilemma between the sameness in gender and the difference in culture.[23] Although my aim here is not to resolve the dilemma, in the rest of the paper I will show why and how the binary understanding of gender and culture as a source of the dilemma is ultimately problematic. Let me first describe the case.

THE DEBATE OVER THE FAMILY-HEAD SYSTEM: AN OVERVIEW

For approximately fifty years, South Korean feminists and South Korean Confucians debated the abolishment of the family-head system.[24] The feminists argued that the system was a primary factor in the perpetuation of South Korean gender inequality, so South Korea should eliminate the related provisions from the country's family law. The Confucians, however, claimed that South Korea should preserve the system in order to preserve all of Korea's "beautiful and good customs" (*mip'ung yangsok*) insofar as the family law was a codification of Confucian family morals. In this section, I will review this heated debate between the South Korean feminists and the South Korean Confucians.

According to the feminists, the principal problem of the family-head system is that the system regulates family relationships in a patriarchal and patrilineal way. The system substantially limits the legal power of women inside as well as outside family structure. Under the system, a married woman is supposed to enter into the husband's family. Given the family-register (*hojŏk*) system based on the family-head system, a married woman must abandon her own family register and enlist herself in her husband's family register. When children are born in the marriage, they are also automatically enlisted in the father's family register. And the system prioritizes the eldest son as successor to the family-headship.[25] From the feminist perspective, such features of the system indicate that the relationship between husband and wife is substantially unequal throughout a family's cycles. Even though the provisions of the constitution guarantee gender equality, the family law violates these provisions, designating the man as a patriarchal head of the family in most business and property transactions and legally legitimizing patrilineage. Simply put, "[T]he system legalizes the patrilineal succession of the family name and family register, patrilocal marriage, and the representation of the families by the patriarch."[26]

The feminists further observed that the system's patriarchal effects, going beyond family relationships, led to other social problems. Patrilineal succession in the family contributes, in South Korea, to generalized patriarchal relationships between males and females, to widespread son preference, to the high abortion rate of female fetuses, and to the related sex-ratio imbalance.[27] In particular, such issues as the high abortion rate of female fetuses and the imbalance in the sex ratio have drawn international media attention. A study revealed that, annually in South Korea, one out of every twelve female fetuses is aborted owing to its sex.[28] Given this estimate, it was expected that by the year 2010, there would be 400,000 more men of marrying age than women. The fact that more boys than girls are born in South Korea (in 1990, the sex ratio reached the level of 1.13) disgraces the country, which—along with China and India—has one of the highest such ratios of any country in the world.[29]

The feminists had been fighting to abolish the family-head system as early as the 1950s.[30] They asked for the elimination of it in the family law even before the original governmental bill was passed in the National Assembly in December 1957. Although some feminists supporting the reform made their voices heard even before the initial enactment of the law in 1960, it was not until the 1970s that South Korean feminists systematically organized themselves to reform the law. In June 1973, sixty-one women's organizations created a federation and launched the Pan-Women's Group for the Revision of the Family Law (PGR).[31] At the founding meeting, it was announced, as part of the federation's declaration, that because "women have suffered from the fetters of age-old traditions and customs," "any institutions that separate women from their humanity must be abolished" and that "institutional reform" was indispensable.[32] According to Yang, the feminists—by identifying tradition as women's "fetters"—grasped that tradition stood in opposition to gender equality.[33]

In July 1989, the feminists organized another large feminist union in order to revise the family law. Forty-one women's organizations forged an alliance, called the Women's Union for Revision of Family Law (WUR), that did not limit itself to the activities of the component feminist groups themselves. The WUR made an effort to attract the general public's attention and to mobilize widespread support. For instance, the WUR started a campaign to organize one million supporters whose combined efforts would publicize feminist goals and augment pro-reform pressures on representatives and officials. As a result of these feminist efforts, family law underwent three stages of revision between the 1950s and the 1980s. The third stage of revision in 1989 significantly weakened the right and duty of the family-head over family members and rendered the family-head system a nominal one, although it remained legal.[34] On the day when the National Assembly passed the legislation from the third stage of revision, Lee Tae-Young, a leading feminist lawyer and president of the WUR, announced, "Today, thirty-seven years of tenacious women's struggles have abolished the [long-standing and] high barriers of human discrimination. . . . [However] I regret very much that . . . the system of family-head remain[s]."[35]

In the 1990s and the 2000s, the feminist revision movement became more active. In 1997, the nationwide campaign for "using both parents' family name," supported by feminist groups, succeeded in re-attracting much attention from the general public as well as from mass media. In 2000, the Citizen Organization for the Abolition of the Family-head System, which was organized to strengthen and augment public support for the abolishment, presented a petition concerning this very issue to the National Assembly. Also, feminist groups recruited suitors from the public to institute a constitutional lawsuit and made systematic efforts to pressure Assembly members to revise the family law. The Ministry of Law, the Ministry of Gender Equality and Family, and Assembly members put together amended bills, which a subcommittee of the National Assembly's Judiciary Committee was reviewing when, in February 2005, the Constitutional Court ruled the family-head system unconstitutional.[36]

Opposed to such a feminist reform movement, the Confucians and other conservatives claimed that the family-head system must be preserved because it was one of Korea's "good and beautiful customs" that had lasted for almost a century. According to these critics, South Koreans should not abandon their precious cultural heritage and should, indeed, vigilantly preserve their own culture, which constitutional provisions guaranteed.[37] The Korean way of governing gender relationships is, according to the conservative critics, culturally and traditionally superior to the Western way and, thus, should remain uncorrupted, especially when the source of corruption comes from feminists' Western ideas. For example, a conservative asserted, allegedly borrowing from the words of Arnold Toynbee, that "the Korean family system is the best one for human beings in the world. I hope that the system is introduced to the West and is preserved eternally. We [the Western people] have lost the ideal family system like the Korean one since the nineteenth century."[38] In short, the conservatives sought to protect Korea's traditional moral and ethical system, which the provisions of South Korea's family law had codified.[39]

In 1975, shortly before the second revision of the family law, Confucian groups and other opponents of reform began to organize themselves to fight against the family-law revision. To this end, they formed the Committee for the Protection of the Family System. They carried on a campaign in which they claimed to have obtained the signatures of one million Confucians, which—in the form of an anti-reform petition—the campaign submitted to the National Assembly.[40] They declared that the amendment bill was an "evil" that would "ruin" Korean tradition and culture. Yi Byung-il, a member of a nationwide Confucian organization (*Yudohoe*), wondered "when we consider today's reality, which is better, Western material happiness or the spiritual happiness of the Korean family?"[41] The general point of interest here is that his question, as an indirect but obvious lamentation, runs counter to the feminist position at that time: whereas the PGR in the 1970s declared that the family-head system was an age-old tradition to be abolished because it hampered women's liberty and equality, the Confucian organization pro-claimed that the system should be preserved because it represented the super-ior spiritual value of Korea.

The second stage of revision in 1977 spurred Confucian groups to orga-nize a nationwide campaign against further reform. They continued to con-duct a signature campaign and began organizing mass rallies. The conserva-tives obtained notable support from 231 local Confucian temples (*hyanggyo*) and 261 branch organizations (*yurim*). The Confucian anti-reform movement enjoyed partial success when, in 1984 and 1986, the feminists' reform bills ended in failure and when, in 1989, the product of the third stage of revision preserved the family-head system.[42] Through the 1990s and until the Court's decision in 2005, Confucian groups made special efforts to draw public attention toward—and mobilize the public against—further reform. To this end, the groups called for a ten-million-signature campaign and publicly tonsured the group leaders as a sign of intensified resistance.[43]

According to a public-opinion poll conducted at the end of 2003, when the National Assembly considered the amended bill, 45.4 percent of those surveyed said that they favored the reform while 46.2 percent of those sur-veyed opposed it.[44] As I stated earlier, this decades-long controversy reached a turning point in 2005, when the Constitutional Court ruled the system unconstitutional and when the National Assembly passed the amended bill, which eliminated the family-head system in the Civil Code. Yet tensions between feminists and Confucians over the family-head system have contin-ued even after the Court's decision. The public and mass media are still able to witness the persisting confrontation.

FEMINIST LOGIC AND RHETORIC: AN ANALYSIS

So far, I have examined the controversy over the issue of South Korea's family-head system. Apparently it is a conflict between the feminists and the Confucians, between gender equality and traditional culture, and between gender universalism and cultural relativism. The relationship between the two camps appears antagonistic and nonnegotiable: as a foreign observer calls it, "a family feud for Confucians and women."[45] The controversy seems to end with a victory for the feminists.

I think that the abolishment of the family-head system can greatly enhance South Korean women's situation and can effectively challenge deeply rooted patriarchy in South Korea. My aim here is to argue that scholars of this hard-won feminist triumph cannot rigorously address the passage of family-law reform if they use, as their framework, the gender-culture binary. By closely examining the feminist logic and the feminist rhetoric developed in the reform movement, I show that gender is constructed by culture and that gender equality can exist within Confucian culture.

The Post-colonial Construction of Culture

Although proponents of the feminist struggle against the family-head system interpret age-old cultures and traditions as "fetters" from which women should be liberated, the feminist demand of gender equality is not a simple rejection of the value of culture. In fact, much of the debate between the feminists and the Confucians concerns the accurate identification of "genuine" or "authentic" Korean culture. That is, the feminists have rejected the family-head system not because it is an exponent of Korean culture but because (according to their view), ironically, it is not.

According to the feminists, the family-head system is not a family custom peculiar to Korea. It is a system that dates from the Japanese Meiji Civil Code during the period of Japanese colonization (1910–1945). Not until the Japanese occupation did Koreans have this kind of family system. After the Meiji Restoration (1868), Japan sought to establish a strong monarchical political structure, which prompted Japan to implement a new family system with which to control the population more effectively. In so doing, Japan instituted the family law (the Civil Code) under which the family-head represented the family, controlled the family, and held a position occupied by a succession of eldest sons through the generations. At the beginning of the Japanese occupation, Japanese colonizers did not attempt to apply their own family law to Korea. Yet, when Japan adopted its assimilation policy in the 1920s, the colonizers extended the Japanese Civil Code to the colonized Koreans. The Japanese colonizers used the family-head system to regulate the Korean population (for example, to draft colonized soldiers and to raise military supplies) and to manage the Japanese occupation.[46] The feminists claimed that the compulsory implementation of the Japanese family system distorted traditional Korean culture. Under the Confucian doctrine of the Chosŏn dynasty, a father's rights over children and a husband's rights over a wife were recognized, but these rights were not identical to those of the family-head. Also, there existed the succession systems over the rights of ritual heirship and the rights to inheritance of property, but there was no succession system, the one over the rights of the family-headship.[47] The feminists contended that, to implant the Japanese family system into the Korean social structure, Japanese colonizers falsely argued that a strong family-head system had already firmly existed in the Chosŏn's traditional law.[48]

The feminists further claimed that even though the Confucians considered the family-head system to be a part of Confucian tradition and not a Japanese import, Confucian tradition itself was not native to Korean culture. The Confucian influence in Korea's family-head system was an import from China and became part of Korean family customs in the early fifteenth century, during the Chosŏn dynasty. Moreover, it was not until the eighteenth century that Confucianism became the full-fledged proponent of the patriarchal and patrilineal family system. Before the eighteenth century, most of the native family customs that persisted throughout the Shilla and Koryŏ periods were neither particularly patriarchal nor particularly patrilineal.[49] The historian JaHyun Kim Haboush presented findings that concern Confucianization in Korea and that support the feminist claim: the bone rank system of the Shilla gave equal importance to both of the parents in determining a child's rank; in the Koryŏ and the early Chosŏn period, daughters inherited the same share of property as their brothers regardless of whether the daughters were married; and during the early Chosŏn period, women were recorded as heads of families.[50] The "patriarchal emphasis" is "very different from native Korean custom."[51] Given such historical findings, the feminists urged that the "unbridgeable" "gap between native tradition and Confucian etiquette" should be acknowledged and that many contemporary Koreans should be awakened from the "mistaken belief that patriarchal family traditions have existed in Korea for thousands of years."[52]

In fact, what feminists actually undertook was a project to clarify and to investigate Korean family tradition, one that is distinct from Japanese or Chinese family traditions. I think, as Yang Hyunah rightly points out, that this feminist logic (as well as the Confucian responses) essentializes the tradition-culture concept and lacks historicization. A more rigorous, more encompassing approach to the concept would treat culture and tradition "as a historical product, ceaselessly reformulated within complex political, economic, and cultural traditions, rather than as unchangeable traits of a nation."[53] That is, the feminist search for authentic Korean culture problematically takes what Uma Narayan calls the "package notion of culture."[54] In

Narayan's account, cultures are not like "neatly wrapped packages, sealed off from each other, possessing sharply defined edges or contours, and having distinctive contents that differ from those of other 'cultural packages.'"[55] Cultures are indeed constructed products,[56] and the boundaries and the labeling among cultures, such as Korean, Japanese, and Chinese cultures, are also constructed.[57] Cultures depend on a "complex discursive process of change," historically informed and contextually sensitive.[58]

My purpose here, however, is to do more than to point out the problematized notion of culture that the participants of the debate employ. I intend, also, to capture the underlying impetus for the feminist effort to identify Korean culture. In the family-law reform movement, the main feminist concern was precisely this effort. For the feminists, both the issue of whether Korean culture is egalitarian and the issue of whether it is indeed compatible with the feminist demand for gender equality seem to be secondary ones. The primary issue is twofold: what Korean culture is and whether such Korean culture is authentic. I argue that this feminist discourse of culture has to do with the colonial legacy of Korea. As many studies on post-colonialism show, colonized nations and people in such nations have participated in the "politics of tradition formation."[59] Narayan states,

> Anticolonial struggles for national independence in many Third World countries not only rejected the legitimacy of Western colonial rule but also often constructed a nationalist political identity by contrasting the indigenous "culture" and "its values" to those of the West, calling for a rejection of the latter. This valorization of the values and practices of "the indigenous culture" of the colony was often a response to colonial attempts to eradicate or regulate customs and practices in the colonies that Western colonial governments found unacceptable or inexpedient.[60]

The colonies rejected "foreign imports" and "Westernized agendas" and tried to discover their own "culturally authentic" values.[61] In so doing, the colonies made a distinction between Western cultures and non-Western cultures or between homeland cultures and foreign cultures. The cultural distinction was constructed as a way to deny colonial power.

In the family-law reform movement, the feminist discourse on culture greatly resembles anti-colonial discourses on culture. The feminist denial of a Japanese colonial heritage is a contemporary (post-colonial) denial of colonial power. Most feminist literature observes that the post-colonial discourse on culture is a tool chiefly of male nationalist elites and that the discourse has affected women negatively, an example thereof being the case of Indian *sati*.[62] This is because the discourse of culture often requires that supporters of the culture preserve the culture's "spiritual distinctiveness," including the culture's distinctive treatment of women, so often operating in the domestic realm. That is, preservation of an indigenous culture rests, in part, on the preservation of women's place in a mostly patriarchal culture. Therefore, it is not surprising that feminist scholars have criticized the masculine and patriarchal nature of post-colonial discourse, arguing that the discourse fuels gender inequality. In this paper, I am arguing that the case of South Korea's family-head system provides a different story. The feminist logic developed in the abolishment of the family-head system engages in the post-colonial discourse of constructing culture, and this engagement has positively served the feminist cause. It is not the case here that the pursuit of gender equality and an embrace of traditional culture are incompatible. [63]

The Post-Confucian Interpretation of Gender Equality

The South Korean Confucians criticized the South Korean feminists by arguing that the abolishment of the family-head system would lead to the destruction of the family system itself; the destruction of the family system would entail the abandonment of ethical and moral values of human beings. The Confucians deplored the possibility that "we Koreans would become animals like dogs and pigs" if the family-head system were abolished. [64] The feminists responded to this Confucian critique by arguing that gender equality in the family would not deny other Confucian family values and that the family rearrangement achieved by the abolishment of the family-head system would, indeed, help to preserve the family, a core institution of Confucianism. In short, they argued, the feminist pursuit of gender equality does not necessarily contradict the values of Confucianism.

The feminists rejected the family-head system because it violated the principle of male-female equality, in particular the egalitarian relationship between a wife and a husband in the family structure. [65] It is true that the feminist egalitarian perspective contradicts the Confucian premise of unequal gender relationships. According to Martina Deuchler, for example, the Confucian view clearly stipulates the order of gender hierarchy that is cosmologically sanctioned. Just as heaven (*yang*) dominates earth (*yin*), so men take precedence over women. [66] Given the law of nature pertaining to human order, women occupy a position inferior to that of men. Women have to obey men's orders; a wife has to obey a husband's orders. At this point, I agree that the feminist critique of the family law is asymmetrical to the Confucian conception of the sexes. Nonetheless, I argue, the feminists did not propose a full-fledged rejection of Confucian family values.

Confucian social values revolve around the five primary social relations. Among them, three are familial relations—between father (parent) and son (child), husband and wife, and elder and younger. The South Korean feminist quest for gender equality has challenged the value revolving around the husband-wife relation. Yet, proponents of the quest have neither underestimated nor disregarded the other two familial relations, including their respective Confucian ethical values such as filial piety (*hyo*) and reverence (*kyŏng*). In the family-law case, the feminists argued that the family-head system ran counter to the familial value of Confucianism. Consider the case where, on the basis of family law, a family named a three-year-old grandson as successor to the family-headship, prioritizing the boy over his mother and his seventy-year-old grandmother. According to the feminists, this case demonstrates that the preservation of the family-head system could undermine the preservation of Confucian family values.[67]

In addition, the feminists argued that the abolishment of the family-head system was not a desecration of the family institution; rather, it was a rearrangement of the institution.[68] Because the family-head system structures the family on the basis of the father's family register and surname, those members of a family who are not formally enlisted in the father's family register and who have surnames different from the father's surname fail to gain legal and social recognition as legitimate family members; also, society often considers the family that comprises these illegitimate family members to be abnormal. For instance, the feminists highlighted the hardships and pains that children of divorced parents suffered under the family-head system. Even in the case where a child actually lived with a remarried mother, the child was enlisted in a divorced father's family register. Also, the feminists observed that a difference between a child's surname and the stepfather's surname could negatively affect the child's welfare in family and school life.[69] The feminist logic for the abolishment of the family-head system endorses a family institution that is based on the love and the trust of the family members rather than on formal paternal lineage. I think, as Chaihark Hahm rightly mentions, the feminist desire to preserve the family is indeed involved in a "deeply Confucian project of trying to redefine the family."[70]

South Korea today is generally considered the most Confucian of all Asian nations.[71] Although Confucianism now cannot claim to be a religion or a political orthodoxy in South Korea, culturally it is deeply ingrained in the public institutions and the private personas of the South Korean people. A government census survey showed that more than 91 percent of those surveyed identified themselves as Confucians in that they performed the basic Confucian rituals and ancestral ceremonies and subscribed to Confucian family values regardless of religious affiliation, whereas those who identified themselves as active Confucians participating in local Confucian temples and associations amounted to less than 2 percent of those surveyed.[72] I am discussing here neither how Confucianism can successfully remain relevant to Korean society nor where the remnants of the Confucian culture reside, although these are significant questions worthy of thoughtful answers. In this paper, I instead examine "how Koreans themselves have perceived Confucianism in this century, and what effect this has had, if any, on these traditional values."[73] In my perspective, the feminist logic in the family-head system constitutes a helpful clue to my questions' answers because the logic shows that, while attacking patriarchy, South Korean feminists, as did Confucians to a greater degree, endorsed the Confucian value of family.[74]

I do not agree with Chaibong Hahm in that he treats the debate between feminists and Confucians in the family-law reform as a contrast between the Confucian tradition of endorsing family values and the modern liberal individualist idea.[75] Proponents of the feminist demand for gender equality might claim that the demand is modern, but they do not necessarily deny the Confucian value of family. The situation is not, as Hahm puts it, "the clash of civilizations."[76] The feminist demand for gender equality concerns neither de-Confucianism nor re-Confucianism.[77] Indeed, it revolves around constant renegotiations with Confucianism, a process that is complex and contesting. A case in point is worth mentioning here. A South Korean female graduate student said that she felt discriminated against on the basis of her sex when she as an eldest daughter did not have the right to perform Confucian ancestral rituals. Her remarks provide an entry into feminist reinterpretations of Confucianism in the post-Confucian context—an entry into the "possibility of Korean style feminism."[78]

The Nationalist Challenge to Neo-colonialism

In the family-law reform movement, the feminists emphasized the fact that South Korea's family law fell short of meeting international standards. That is, the feminists argued that because the inequality between South Korean women and South Korean men was more pronounced than comparable inequalities in the West, the South Korean situation symbolized the deficient status of South Korea in the international context. The feminist logic and the feminist rhetoric in question voiced this concern to motivate popular support for the reform and to influence the development of the family-law reform.

Consider the Convention on the Elimination of All Forms of Discrimination against Women (CEDAW) adopted in the General Assembly of the United Nations in 1979. The CEDAW demanded the same rights, the same standards, and the same treatment for women as for men regarding family relationships, an area previously left unregulated by international law. It addressed the political, social, economic, civil, and family rights of women and is the most comprehensive international instrument on women's rights to date. While South Korea's Confucian society vehemently opposed South Korea's signing of the CEDAW, South Korean feminist groups urged their country to sign it. Not until 1985 did the South Korean government ratify the convention, with some qualification when the terms of the convention conflicted with South Korean domestic legal systems or with traditional culture. And until recently, the government reserved the qualification of the provisions concerning marriage and family relationships.[79]

I will now focus my attention on the feminist logic and the feminist rhetoric that the feminist groups used both to criticize the lukewarm response of the government and to encourage the government to unreservedly sign the convention. Erin Cho interprets the feminist reasoning as follows:

> The Women's Alliance for the Revision of the Family Law [earlier in this paper, I refer to it as the WUR] countered such culturally relativistic arguments by asserting that Korea must sign onto the Convention *if it wanted to attain international recognition and respect commensurate with the country's growing economic power*. They argued that the Convention like the family law revision movement is not aimed at adopting Western standards of thinking and conduct or an instrument to promote Western imperialism, but rather aimed at allowing women to recover rights they already possessed under the 1948 Constitution. [80]

The feminist emphasis was not limited to the fact that the unrevised family law was harmful to South Korean women. Interestingly, the feminists further pointed out that the unrevised family law was also harmful to national pride. Using the nationalistic rhetoric, the feminists tried to stimulate "the state's awareness about women in Korea," which was "more sensitive to global trends than to the demands of Korean women themselves."[81]

Nationalism has played an important role in feminists' rhetoric. Since national independence (1945) and the Korean War (1950–1953), South Korea has evolved from a poor state to an economic and sociopolitical power reinforced by rich Western countries. To recover its national pride and to challenge neo-colonial domination, South Korea—both the state and the general public—has engaged in nationalist discourse. In the 1960s and the 1970s, the state generated a nationalist discourse primarily in order to attain economic growth, and in the 1980s and the 1990s, the public often advanced a nationalist discussion in order to achieve democracy under the authoritarian government. Interestingly, feminist nationalist rhetoric characterized the discourse on both of the occasions. For example, in the beginning of the economic-growth movement (in the 1960s and the 1970s), feminists claimed that the family-head system contributed to South Korea's overpopulation, a social problem that hampered economic growth. Because people kept having babies until they had a boy, according to the feminists, the abolishment of the family-head system would not only be compatible with the state's population-control policy but also contribute to the state's economic growth overall.[82] In the democratic reform movement (throughout the 1980s and the 1990s and until recently), the feminists argued that the abolishment of the family-head system would strengthen the prospects of democracy. According to this argument, a society whose family institution is patriarchal cannot guarantee individual freedom and equality, or the basic principles of democracy. Thus the abolishment of the family-head system would help not only liberate South Korean women from sexism, but also establish and protect South Korea's democracy. [83]

The case of the family-head system illuminates the relationship between nationalism and feminism. Many studies on post-colonial (and anti-colonial) nationalism discuss the gendered nature of nationalism in the anti-colonial struggle; they observe the "often uncompromising tension" between feminism and nationalism in the post-colonial context. [84] The works of Partha Chatterjee, for example, recognize the construction of the gendered discourse of "official" Indian nationalism. [85] Given the gendered nature of nationalism, Chatterjee concludes that "unlike the women's movement in nineteenth- and twentieth-century Europe or America, the battle for the new idea of womanhood in the era of nationalism was waged in the home [in India's homes]." [86] In a similar vein, some South Korean scholars highlight the masculine image of nation—the gendered nationalism—in South Korea's anti-colonial discourse as well as South Korea's neo-colonial discourse. [87] "The dominant discourse of nationalism in postcolonial Korea strategically chooses to suppress women's equivocality to privilege the masculine subject of the nation." [88] For instance, South Korea's economic-growth policy of the 1970s and the 1980s relied on gendered nationalism by idealizing self-sacrificing women and by, in this way, successfully subjugating women, especially in the case of young female factory workers. Also, South Korea's androcentric nationalism silenced the voices of comfort women. [89]

Of course, as Seungsook Moon persuasively argues, the feminist family-law reform movement challenges androcentric nationalism in that the reform movement undermines "the patrilineal family as the basic unit of the nation." [90] According to Moon, the nationalist discourse uses the patrilineal family as a basis for a nation where paternalistic harmony dominates. So the feminist rejection of the patrilineal family system challenges not only a patriarchal form of the family but also the image of the nation as a whole. I do not intend to deny or underestimate this observation. Nonetheless I argue that the case of the family-head system analyzed in this paper suggests another notable aspect of the nationalist discourse that is not necessarily antagonistic to feminism. Nationalism may have potential for generating economic growth and promoting democracy as well as the feminist cause. [91]

CONCLUSION: LOCATING SOUTH KOREAN FEMINISM

A rigorous analysis of the struggle between South Korean feminists and South Korean Confucians contradicts the assertion that the feminists simply rejected the value of culture and tradition. The feminists challenged the patriarchal system of gender in the family structure while (re)constructing and (re)identifying culture. To grasp the role that gender inevitably plays in the larger framework of culture, scholars must first analyze the role beyond the limiting and distorting effects of the gender-culture binary. In this paper, I have attempted to move beyond this binary by considering, for example, the legacy of colonialism, reinterpreted Confucian ideology, and the socioeconomic and political status of South Korea. At this moment, any effort to find a genuine source of Korean feminism is not only useless, but meaningless as well. This is because the source is present neither in ahistorical Korean culture nor in alien Western influences.

In conclusion, the above analysis of the family-head system enables me to identify four important features of South Korean feminism that could provide some interesting lessons for current feminist scholarship. First, contrary to the conventional feminist understanding that the discourses of culture/tradition, Confucianism, and nationalism are detrimental to feminism in general, the case reveals that these discourses can support the feminist cause. In the case at hand, we see the possibility that the relationship between culture and feminism, between Confucianism and feminism, and between nationalism and feminism are not only compatible but also reciprocally empowering.

Second, no single approach can adequately characterize the many facets of South Korean feminism. It is worth mentioning, in regard to these many facets, Mohanty's observation on feminism: "no non-contradictory or 'pure' feminism is possible."[92] South Korean feminism, like other feminisms, is indeed complex and contesting.

Third, Kumari Jayawardena, in her pioneering work *Feminism and Nationalism in the Third World*, argues that "[Third World] feminism was *not* imposed on the Third World by the West" but arose in the historicized context of "material and ideological changes that affected women."[93] Yet she adds that early Indian feminism lacked "a revolutionary feminist consciousness" in the movement because it was not like a form of autonomous women's movement (like that in the West) but mingled within the backgrounds of nationalist struggles, working-class agitation, and peasant rebellions.[94] However, I think that the case of South Korean feminism provides a somewhat different interpretation. Contextualized Korean feminism does not necessarily lack autonomous or radical features. Rather, the search for genuine "autonomous" and "radical" features may lead us to dismiss the historicized and contextualized process of the (re)production of feminism.

Finally, I find that South Korean feminism holds many possibilities for global feminism. By "global feminism," I do not mean a homogenized, monolithic vision of gender equality that cuts across cultural borders. For me, the term carries with it justified skepticism regarding the assertion that both Western and non-Western (or third- and first-world) women share ahistorical experiences.[95] As a feminism that transcends national and cultural circumstances, global feminism unites women who find themselves enmeshed in their respective cultures which differ from one another, and who

nevertheless engage in discourse with and forge coalitions with other wom-
en—who, in short, come together while historicizing and contextualizing
their own feminist movements.[96] By considering the continuing effects of a
colonial history, of a Confucian heritage, and of neo-colonial socioeconomic
and political relationships, South Korean feminists can acquire perspectives
that facilitate open—not closed—communication with other feminists and
with other perspectives.

NOTES

*The earlier version of this chapter has been published in Hee-Kang Kim, "Locating Feminism
beyond Gender and Culture: A Case of the Family-head System in South Korea," *Discourse
201* 10, no. 1 (2007), pp. 245–90. I am grateful to Jung-in Kang and Hyunah Yang for
comments on an earlier draft.

    1. Article 778, Article 781(1), and Article 826(3) stipulate, respectively, that "[A] person
who succeeds to the family lineage, or [who] has set up [a] branch family, or who has established a new family, or [who] has restored a family for any other reason, shall become the head
of the family"; "[a] child shall assume its father's surname and the origin of the surname and
shall have the name entered in its father's family register"; and "the wife shall have her name
entered in her husband's family register. When the wife is the head or the successor of headship
of her parents' family, the husband may have his name entered in his wife's family register
(Amended by Act No. 4199. Jan. 13, 1990)." The Civil Code consists of five parts, and the
fourth and fifth parts where these provisions are provided are known as the family law. It is
generally said that the earlier parts of the Civil Code drew their influence from French and
German law and that the latter parts, or the family law, reflected Korean family traditions
traceable back to the Chosŏn dynasty (1392–1910). See Erin Cho, "Caught in Confucius'
Shadow: The Struggle for Women's Legal Equality in South Korea," *Columbia Journal of
Asian Law* 12, no. 2 (1998), pp. 125–89, 147; Sang Hyun Song, "Special Problems in Studying
Korean Law," in his *Korean Law in the Global Economy* (Seoul: Pagyŏngsa, 1996).

    2. Judgment of Feb. 3, 2005 (2001Hun-Ga9-10, 2001Hun-Ga11-15, and 2004Hun-Ga5).
The ruling declared that the Civil Code's above provisions ran counter to Article 36, section 1
of the Constitution, "[M]arriage and family life shall be entered into and sustained on the basis
of individual dignity and equality of the sexes, and the State shall do everything in its power to
achieve that goal."

    3. Ah-young Chung, "Current Family Registry System Incompatible with the Constitu-
tion," *Korean Times*, Feb. 3, 2005; Ji-won Chun and Jung-min Dong, "*Yeoseonggye-yurim
baneung*" [Feminist-Confucian Responses], *Donga Ilbo*, Feb. 3, 2005.

    4. Susan Okin, "Gender Inequality and Cultural Differences," *Political Theory* 22, no. 1
(1994), pp. 5–24; Okin, "Inequalities between the Sexes in Different Cultural Contexts," in
Women, Culture and Development: A Study of Human Capabilities, eds. Martha Nussbaum and
Jonathan Glover (Oxford: Clarendon Press, 1995); Okin, "Feminism, Women's Human Rights,
and Cultural Differences," in *Decentering the Center: Philosophy for a Multicultural, Postco-
lonial, and Feminist World*, eds. Uma Narayan and Sandra Harding (Bloomington: Indiana
University Press, 2000); Martha Nussbaum, "Human Capabilities, Female Human Beings," in
Women, Culture and Development: A Study of Human Capabilities, eds. Martha Nussbaum and
Jonathan Glover (Oxford: Clarendon Press, 1995); Nussbaum, *Sex and Social Justice* (New
York and Oxford: Oxford University Press, 1999), chap. 1; Martha Chen, "A Matter of Survi-
val: Women's Right to Employment in India and Bangladesh," in *Women, Culture and Devel-
opment: A Study of Human Capabilities*, eds. Martha Nussbaum and Jonathan Glover (Oxford:
Clarendon Press, 1995); Hanna Papanek, "To Each Less Than She Needs, from Each More
Than She Can Do: Allocations, Entitlements, and Value," in *Persistent Inequalities: Women
and World Development*, ed. Irene Tinker (New York: Oxford University Press, 1990). Following Alison Jaggar, I am using the term "Western" to refer to the wealthy industrialized or post-

industrial capitalist nations, located mainly in Western Europe, Australasia, and North America, and I am using the term "non-Western" to refer to the poor or industrializing nations, located mainly in Africa, Latin America, the Caribbean, and South and East Asia. See Alison M. Jaggar, "Globalizing Feminist Ethics," in *Decentering the Center: Philosophy for a Multicultural, Postcolonial, and Feminist World*, eds. Uma Narayan and Sandra Harding (Bloomington: Indiana University Press, 2000), p. 11, n5.

5. Okin, "Gender Inequality," p. 11; Okin, "Inequalities between the Sexes," p. 275, original emphasis.

6. Okin, "Gender Inequality," pp. 20–21.

7. Okin, "Feminism, Women's Human Rights," p. 31; Uma Narayan, "Essence of Culture and a Sense of History: A Feminist Critique of Cultural Essentialism," in *Decentering the Center: Philosophy for a Multicultural, Postcolonial, and Feminist World*, eds. Uma Narayan and Sandra Harding (Bloomington: Indiana University Press, 2000), pp. 90–93.

8. Nussbaum, "Human Capabilities"; Nussbaum, *Sex and Social Justice*, chap. 1; Nussbaum, *Women and Human Development: The Capabilities Approach* (Cambridge: Cambridge University Press, 2000), chap. 1. Nussbaum declares, "My proposal is frankly universalist and 'essentialist.' That is, it asks us to focus on what is common to all, rather than on differences (although, as we shall see, it does not neglect these), and to see some capabilities and functions as more central, more at the core of human life, than others" ("Human Capabilities," p. 63).

9. Nussbaum, *Sex and Social Justice*, p. 47.

10. Okin, "Feminism, Women's Human Rights," p. 39.

11. Ibid., p. 31.

12. Cited from ibid., p. 39.

13. Chandra Talpade Mohanty, *Feminism without Borders: Decolonizing Theory, Practicing Solidarity* (Durham, NC: Duke University Press, 2003), p. 22.

14. Mohanty, "Feminist Encounters: Locating the Politics of Experience," in *Destabilizing Theory: Contemporary Feminist Debates*, eds. Michele Barrett and Anne Phillips (Stanford, CA: Stanford University Press, 1992); Kathy Rudy, "Difference and Indifference: A U.S. Feminist Response to Global Politics," in *Feminisms at a Millennium*, eds. Judith A. Howard and Carolyn Allen (Chicago: University of Chicago Press, 2000).

15. Ruth Anna Putman, "Why Not a Feminist Theory of Justice?" in *Women, Culture and Development: A Study of Human Capabilities*, eds. Martha Nussbaum and Jonathan Glover (Oxford: Clarendon Press, 1995); Lorraine Code, "How to Think Globally: Stretching the Limits of Imagination," in *Decentering the Center: Philosophy for a Multicultural, Postcolonial, and Feminist World*, eds. Uma Narayan and Sandra Harding (Bloomington: Indiana University Press, 2000); Ofelia Schutte, "Cultural Alterity: Cross-Cultural Communication and Feminist Theory in North-South Contexts," in *Decentering the Center: Philosophy for a Multicultural, Postcolonial, and Feminist World*, eds. Uma Narayan and Sandra Harding (Bloomington: Indiana University Press, 2000), pp. 49–50.

16. Schutte, "Cultural Alterity," p. 49.

17. Paul Feyerabend, "Notes on Relativism," in his *Farewell to Reason* (London: Verso, 1987), p. 19.

18. Mohanty, *Feminism without Borders*, pp. 39–40; Uma Narayan, *Dislocating Cultures: Identities, Traditions, and Third World Feminism* (New York and London: Routledge, 1997), chap. 1.

19. Okin, "Gender Inequality," p. 19.

20. Cheryl Johnson-Odim, "Common Themes, Different Contexts: Third World Women and Feminism," in *Third World Women and the Politics of Feminism*, eds. Chandra Talpade Mohanty, Ann Russo, and Lourdes Torres (Bloomington: Indiana University Press, 1991), p. 322; Angela Gilliam, "Women's Equality and National Liberation," in *Third World Women and the Politics of Feminism*, eds. Chandra Talpade Mohanty, Ann Russo, and Lourdes Torres (Bloomington: Indiana University Press, 1991), pp. 218–19; Mohanty, *Feminism without Borders*, p. 24.

21. Sander L. Gilman, "'Barbaric' Rituals?" in *Is Multiculturalism Bad for Women?* eds. Joshua Cohen, Matthew Howard, and Martha Nussbaum (Princeton, NJ: Princeton University Press, 1999), p. 58.

22. Rudy, "Difference and Indifference," p. 60. The recent popularized debate between feminism and multiculturalism also reflects this conflict between, on the one hand, "aiming to promote the equal dignity of and respect for women" and, on the other, "aiming to support and protect many cultures." See Okin, "Multiculturalism and Feminism: No Simple Question, No Simple Answers," in *Minorities within Minorities: Equality, Rights and Diversity,* eds. Avigail Eisenberg and Jeff Spinner-Halev (Cambridge: Cambridge University Press, 2005), p. 67. Okin rejects the conventional view that feminism and multiculturalism are "both good things which are easily reconciled," and points out that there is "a deep and growing tension" in the relationship between feminism and multiculturalism. See Okin, "Is Multiculturalism Bad for Women?" in *Is Multiculturalism Bad for Women?* eds. Joshua Cohen, Matthew Howard, and Martha Nussbaum (Princeton, NJ: Princeton University Press, 1999), p. 10. For studies on the debate between feminism and multiculturalism, see Okin, "Feminism and Multiculturalism: Some Tensions," *Ethics* 108, no. 4 (1998), pp. 661–84; Okin, "Is Multiculturalism Bad for Women?"; Okin, "Multiculturalism and Feminism"; Ranjoo Seodu Herr, "A Third World Feminist Defense of Multiculturalism," *Social Theory and Practice* 30, no. 1 (2004), pp. 73–103; Ayelet Schachar, *Multicultural Jurisdictions: Cultural Differences and Women's Rights* (Cambridge: Cambridge University Press, 2001); Jeff Spinner-Halev, "Feminism, Multiculturalism, Oppression, and the State," *Ethics* 112 (2001), pp. 84–113; Monique Deveaux, "Conflicting Equalities? Cultural Group Rights and Sex Equality," *Political Studies* 48, no. 3 (2000), pp. 522–39.

23. Narayan, "Essence of Culture"; Jaggar, "Globalizing Feminist Ethics"; Schutte, "Cultural Alterity"; Rudy, "Difference and Indifference."

24. The feminist position was largely shared with so-called liberals while the Confucian position was largely shared with so-called conservatives.

25. Cho, "Caught in Confucius' Shadow," pp. 175–77.

26. Hyunah Yang, "Unfinished Tasks for Korean Family Policy in the 1990s: Maternity Protection Policy and Abolition of the Family-Head System," *Korea Journal* 42, no. 2 (2002), pp. 68–99, 72–73.

27. Ibid., 86; Yang, "Chŏntonggwa yŏsŏngui mannam: Hojujedo wihŏnsosonge kwanhan munhwa" [Questions of 'Tradition' and 'Women': Cultural Analysis of the Lawsuit about Unconstitutionality of the Family-head (*hoju*) System], *Pŏpsahak yŏn'gu* [Legal Sociology Studies] 25 (2002), pp. 105–30, 123–27; Yang, "Hojujedo wihŏnsosonge kwanhan bŏpsahoehakchŏk koch'al" [A Study of the Lawsuit about Unconstitutionality of the Family-head (*hoju*) System from the View of Sociology of Law: Changes of 'the Families' in Korea] *Hang'uk sahoehak* [Korean Sociological Review] 36, no. 5 (2002), pp. 201–29, 218–20.

28. In the *New York Times* article entitled "Korean Women Still Feel Demands to Bear a Son," WuDunn points out that favoritism toward sons persists in South Korea, even though the government legally prohibited discrimination against women in the areas of property inheritance. See Sheryl WuDunn, "Korean Women Still Feel Demands to Bear a Son," *New York Times,* Jan. 14, 1997.

29. Cho, "Caught in Confucius' Shadow," pp. 182–83; Chai Bin Park and Nam-Hoon Cho, "Consequences of Son Preference in a Low-Fertility Society: Imbalance of the Sex-Ratio at Birth in Korea," *Population and Development Review* 21, no. 1 (1995), pp. 59–84.

30. For detailed histories and analyses of feminist reform movements, see Tae-Young Lee, *Kajokpŏp kaejŏngundong 37nyŏnsa* [The 37 Year Movement to Revise Korea's Family Law] (Seoul: Korea Legal Aid Center for Family Relations Press, 1992); Cho, "Caught in Confucius' Shadow"; Hyunah Yang, "Gender Equality vs. 'Tradition' in Korean Family Law: Toward a Postcolonial Feminist Jurisprudence," *Review of Korean Studies* 6, no. 2 (2003), pp. 85–118.

31. Yang, "Gender Equality vs. 'Tradition,'" pp. 89–90; Lee, *Kajokpŏp kaejŏngundong,* pp. 149–54; Cho, "Caught in Confucius' Shadow," pp. 152–53.

32. Yang, "Gender Equality vs. 'Tradition,'" p. 91; Lee, *Kajokpŏp kaejŏngundong,* p. 151.

33. Yang, "Gender Equality vs. 'Tradition,'" p. 92.

34. Ibid., pp. 98–111; Cho, "Caught in Confucius' Shadow," pp. 163–70. The WUR originally drafted the amended bill of 1988 to abolish the family-head system. During the deliberation process in the National Assembly, however, the National Assembly adopted an alternative bill. The alternative bill included amended provisions that would change the inheritance system of the family-headship into a succession system and that would weaken the rights and the duties

of the family-head over family members. See Kyung-hee Kim, "Hojuje p'yejiui nonjaenggwa chŏnmang" [The Debate on the Abolition of the Family-Head System and Anticipation], *Yŏsŏnggwa sahoe* [Women and Society] 15 (2004), pp. 379–92, 381–82.

35. Yang, "Gender Equality vs. 'Tradition,'" p. 111; Lee, *Kajokpŏp kaejŏngundong*, p. 379.

36. Kim, "Hojuje p'yejiui nonjaenggwa chŏnmang," pp. 379–80.

37. Article 9 of the Constitution provides that "the State shall strive to sustain and develop cultural heritages and to enhance national culture." In the preamble, it also states, "[W]e, the people of Korea, proud of a resplendent history and traditions dating from time immemorial."

38. Cited from Lee, *Kajokpŏp kaejŏngundong*, p. 174.

39. Cho, "Caught in Confucius' Shadow," pp. 170–72.

40. Yang, "Gender Equality vs. 'Tradition,'" p. 93; Cho, "Caught in Confucius' Shadow," pp. 171–72.

41. Cited from Yang, "Gender Equality vs. 'Tradition,'" pp. 93–94.

42. Cho, "Caught in Confucius' Shadow," pp. 170–72.

43. In-kyung Yu, "Chindan 2003 han'guk: Hojuje p'yeji yurimdŭng pandaeron kŏse" [Diagnosing 2003: *Yurim*'s Strong Rejection against the Abolishment of the Family-Head System], *Kyunghyang Sinmun*, June 2, 2003.

44. Kim, "Hojuje p'yejiui nonjaenggwa chŏnmang," p. 380.

45. John McBeth, "A Family Feud for Confucians and Women," *Far Eastern Economic Review*, Feb. 26, 1987, pp. 38–41, 38.

46. Seongwoo Lee, "Kajokpŏpgwa kachokchuŭi: Hojuchedorŭl chungsimŭro" [Feminism in Korean Family Law], *Yugyosasang munhwa yŏn'gu* [Confucian Thought Studies] 20 (2004), pp. 67–96, 72–76.

47. Ibid., pp. 76–78.

48. WhaSook Lee, "Hojujedoga kwŏnwijuŭijŏgin kungminŭisiggwa namnyŏch'abyŏlpŏbe mich'inŭn yŏnghyang" [The Head of Family System, Its Patriarchal Thought and Discriminational Factors], *Yŏnse pŏp'ak yŏn'gu* [Yonsei Law Review] 10, no. 2 (2004), pp. 17–40, 20–22; Cho, "Caught in Confucius' Shadow," pp. 140–43.

49. Cho, "Caught in Confucius' Shadow," pp. 133, 188.

50. JaHyun Kim Haboush, "The Confucianization of Korean Society," in *The East Asian Region: Confucian Heritage and Its Modern Adaptation*, ed. Gilbert Rozman (Princeton, NJ: Princeton University Press, 1991), pp. 104–5.

51. Ibid., p. 104.

52. Cho, "Caught in Confucius' Shadow," pp. 133, 188.

53. Yang, "Gender Equality vs. 'Tradition,'" p. 113.

54. Uma Narayan, "Undoing the 'Package Picture' of Cultures," in *Feminisms at a Millennium*, eds. Judith A. Howard and Carolyn Allen (Chicago: University of Chicago Press, 2000).

55. Ibid., p. 89.

56. See also Seyla Benhabib, *The Claims of Culture: Equality and Diversity in the Global Era* (Princeton, NJ: Princeton University Press, 2002); Lisa Wedeen, "Conceptualizing Culture: Possibilities for Political Science," *American Political Science Review* 96 (2002), pp. 713–28; Eric Hobsbawm and Terence Ranger, eds., *The Invention of Tradition* (Cambridge: Cambridge University Press, 1992).

57. Narayan, *Dislocating Cultures*, "Essence of Culture," pp. 86–90.

58. Narayan, "Essence of Culture," p. 87.

59. Narayan, *Dislocating Cultures*, p. 61; Partha Chatterjee, *Nationalist Thought and the Colonial World: A Derivative Discourse?* (Minneapolis: University of Minnesota Press, 1986); Narayan, *The Nation and Its Fragments: Colonial and Postcolonial Histories* (Princeton, NJ: Princeton University Press, 1993); Inderpal Grewal, "Autobiographic Subjects and Diasporic Locations: Meatless Days and Borderlands," in *Scattered Hegemonies: Postmodernity, and Transnational Feminist Practices*, eds. Inderpal Grewal and Caren Kaplan (Minneapolis: University of Minnesota Press, 1994).

60. Narayan, *Dislocating Cultures*, p. 14.

61. Ibid., p. 12.

62. Ibid., chap. 2; Chatterjee, *Nationalist Thought and the Colonial World*; Chatterjee, *The Nation and Its Fragments*, chap. 6.

63. See also Herr, "A Third World Feminist," pp. 94–100.

64. Yu, "Chindan 2003 han'guk."

65. Korea Legal Aid Center for Family Relations, *Algi shwiun hojuje p'yeji: Ch'abyŏrŭi kullerŭl pŏtkko p'yŏngdŭngŭi shidaero* [An Easy Introduction of the Abolishment of the Family-head System (A Leaflet)] (Seoul: Korea Legal Aid Center for Family Relations Press, 2005), pp. 3–4.

66. Martina Deuchler, *The Confucian Transformation of Korea: A Study of Society and Ideology* (Cambridge, MA: Harvard University Press, 1992), p. 231.

67. Lee, "Hojujedoga kwŏnwijuŭijŏgin kungminŭisiggwa namnyŏch'abyŏlppŏbe mich'inŭn yŏnghyang," pp. 27–28.

68. Korea Legal Aid Center for Family Relations, *Algi shwiun hojuje p'yeji*, pp. 7–9.

69. Yang, "Chŏntonggwa yŏsŏngui mannam," pp. 119–25; Yang, "Hojujedo," pp. 220–24.

70. Chaihark Hahm, "Law, Culture, and the Politics of Confucianism," *Columbia Journal of Asian Law* 16, no. 2 (2003), pp. 254–301, 296.

71. Wei-ming Tu, "The Search for Roots in Industrial East Asia: The Case of the Confucian Revival," in *Fundamentalisms Observed*, eds. Martin Marty and R. Scott Appleby (Chicago: Chicago University Press, 1991), p. 761.

72. Byong-ik Koh, "Confucianism in Contemporary Korea," in *Confucian Traditions in East Asian Modernity*, ed. Tu Wei-ming (Cambridge, MA: Harvard University Press, 1996), pp. 191–93; Kwang-ok Kim, "The Reproduction of Confucian Culture in Contemporary Korea," in *Confucian Traditions in East Asian Modernity*, p. 204.

73. Michael Robinson, "Perceptions of Confucianism in Twentieth-Century Korea," in *The East Asian Region: Confucian Heritage and Its Modern Adaptation*, ed. Gilbert Rozman, (Princeton, NJ: Princeton University Press, 1991), p. 204.

74. It is true that the feminists and the Confucians do not agree with each other on the matter of a specific form of family they endorse (for example, the Confucians support a traditional form of family comprising a husband, a wife, and children, whereas the feminists justify various kinds of family, including a female-head family). In spite of such a difference, it is worth noting that they both emphasize the value of family as a basis of their logic.

75. Chaibong Hahm, "Family versus the Individual: The Politics of Marriage," in *Confucianism for the Modern World*, eds. Daniel A. Bell and Chaibong Hahm (Cambridge: Cambridge University Press, 2003).

76. Ibid., p. 358.

77. Rozman, ed., *The East Asian Region*, p. v.

78. Hahm, "Family versus the Individual," p. 23, n19.

79. Cho, "Caught in Confucius' Shadow," pp. 177–78; Yang, "Unfinished Tasks," p. 85; Lee, "Hojujedoga," p. 30.

80. Cho, "Caught in Confucius' Shadow," p. 179.

81. Yang, "Unfinished Tasks," p. 92.

82. Man'gil Kang, "Contemporary Nationalist Movements and the Minjung," translated by Roger Duncan, in *South Korea's Mingjung Movement: The Culture and Politics of Dissidence*, edited by Kenneth Wells (Honolulu: University of Hawai'i Press, 1995); Kenneth Wells, "Introduction," in *South Korea's Mingjung Movement: The Culture and Politics of Dissidence*, ed. Kenneth Wells (Honolulu: University of Hawai'i Press, 1995).

83. See Lee, "Hojujedoga," p. 31; Korea Legal Aid Center for Family Relations, *Algi shwiun hojuje p'yeji*, pp. 3–4.

84. Chungmoo Choi, "Nationalism and Construction of Gender in Korea," in *Dangerous Women: Gender and Korean Nationalism*, eds. Elaine H. Kim and Chungmoo Choi (London: Routledge, 1998), p. 28.

85. Chatterjee, *Nationalist Thought*; Chatterjee, *The Nation and Its Fragments*.

86. Chatterjee, *The Nation and Its Fragments*, p. 133.

87. Elaine H. Kim and Chungmoo Choi, "Introduction," in *Dangerous Women: Gender and Korean Nationalism*, eds. Elaine H. Kim and Chungmoo Choi (London: Routledge, 1998); Choi, "Nationalism and Construction of Gender"; Seungsook Moon, "Begetting the Nation: The Androcentric Discourse of National History and Tradition in South Korea," in *Dangerous Women: Gender and Korean Nationalism*, eds. Elaine H. Kim and Chungmoo Choi (London:

Routledge, 1998); Hyunah Yang, "Remembering the Korean Military Comfort Women: Nationalism, Sexuality, and Silencing," in *Dangerous Women: Gender and Korean Nationalism*, eds. Elaine H. Kim and Chungmoo Choi (London: Routledge, 1998).

88. Choi, "Nationalism and Construction of Gender," p. 28.

89. Yang, "Remembering the Korean Military Comfort Women."

90. Moon, "Begetting the Nation," p. 54.

91. Miriam Ching Yoon Louie, "Mingjung Feminism: Korean Women's Movement for Gender and Class Liberation," *Women's Studies International Forum* 18, no. 4 (1995), pp. 417–30; Ranjoo Seodu Herr, "The Possibility of Nationalist Feminism," *Hypatia* 18, no. 3 (2003), pp. 135–60; Bang-Soon L. Yoon, "Democratization and Gender Politics in South Korea," in *Gender, Globalization and Democratization*, eds. Rita Kelly, Jane Bayes, Mary Hawkesworth, and Brigitte Young (Lanham, MD: Rowman & Littlefield, 1995).

92. Chandra Talpade Mohanty, "Cartographies of Struggle: Third World Women and the Politics of Feminism," in *Third World Women and the Politics of Feminism*, eds. Chandra Talpade Mohanty, Ann Russo, and Lourdes Torres (Bloomington: Indiana University Press, 1991), p. 20.

93. Kumari Jayawardena, *Feminism and Nationalism in the Third World* (London and New Jersey: Zed Books, 1986), p. 2.

94. Jayawardena, *Feminism and Nationalism*, pp. 107–8.

95. Code, "How to Think Globally"; Jaggar, "Globalizing Feminist Ethics."

96. Rudy, "Difference and Indifference," p. 5; Uma Narayan and Sandra Harding, eds., *Decentering the Center: Philosophy for a Multicultural, Postcolonial, and Feminist World* (Bloomington: Indiana University Press, 2000), p. viii.

Chapter Four

Civil Confucianism in South Korea

*Liberal Rights, Confucian Reasoning,
and Gender Equality*

Sungmoon Kim

Given the fact that Korea was the most thoroughly Confucianized during the Chosŏn dynasty (1392–1910), especially since the late seventeenth century when Confucian rituals and moral precepts were fully localized in every nook and cranny of Korean society,[1] it is hardly surprising that many scholars still observe Korean society as the most Confucian of all Asian societies. Most tellingly, Tu Wei-ming states that "South Korea today is more Confucian than her East Asia neighbors in cultural orientation, social structure, political ideology, and economic strategy."[2] Furthermore, the most recent empirical data culled from a public opinion poll echoes this common observation that Koreans are still deeply saturated with Confucian values and norms.[3]

Quite surprisingly, however, this received truism has almost no resonance with the general Korean public, for many of whom Confucianism is nothing more than a relic of the old regime and the very source of its downfall. Even when they uphold values such as filial piety and respect for elders, and conduct ritual memorial ceremonies for their ancestors—values and practices commonly associated with Confucianism—they strongly deny any association of their values and practices with the traditional cultural system of Confucianism, because for them the Confucian part of tradition is a stumbling block to overcome, certainly not something to be proud of. For Koreans (especially young Koreans), concepts like "Confucian democracy" or "Confucian constitutionalism" signal an anachronism, even bad faith. For them, such concepts make no sense in light of the actual development of Korean democracy and constitutionalism since the late 1980s because, in their view, the consolidation of Korean constitutional democracy was accelerated in the past two decades precisely by legally uprooting the residues of pre-modern Confucian culture when the Constitutional Court declared unconstitutional two core Confucian legal practices—prohibition of marriage between persons who have the same surname (*tongsŏng* 同姓) and the same ancestral seat (*tongbon* 同本) in 1997[4] and the family-head system in 2005.[5] The Court's decisions reinforced the entrenched social perception that liberal values such as individual dignity and gender equality, to which Korea is constitutionally committed, are critically opposed to traditional Confucianism, at the heart of which lie patriarchy, rigid social hierarchy, nepotism, collectivism, male-centrism, and, most fundamentally, disrespect of individuality. Therefore, given the long-standing struggle of Koreans to overcome Confucianism, the observation (often by Western scholars) that Korean culture is still predominantly Confucian is likely to be taken as an anathema.

Are Confucian values really incompatible with liberal-democratic values and institutions?[6] Can liberal democracy be attained only if Confucian values are superseded by liberal rights and the social values affiliated with them? If Koreans are still deeply soaked in Confucian values and practices, as many scholars observe, even when they subscribe to diverse moral systems and religious faiths as private individuals and are formally committed to the liberal-democratic constitution, is compatibility between Confucian *doxa* and liberal *episteme* practically possible?[7] If practical compatibility is what characterizes the complex relationship between Confucianism and liberalism in contemporary Korea, how can we make sense of the process of cultural interactions between them that ensues inevitably? Finally, how can we make sense of the products of such interactions, mainly negotiations, as shall be shown later, which are neither traditionally Confucian nor purely liberal?[8]

In this chapter, I examine how cultural negotiations between traditional Confucian values/practices and liberal rights/values actually take place in contemporary Korea by focusing on a landmark decision made by the Supreme Court in 2005, which, along with the Constitutional Court, many Koreans consider the bulwark of liberal rights and freedoms. In this case, the court ruled that women are entitled to formal membership with all accompanying rights of their paternal clan organization (*chongjung* 宗中), overturning a 1958 decision that admits only adult men as full members. Contrary to the popular view that this case is a victory for liberalism (particularly liberal feminism) over archaic patriarchal Confucianism *tout court*, I argue that in this case, the Supreme Court offered itself as an institutional venue in which traditional Confucian values/practices and liberal rights/values could be negotiated with and accommodated by each other, thereby reinventing traditional Confucianism into a mode of Confucianism—what I call civil Confucianism—that is plausible under the modern Korean social and legal circumstances. I then draw normative implications, though preliminary, from this case study for constructing a political theory of Confucian constitutionalism.

THE DAUGHTERS' REBELLION: THE CASE

Background

In 1999, the clan organization of the Samaenggong Branch of the Lee Clan from the ancestral seat of Yong'in distributed among its members dividends resulting from a sale of the clan's land property.[9] According to its internal regulations predicated on traditional Confucian patrilineal clan law (c. *zongfa* 宗法), governed by Zhu Xi's *Family Ritual* (c. *Jiali* 家禮), which admits only adult men as full members in the capacity of sons, the association gave adult male members 150 million won (approximately US$150,000) and male members under the age of 20, regarded as associate members, between 16.5 and 55 million won (approximately between US$15,000 and $50,000) each. Though not recognized as "formal" members in light of clan law, female members of the clan, namely unmarried daughters as well as daughters-in-law, who are responsible for, among other things, preparing the food for family rituals and clan activities, also each received 2.2 million won (approximately US$2,000) and 3.3 million won (approximately US$3,000) respectively, not in terms of dividends, which are only given to formal members, but in terms of "inheritance."[10] In the course of distributing the clan's wealth, however, married daughters (i.e., the clan's daughters who had married members of another clan) were completely excluded based on the traditional patriarchal Confucian custom that regards daughters as "outsiders" upon marriage (in Korean words, *ch'ulgaoein* 出嫁外人).[11]

Infuriated, more than a hundred married daughters openly protested the clan council's decision and demanded their "due" share as members of the clan, pointing to the clan association's somewhat equivocal definition of membership as pertaining to "*any* descendant of the Samaenggong branch when one comes of age." In the face of unflagging protests from the married daughters, the clan council eventually offered each married daughter 2.2 million won (approximately US$2,000), also in terms of inheritance, hence not recognizing their formal membership. However, this decision fell far short of assuaging the anger and frustration of the protestors, who soon found out that the clan's daughters-in-law had received more money than they did. As one of the participants in this protest expressed later, what frustrated them the most was not so much the amount of money but the clan's patriarchal tradition that systematically discriminated against the married daughters simply because they were women (and admitted women's partial membership only in their capacity as the wives of the clan's sons).[12] Recognizing that verbal protests would not be sufficient to gain formal acceptance into the clan association as members, in 2000, some of these women brought the case to the district court, asking the court to adjudicate the legality of the clan's stipulations regarding membership. After losing in both district and appellate courts, five of the married daughters from Samaenggong, together with three of the married daughters from the Hyeryŏnggong branch of the Shim Clan from Ch'ŏngsong, who had suffered the same defeats in lower courts, appealed to the Supreme Court. After a long deliberation accompanied by a public hearing, the first of its kind in the history of Korean jurisprudence, the Court, attended by all thirteen justices, made a landmark decision in 2005 by ruling for the plaintiffs, thereby redefining the membership of clan organizations. [13]

The Court's Decision

In Korea, cases advanced to the Supreme Court are usually assigned to sections (*pu* 部), each consisting of three justices, and most cases are adjudicated by one section. However, for cases that are likely to entail immense social consequences or to overturn previous decision(s), all members of the Court participate in the deliberation and decision-making. As noted, the full-member court participated in the present case, implying its significance in the Korean social context. The key message of the Court's ruling (i.e., the majority opinion) can be recapitulated as the following:

1. The long-standing customary practice of clan associations admitting only adult men as members and denying women formal membership has become less legally certain among the members of our society.

2. Above all, our entire legal order, in which the Constitution has the highest normative authority, not only ensures a family life based on individual dignity and gender equality, but it also does not tolerate gender inequality in the exercise of rights and duties within the family. It has progressed by abolishing discrimination against women in all spheres of life—political, economic, social, and cultural—thereby realizing gender equality, and it will continue to make sure that the norm of gender equality is firmly maintained.

3. Clan organizations (*chongjung*) are family clans, whose purpose is to maintain the tombs of common ancestors, carry out memorial ceremonies, and promote intimate relationships among their members, and they arose naturally by the efforts of descendants upon the demise of their common ancestor(s).

4. The customary practice of clan organizations to admit, among the descendants of common ancestors, only adult men as members and to exclude women from formal membership does not correspond with our entire legal order, which has significantly changed as explained

above and thus lacks justification and reasonableness, because it endows and denies the opportunity to participate in clan activities, such as maintenance of the tombs of common ancestors and memorial ceremonies, solely on the basis of sex.

5. Therefore, the customary practice of limiting formal membership in the clan exclusively to its male adults is no longer legally valid.[14]

Confucianism versus Liberalism?

Mass media immediately framed the whole case in terms of a grand show-down between traditional Confucianism and progressive modernity, in the same way that it had presented a decision by the Constitutional Court a few months prior on the family-head system.[15] Not surprisingly, progressives and liberal feminists on one side and (conservative) Confucians and traditionalists on the other responded to the decision in diametrically different ways. For instance, Kwark Bae-hee, president of the Korea Legal Aid Center for Family Relations, said, "Along with the scrapping of the family-head system, this decision will become another cornerstone as our society truly moves toward gender equality." Nam Yun In-soon, the head of Korea Women's Associations United, hailed the decision by saying that it will greatly help eliminate discrimination between sons and daughters. In marked contrast, traditionalist Confucians (*yurim* 儒林) and conservatives were in an uproar, slamming the decision that in their view would not only bring irrevocable disorder to the traditional structure of the family, but more fundamentally, destroy the very meaning of the (Confucian) family undergirded by different social roles and statuses according to gender. This point was most clearly pronounced by Lee Seung-gwan, the head of the Sungkyunkwan[16] committee on Confucian ritual, when he said, "Women can't participate in the family clan, a special organization inherited from our ancestors. If married women get to participate in the clan organizations of their maiden homes, does this mean [that] men have to assume responsibilities in their wives' family clans as well?"[17]

There is no denying that though not directly alluding to liberalism, the Court vindicated liberal moral principles championed by liberal feminists and progressives, and thus there was indeed good reason for Confucians and traditionalists to complain that the justices of the Court (particularly the seven justices upholding the decision) did not give full consideration to the legal status of customary practice in Korean society, which precedes the establishment of the (modern) constitution in 1948. However, it is worth noting that while the clan organizations' customary practice is largely at odds with contemporary Korea's constitutional commitment to individual dignity and gender equality, the Court never espoused substantively "liberal" notions of individual dignity and gender equality or abandoned core Confucian val-

ues such as filial piety, respect for elders, ancestor worship, and ritual propriety completely. Quite the contrary, as clearly revealed in Justice Ko Hyŏn-
chŏl's supplementary opinion to the majority opinion, the Court's true intention was rather to succeed and further develop the traditional clan system in a
way compatible with Korea's constitutional norms and principles, such as
individual dignity and gender equality, by allowing both men (as sons) and
women (as daughters) to participate in the clan activities.

In this regard, the public hearing held two years before the decision was
made is worthy of special attention because it helps us to better understand
what kind of reasoning was used when the Court later upheld equal membership within the clan organizations. During the hearing, Justice Yu Chi-tam
asked the legal representative of the defendants (i.e., the clan organizations)
whether, for example, it would be fair for the clan to prohibit formal membership to women simply because they are women, even though they are
earnest filial daughters, while automatically admitting any adult man as a
member regardless of his filial commitment to his ancestors. In addition,
turning to the legal representative of the plaintiffs (the married daughters),
Justice Cho Muje asked whether or not the plaintiffs had fulfilled their duties
faithfully, the kinds of duties required of every clan member, such as pay-
ment of membership fees and participation in memorial ceremonies.

While the question Justice Yu raised to the defendants concerned the
injustice of gender inequality perpetrated by the clan organizations in the
name of customary practice, the reasoning behind it is undeniably Confucian.
If unpacked and reconstructed, Justice Yu's reasoning seems to consist of the
following propositions:

1. Clan organizations in Korea are Confucian institutions;
2. As Confucian institutions, the operating moral principles of the clan
   organizations must be grounded in Confucian ethics;
3. According to Confucian ethics, *ren* 仁 is the moral virtue par excel-
   lence and filial piety is thought to be the root of *ren*;[18] therefore,
4. The quintessential criteria for Confucian clan membership must be the
   candidate's filial piety toward his or her ancestors, which would determine his or her overall commitment to the purposes for which the clan
   exists.[19]

According to this line of reasoning, the injustice involved in this case has
little (almost nothing) to do with the clans' failure to become a liberal voluntary association or to promote gender equality as the liberal critics claimed.[20]
The true source of injustice is that the clan organizations have excluded
female members from formal membership, violating their norm of filial piety, a virtue which must be possessed by both men and women according to
Confucianism.[21] In other words, the injustice *depends on* the nature of the

clan organization and particularly its essential aims and practices, and they are characteristically and unambiguously Confucian.

Of course, one caveat in making filial piety the sole criterion of clan membership is the practical difficulty of actually using it. Without an explanation by Justice Yu, it is difficult to know what he really had in mind when he raised the question about filial piety. After all, when the decision was made two years later, Justice Yu himself did not join the majority opinion. Rather, along with five other members, including Chief Justice Ch'oe Chong-yŏng, he formed a minority opinion in consideration of other equally (perhaps more) pressing legal problems that in his view were more directly relevant to clan membership than gender equality, such as, among others, the (private) organization's constitutional right to freedom of association, though without disagreeing with one of the conclusions by the majority opinion that membership should be given to the plaintiffs. I will examine the Court's minority opinion in the next section. In the present context in which the Court's reasoning behind its decision is being examined, however, questions such as what Justice Yu actually intended to ask or whether the justice changed his mind over two years of adjudication, assuming that his original reasoning was roughly along the lines of my reconstruction, are less important. What is important is what kind of reasoning was being used during the lengthy processes of adjudication and decision-making, and my point is that the question raised by Justice Yu and the moral reasoning implied in it enable us to question the popular view that the Court's eventual vindication of gender equality reflects its endorsement of Western-liberal notions of gender equality, because the same, ostensibly liberal, conclusion can also be supported by Confucian reasoning.

Yet, there is another way to derive the same conclusion from Justice Yu's question, without being entangled in the caveat mentioned above. Irrespective of the justice's real intention, to make filial piety the sole criterion of clan membership is an unrealistic demand for the defendants to accept, not only because of the practical difficulty in measuring it, but also due to the *natural* origin of clan organizations. A more practical suggestion could be as follows: since the current practice admits only adult male descendants as legitimate members solely by virtue of family ties, regardless of their actual possession of filial piety, which in principle should be considered the most important criterion for membership, then, in fairness, family ties alone, not gender, should be employed as the criterion to determine whether one is eligible for formal membership.

At any rate, regardless of which criterion is employed (filial piety or family ties), the current practice is problematic in light of Confucianism, which is the basis upon which the clan operates. Although Justice Yu eventually joined the minority opinion, the question he raised makes this type of reasoning possible. In fact, the Court seems to have employed this line of reasoning when it said (4): "The customary practice of the clan organizations to admit, among the descendants of the same ancestors, only adult men as members, and to exclude women from formal membership . . . lacks justification and reasonableness, because it endows or denies the opportunity to participate in clan activities such as maintenance of the tombs of common ancestors and memorial ceremonies solely on the basis of sex."

Unlike Justice Yu's case, Justice Cho's reasoning does not directly involve Confucianism, but it does not appeal to the liberal notions of individual dignity and gender equality either. [22] His question focuses on a member's duty, in return for which she can claim the affiliated right, in this case, to property. What is at stake, however, does not seem to merely rectify the asymmetry between duty (fulfilled) and right (not granted). The more important point has to do with what is implied in the justice's question, which is that at the heart of clan membership is a member's voluntary participation in various kinds of clan activities, mostly rites-related. Thus, the underlying reasoning is that only those who are participating in the rites are entitled to claim rights. [23] In response, Hwang Dŏk-nam, representing the plaintiffs, said that the plaintiffs indeed had rarely participated in memorial ceremonies for ancestors beyond their great-grandparents, but argued that the reason for the lack of participation had mainly to do with denial of their formal clan membership. [24]

In a sense, Justice Cho's question is full of irony because he is asking about duties where there are no recognized rights. In the absence of recognized membership, how can we think about "rights," to which only members are entitled? Wasn't the case precisely about recognizing daughters as formal members of the clan? Once again, available data does not tell us exactly what the justice had in mind when he raised the question. His intention could be sheer fact-checking, to see if the plaintiffs had fulfilled their duties (both financial and, more importantly, ritual) as de facto members by virtue of family relations. However, strong emphasis on duty or exclusive focus on the asymmetry problem in adjudicating the question of membership does not so much solve the problem as generate another one, a problem more intractable, that is, what to do with male descendants who are negligent of their duties. Given that the duties at issue here cannot be thought of independently from filial piety, the virtue that generates duties on the part of the descendants— the whole conundrum associated with Justice Yu's question—is likely to be reintroduced.

In my view, the best way to make sense of Justice Cho's question while avoiding the filial piety-duty-right conundrum is to see it as a normative statement. The question then is seen in a fresh light as involving several propositions:

1. Clan membership involves both rights and duties;

2. Rights, including property rights, *ought* to depend upon the practice of rites (and other duties necessary for the sustenance of the clan);

3. However, the plaintiffs have been systematically deprived of formal clan membership (and only as a member can one fulfill his or her rightful duties); therefore,

4. Should the Court decide for the plaintiffs, both sons and daughters ought to be equally obligated to fulfill their duties.

According to this reasoning (i.e., Confucian public reasoning), equal formal membership is granted according to one's birth right regardless of gender, but the real point is the way in which gender equality is realized within the clan structure. It is not by imposing the Western-liberal notion of gender equality on clan members but by virtue of equal participation in the rites and fulfillment of duties.

This line of reasoning is not incidentally compatible with the Court's decision. There is a good reason to suspect that the Court indeed purposely employed this very line of reasoning. [25] After all, the Court never alluded to, let alone imposed, any substantively liberal notion of gender equality, nor did it uphold a mechanical equality between men and women on the grounds of a liberal political theory such as social contract theory, irrespective of differences in roles that they have traditionally played as sons and daughters. The Court never took issue with the clan law, by which clan organizations operate and which stipulates various sorts of gendered ritual roles and obligations that many liberals and feminists find patriarchal and androcentric. [26] Moreover, by recognizing clan organizations as naturally originated, the Court endorsed the popular Confucian (hence non-contractual) understanding of them as extended families. Again, what the Court ruled problematic was the clan organizations' customary practice to endow and deny solely on the basis of gender the *rightful* opportunity to participate in clan activities and fulfill duties affiliated with that right. The plaintiffs took the decision precisely in this way, when Hwang said, "The decision means that women have [now] been given their proper position in light of gender equality, but it also means that women must carry out their share of duties as clan members." [27]

Seen in this way, the popular view of the court decision as a victory of liberalism over Confucianism should be reconsidered. The gender equality and individual dignity that the Court seemingly vindicated were based on equal rights to formal clan membership between men and women as *sons and daughters*. From a purely legal perspective, the Court derived the right to equal formal membership solely from the candidates' family ties. A close reading of the decision, however, tells us that the Court's real intent was to point out the substantive meaning of membership rights, fully justifiable in light of the (Confucian) purpose for which the clan organizations exist. In upholding gender equality, the Court, instead of appealing to the abstract

notion of rights or enlisting the authority of any particular liberal notion of
rights, vindicated a right that is most apposite in the given context by enabling female members to actively participate in clan activities. In other
words, the Court negotiated rights, the backbone of liberalism, with rites (and
associated duties), thereby creating *Confucian rights* that can undergird the
moral ideals of individual dignity and gender equality, commonly known as
liberal values.

CLAN ORGANIZATIONS AS VOLUNTARY PRIVATE ASSOCIATIONS?

My claim that the Supreme Court's decision cannot be framed in terms of
liberalism versus Confucianism or modernity versus tradition is in part vindicated by the fact that the decision was a very close call. Seven out of thirteen
justices formed the majority, while the remaining six, including Justice Yu
Chi-tam, whose views I discussed earlier, submitted a minority opinion,
which the media largely sidelined, thus depriving the Korean public of the
chance to make better sense of what was further at stake in this case.

The minority opinion raised a question about the majority opinion's conclusion. The key points of the minority opinion can be recapitulated as follows:

1. In general, we agree that our patrilineal customary practice needs to be
   revisited and reevaluated. However, considering the fact that the pro-
   genitors of the clans are all male ancestors, the scope and limit of
   gender equality within clan organizations require a more careful approach.
2. Admittedly, [Confucian-style] clan organizations are uniquely Korean
   traditional cultural assets and Article 9 of the Constitution requires us
   to strive to succeed and develop them in ways harmonious with contemporary legal order.
3. In principle, the most important obligation of the clan members is to
   continue the ritual ceremonies of worshiping their common ancestors
   and [properly conducting this task] requires several associated services to the clan, including maintenance of family ancestral burial
   grounds and mountains . . . which are not so much duties coerced by
   law but only moral or ethical obligations. Since there is no relevant
   case of legal infringement upon the members' rights, public law has
   no reason to interfere with the clans' [international operations]. Likewise, from a legal point of view, the customary practice that an adult
   man automatically acquires clan membership regardless of his willingness is not problematic.

4. While the majority opinion states that the customary law in question has become incompatible with our "entire" legal order, in reality it evaluates the customary law governing clan organizations solely from the standpoint of the gender equality principle. We do not agree with this mechanical application of the gender equality principle to the current case.

5. Moreover, in adjudicating the question of clan membership from the standpoint of Korea's entire legal order, clans which are associations for ancestral worship and familial intimacy in terms of their functions, hence essentially private voluntary associations, the more pressing legal issue to consider than the principle of gender equality is how clan membership can be understood in light of freedom of association in Article 22-1 of the Constitution. . . . Also, since there can be various attitudes toward sacrificial rites, from the view that it is a long-established fine custom (*mipungyangsok* 美風良俗) to the extremely negative view that it is a superstition, the clan membership question should be considered in relation to freedom of conscience (Article 19) as well as freedom of religion (Article 20).

6. As for membership in private voluntary associations, it cannot be that someone should be included as a member, artificially or coercively, irrespective of his or her voluntary consent.

7. Since the problem of the customary law governing clan organizations is limited to the case that those adult women who explicitly expressed their willingness to join their clans have been denied formal membership . . . and since an increasing number of women want to participate in clan activities, open for only formal members, corresponding with their increasing self-awareness of the right and desire for clear self-identity, unless there is a justified and rational reason to deny membership (for instance, no familial ties with the clan's progenitor), an adult woman can acquire membership by expressing her willingness to become a member.

8. Seen in this way, the majority opinion's conclusion that descendants who share with their common ancestors the same surname (*sŏng* 姓) and ancestral seat (*pon* 本) are automatically entitled to formal clan membership once they come of age, regardless of sex, is problematic.

Roughly, the minority opinion has two parts: while the first part (1 through 4) is focused on the reasonableness of the clan organizations' customary practices, especially with regard to membership, the second part (5 through 8) is concerned mainly with an argument from the perspective of the constitutional right to freedom of association. Whether these two parts logically cohere with each other, however, is unclear. The first part finds the customary law (*kwansŭppŏp* 慣習法) governing clan organizations reasonable, because it does not violate anyone's rights, and clan organizations are also found worthy of public protection because they are an important part of the cultural heritage and/or national culture which Korean Constitution Article 9 aims to protect.[28] Worth noting here is that clan organizations are understood as *natural* kin groups, as customary law defines them, and it is such customarily defined clan organizations whose internal operation the minority opinion finds largely reasonable. The second part of the opinion, however, redefines the clan organization, in a way making sense in modern legal terms, by calling it a *private voluntary association*. This redefinition of clan organizations is of crucial significance because it shifts the focus of jurisprudence from the question of "customary law versus modern constitutional law" to that of "a cultural group's autonomy vis-à-vis the constitution."

As we have seen earlier, the Court's majority opinion revolves around the first framework, the question of how to balance between customary law, represented by the ongoing practices of the clans, understood as natural kin groups, and Korea's modern constitutional law. Navigating within this framework, the majority opinion implies that Koreans, as long as they are of aristocratic origin,[29] are all (potential) members of their respective clans, regardless of whether they actually participate in them or not. And it is in part for this reason that the mass media understood the Court's (majority) decision as dismantling one of the country's oldest customary laws and thus covered it extensively and with great enthusiasm, as if it concerned the entire Korean population.[30] Certainly, the Court did not subscribe to the pre-formulated framework of "liberalism versus Confucianism" as noted earlier, but it was clearly aware that its decision in favor of the plaintiffs would make the entire Korean legal order more modern as well as progressive.

In the second part, however, the dissenting justices are seemingly chastising the majority opinion's grand ambition to transform traditional Confucianism into a Confucianism safe in modern Korea, constitutionally predicated on liberal values and principles, even though they generally concur with the rationale that traditional Confucianism and its underlying institutions need to be properly reconstructed, as evidenced in statements 1 and especially 2. In the dissenting opinion's view, a critical mistake of the majority opinion was to misunderstand the nature of clan organizations within the contemporary Korean constitutional structure. Historically speaking, clan organizations might have originated naturally. However, under the current (liberal) constitutional structure we are not equipped with proper legal language and concepts to make meaningful legal sense of them, *unless* we consider them private voluntary associations by focusing on the members' shared practical goal of organizing ritual ceremonies for ancestor worship as well as promoting familial intimacy among themselves.[31]

Thus reformulated, then, the case at hand should not necessarily be about progressing the Korean constitutional order by reforming the customary law that putatively concerns *all* Korean citizens. Rather, the Court's task should be far more modest, namely, to adjudicate the question of who is qualified to be a member in a private voluntary association called *chongjung* in light of Korea's liberal constitution. Hence, a completely different reasoning is evident in the dissenting opinion:

1. Clan organizations are private voluntary associations;
2. As private voluntary associations, membership in clan organization is determined by the candidate's voluntary consent to become a member; therefore,
3. It is a violation of the constitutional right to freedom of association that a person is forced to become a member of the clan organization.

According to this reasoning, the target of the Court's decision is not so much women as *citizens* but women as *members* of the particular clans. Eventually, the dissenting justices concluded that only those adult women who want to be formal members of the clan organization should be given membership rights.

From a liberal political standpoint, and if we agree, for argument's sake, that clan membership is a *private* associational membership, the difference between the majority and minority opinions regarding private membership vis-à-vis the liberal-democratic constitution seems to track remarkably well the difference between political liberalism (or public reason liberalism) and liberal pluralism in contemporary liberal political theory. Here let me briefly recapitulate the core tenets of each theoretical position. Political liberalism, championed most notably by John Rawls and Stephen Macedo, understands the essential characteristic of modern liberal democratic society in terms of pluralism, that a liberal society consists of individuals and groups holding different moral, philosophical, or religious doctrines. [32] Given pervasive pluralism marked by different comprehensive doctrines and moral disagreement among individuals and groups, the most pressing political question in a liberal-constitutional democracy, according to political liberals, is how to maintain social stability and constitutional order in the face of pluralism. As is well known, the political-liberal solution to this problem relies on overlapping consensus among groups and individuals on the principles of justice (i.e., the political conception of justice) governing the constitutional essentials and society's basic structure, but not the background culture of civil society. [33] The practical implication is that political liberalism puts greater emphasis on overlapping consensus and the common liberal-democratic citizenship that it undergirds than diversity (and various associational memberships composing it) as such. [34] From the constitutional standpoint of political liberalism, public institutions (including the courts as well as schools) should play a more active role in forming and reproducing liberal-democratic citi-

zenship applicable to all reasonable citizens who otherwise belong to different moral, religious, or cultural communities as private individuals.[35]

Liberal pluralists, however, find political liberalism's perfectionist constitutional ambition to form or mold a common democratic citizenship over-
bearing and object to the congruence between the broader society's liberal-
democratic principles and the principles that govern the internal affairs of
private associations. Their central argument is that, for the most part, associations in civil society should be left insulated from state interference and
enjoy their self-governing rights derived from the constitutional right to freedom of association, unless they vitally harm other groups upholding different
comprehensive doctrines, thereby destabilizing the overall constitutional order seriously.[36]

Returning to our case, the structural affinity between the Supreme Court's
majority decision and political liberalism is not difficult to see. The Court's
decision upholds the congruence thesis, by claiming that the clan organizations' associational freedom should adapt to the constitutional principles of
gender equality and individual dignity concerned with *all* Korean citizens. In
this reasoning, clan organizations can exercise their constitutional right to
freedom of association *as long as* the moral principles governing their internal affairs—particularly the way they define membership—are congruent
with the principles of gender equality and individual dignity. Of course, there
is an important caveat in drawing this implication from the majority opinion,
because as I showed earlier, the Court achieved this seemingly "liberal"
congruence by negotiating liberal rights with Confucian rites, rather than
imposing substantively liberal notions of gender equality and individual dignity upon the clan organizations that operate mainly on Confucian laws and
rituals. Thus, although the Court's majority decision tracks well the mode of
political reasoning characteristic of political liberalism, its *liberal* dimension
is significantly qualified by Confucian moral reasoning.

Whether the minority decision also tracks liberal pluralism well, however,
is less clear, although apparently the dissenting justices' attention to freedom
of association in determining membership in a free association strongly reso-
nates with liberal pluralism. From the perspective of liberal pluralism, it is
troubling, as much as the majority opinion's congruence thesis, that the minority opinion does not fully endorse the clan organizations' freedom of
association and the right to self-government that follows. Why do the dissenting justices still conclude that the clan organizations should accept wom-
en (who want to be members) as members, when the defendants' core claim
is that acceptance of women *critically* threatens their traditional Confucian
way of life? Does the clans' right to self-government in accordance with their
tradition, which precedes the establishment of the modern legal system, *seriously* or *vitally* threaten the constitutional order of the Korean polity? Corre-
spondingly, what is the *compelling* reason for the state to intervene with

internal affairs of the clan organizations, which the minority opinion understands as private voluntary associations, given the very small number of the Korean populace who even belong to clan organizations in contemporary Korea? Put differently, if the minority opinion recognizes the clan organizations as private voluntary associations, why does it still force them to embrace, albeit partially, the liberal ideal of gender equality, when they actively reject a liberal way of life? Shouldn't Korea's liberal-democratic constitution protect this non-liberal way of life in the very name of liberty (i.e., freedom of association) as long as it does not vitally threaten the foundation of the constitutional order?

There is yet another problem. Even if it is granted, contrary to the majority opinion, that the clan organizations are private associations and thus it is problematic for the majority opinion to treat the clan organizations' internal way of life as if it concerned all Korean citizens, it is unclear why the minority opinion regards the clan organizations as purely voluntary associations. If the clan organizations were purely voluntary private associations, why didn't the dissenting justices find the involuntary nature of (established) male membership equally problematic, while forcing the organizations to accept women on a voluntary basis? In this regard, the Court's decision was not entirely wrong when it defines the clan organizations as *natural* associations, of course, if by natural the court meant to stress the involuntary nature of membership, which applied to both men and women.

In the end, notwithstanding more attention to liberty through the invocation of freedom of association, the minority opinion also turned out to be not fully *liberal* in its intended sense (i.e., liberal pluralism), because it still upheld the moral principle of gender equality in clan membership by applying contractrian reasoning to clan organizations, which are in fact involuntary associations whose membership is formed by virtue of family ties.[37] Nor did it uphold the more substantively liberal meaning of freedom of association, namely the compelling moral and constitutional justification of the state to intervene in internal affairs of private associations, particularly involuntary associations formed by cultural and religious groups.[38]

CONCLUSION

So, what does all this mean? What I wish to point out is that neither the majority opinion nor the minority opinion was unambiguously liberal in terms of both reasoning and conclusion. The minority opinion, despite its ostensibly greater commitment to liberal constitutionalism, at the core of which lies protection of core liberties (including freedom of association), was more problematic precisely because of its liberal commitment. Not only did it fail to recognize the clan organizations' self-governing rights according to their traditional way of life (which does not vitally threaten the constitutional order) by the logic of freedom of (involuntary) association, but more problematically, it wrongly assumed that freedom of association is applicable only to voluntary associations while actually applying this right to clan organizations which it deemed as naturally originated. Interestingly, because of its weaker sensitivity to the constitutional value of liberties, the majority opinion was able to avoid altogether the liberal moral and legal conundrum and arrive at the conclusion that in my view could accommodate the growing moral sensitivity among the Korean public toward gender equality and individual dignity without reconstituting the clan organizations in substantively liberal terms, thus still leaving their internal order and way of life substantively Confucian.

Thus understood, what is actually taking place in contemporary Korea is far more complex than what the triumph of liberalism over Confucianism thesis commonly stipulates. The reality can be better grasped in terms of ongoing dialectic processes of negotiations and renegotiations between rights and rites, between (individual/associational) liberties and (common democratic) citizenship, and between liberal constitutionalism and Confucian moral reasoning. Still, for many Koreans, Confucian rituals, norms, and laws are not merely the private matters of those who insist on living directly under them as members of clan organizations or traditional extended families. They still hold a strong grip on the Korean people as a sort of "habit of the heart," through which they can come to terms with liberal rights, liberties, values, and institutions. And it is for this reason (unwittingly, I think) that the Supreme Court treated the case of formal clan membership, otherwise a purely private matter concerning only the actual and potential members of the clan organizations, as a constitutional question that concerned all Korean citizens. As we have seen, the result of such complex processes is a new Confucianism made sense of through the use of various concepts in contemporary literature, such as Confucian rights, Confucian constitutionalism, and Confucian democracy. In such processes, traditional Confucianism, with its morally comprehensive characteristics, is constantly being adapted to liberal-democratic institutions and values, rather than merely being superseded by them, re-articulated in democratic-constitutional and liberal-democratic terms—especially (but not exclusively) in the courts—and re-created as a new mode of Confucianism that is far less comprehensive and much more civic and civil, providing the Korean people with resources from which they draw moral reasoning publicly available to other citizens. [39]

This does not mean that we can pinpoint exactly what this new Confucianism is or what it consists of. The Confucianism at issue here (and the Confucian public reasons it furnishes) is open to public debate and democratic contestation regarding both its nature as *Confucianism* and its complex relations to liberal-democratic and liberal-constitutionalist structures of the

Korean society. Traditional Confucians may find it to simply be another version of liberalism, while liberals for their part may point to the remnants of traditional Confucianism still attached to it, complaining that this "Confucianism" only corrodes the liberal authenticity of Korean democracy and constitutionalism. But can't we envision Korean democracy and constitutionalism from the perspective of this reformed Confucianism, not from either the abstract notion of liberal democracy or a substantively Western liberal-style democracy?[40] It is a daunting task, to be sure, but I believe it can offer Koreans modes of democracy and constitutionalism (or ideally a coherent mode of democratic constitutionalism) that are more culturally relevant and socially practicable. This constructive project begins with a thorough investigation of the new mode of Confucianism, namely *civil Confucianism*, which I have only been able to introduce in this essay.[41]

NOTES

This research was supported by an Academy of Korean Studies Grant funded by the Korean Government (MEST) (AKS-2011-AAA-2102).
 1. Martina Deuchler, *The Confucian Transformation of Korea: A Study of Society and Ideology* (Cambridge, MA: Harvard University Press, 1992).
 2. Tu Wei-ming, "The Search for Roots in Industrial East Asia: The Case of the Confucian Revival," in *Fundamentalisms Observed*, eds. Martin E. Marty and R. Scott Appleby (Chicago: University of Chicago Press, 1991), p. 761. Also see Byung-ik Koh, "Confucianism in Contemporary Korea," in *Confucian Traditions in East Asian Modernity: Moral Education and Economic Culture in Japan and Four Mini-Dragons*, ed. Tu Wei-ming (Cambridge, MA: Harvard University Press); Geir Helgesen, *Democracy and Authority in Korea: The Cultural Dimension in Korean Politics* (Surrey: Curzon, 1998).
 3. Doh Chull Shin, *Confucianism and Democratization in East Asia* (New York: Cambridge University Press, 2012). Doh's operationalization of "Confucianism," however, is question-begging because he understands Confucianism in terms of collectivism, hierarchy, familism, and meritocracy, thereby blurring the line between Confucianism and the non-Confucian collectivistic-hierarchical value system. Despite this methodological problem, Shin's research still shows a strong hold of (a certain aspect of) Confucianism in contemporary Korea. Also see Mun-jo Bae and Se-jeong Park, "Taehaksengŭi hyoedaehan inshikkwaa kachokgach'igwane yŏnghyang'ŭl mich'inŭn pyŏnin" [Consciousness of Filial Piety and Family Values among College Students], *Journal of the Korean Contents Association* 13 (2013), pp. 275–85; Su-young Ryu, "Han'gukinui yugyojeok gachicheukjeongnunhang gaebal yeon'gu" [Item Development for Korean Confucian Values], *Korean Journal of Management* 15 (2007), pp. 171–205.
 4. For legal and political theoretical analyses of this case, see Chaihark Hahm, "Law, Culture, and the Politics of Confucianism," *Columbia Journal of Asian Law* 16, no. 2 (2003), pp. 253–301, at pp. 287–296; and Chaibong Hahm, "Family versus the Individual: The Politics of Marriage Laws in Korea," in *Confucianism for the Modern World*, eds. Daniel A. Bell and Chaibong Hahm (Cambridge: Cambridge University Press, 2003) respectively.
 5. In addition, in 1998, the Constitutional Court declared unconstitutional parts of Law Concerning Family Rituals (*Kajŏng Ŭirye-e kwanhan Pŏmnyul*) (Law No. 4367), a form of Confucian sumptuary law, because it violated an individual's right to happiness. See Hahm, "Law, Culture, and the Politics of Confucianism," pp. 280–287. Unless otherwise noted, all transliterations of the Chinese characters in this paper are based on the Korean pronunciation.
 6. Many contemporary Confucian political philosophers uphold this incompatibility thesis. See, for instance, Chenyang Li, "Confucian Value and Democratic Value," *Journal of Value*

Inquiry 31 (1993), pp. 183–93; Henry Rosemont, Jr., "Why Take Rights Seriously? A Confucian Critique," in *Human Rights and the World's Religions*, ed. Leroy Rouner (Notre Dame, IN: University of Notre Dame Press, 1988), pp. 167–82.

7. For a discussion about Confucianism as the Korean *doxa* through which Koreans are socialized, often unconsciously, into their unique cultural values, social norms, and moral precepts, see Byung-kook Kim, "Panyugyojŏk yugyojŏngch'i" [Confucian Politics That Are Anti-Confucian], *Chŏntong-gwa Hyŏndae* [Tradition and Modernity] 1 (1997), pp. 50–73.

8. For an illuminating study on such cultural negotiations, see Chaihark Hahm, "Negotiating Confucian Civility through Constitutional Discourse," in *The Politics of Affective Relations: East Asia and Beyond*, eds. Chaihark Hahm and Daniel A. Bell (Lanham, MD: Lexington Books, 2003), pp. 277–308.

9. In Korea, a clan association consists of male descendants sharing the same surname, same ancestral seat, and (often, but not necessarily) the same branch. In the present case, the clan association is composed of those whose surname is Lee, whose ancestral seat is Yong'in, and whose branch is Samaenggong. While the ancestral seat (*pon* 本 or *pon'gwan* 本貫) refers to the regional origin of the clan's founder, the branch (*p'a* 派) refers to a subgroup within the entire clan sharing the same ancestral seat and is often created by someone who either held a high governmental post or was hailed as a prominent Confucian scholar.

10. Originally, the clan council was going to distribute the dividends only to the formal members of the clan, but upon vehement complaints from various "members" excluded from a share of the wealth, it eventually decided to give a certain amount of money to some female members, including daughters-in-law.

11. This Confucian norm was widely disseminated in Korean society after the *Family Ritual* by Zhu Xi (1130–1200), the authoritative compiler of Cheng-Zhu Neo-Confucianism or the Learning of the Way (c. *Daoxue* 道學) during the Song dynasty, had become the orthodox guidelines regulating the *yangban* aristocratic families. Regarding the married women's inheritance rights during the Chosŏn period, Martina Deuchler writes, "The integration of women into their husbands' descent group as demanded by Confucian ideology is impressively illustrated by the daughters' gradual loss of inheritance rights. . . . [B]y the middle of the dynasty daughters who upon marriage left their natal family were deprived of their stake in their families' ancestral property and entered their husbands' home without the land and slaves they had brought in earlier. . . . Women thus lost the economic independence they had enjoyed at the beginning of the dynasty. This development was closely connected with the gradual acceptance of the rule of primogeniture that concentrated a descent group's ancestral land and slaves in the hands of its primary agnatic heir" (*The Confucian Transformation of Korea*, p. 266).

12. *Han'gyŏre Shinmun*, July 21, 2005.

13. To avoid a disruption in legal order and continuity, however, the Court noted that the decision was not retroactive, leaving unaffected male-only votes on clan leaders and clan property distribution made prior to this decision.

14. Korean Supreme Court, judgment of July 21, 2005, 2002ta13850.

15. On the Constitutional Court's abolition of the family-head system, see Hyunah Yang, "Vision of Postcolonial Feminist Jurisprudence in Korea: Seen from the 'Family-Head System' in Family Law," *Journal of Korean Law* 5, 2 (2006), pp. 12–28.

16. Sungkyunkwan 成均館 used to be the National Academy during the Chosŏn dynasty, and was and still is considered Korea's Confucian sanctuary.

17. All direct and indirect quotations in this paragraph are adopted from the English version of *Chosun Ilbo* (July 21, 2005). Note that the romanization of the Korean names here follows the Ministry of Education system promulgated in 2000. In other places in this chapter, I employ the McCune-Reischauer system.

18. "The gentleman (*junzi* 君子) devotes his efforts to the roots, for once the roots are established, the Way will grow therefrom. Being good as a son and obedient as a young man is, perhaps, the root of a man's character" (*Analects* 1:2). The English translation is adopted from D. C. Lau, trans., *The Analects* (New York: Penguin, 1979). On the fundamental importance of filial piety to *ren*, see Sin Yee Chan, "Filial Piety, Commiseration, and the Virtue of *Ren*," in *Filial Piety in Chinese Thought and History*, eds. Alan K. L. Chan and Sor-hoon Tan (London: RoutledgeCurzon, 2004); Chenyang Li, "Shifting Perspectives: Filial Morality Revisited," *Phi-*

losophy East and West 47 (1997), pp. 211–32; Philip J. Ivanhoe, "Filial Piety as Virtue," in *Working Virtue: Virtue Ethics and Contemporary Moral Problems*, eds. Rebecca L. Walker and Philip J. Ivanhoe (Oxford: Oxford University Press, 2007).

19. I admit that only the last proposition is inferable directly from Justice Yu's question and the other propositions are my own reconstruction, which may not have been intended by the justice himself. However, there seems to be no better way to make sense of the reasoning that led to Justice Yu's question.

20. For instance, see Whasook Lee, "Married Daughters Should Be Recognized as 'Jong-jung' Members," *Munhwa Ilbo*, December 17, 2003 (English version).

21. It is worth noting that during the late eighteenth and early nineteenth centuries, some Korean female Neo-Confucian scholars such as Im Yunjidang (1721–1793) and Kang Chŏngildang (1772–1832) advanced the idea of moral equality between men and women by revisiting classical Confucian texts such as the *Analects* of Confucius, the *Mencius*, and the *Doctrine of the Mean*. See Ŭn-sŏn Yi, *Irŏbŏrin ch'owŏrŭl ch'ajasŏ* [In Search of Transcendence That Has Been Lost] (Seoul: Mosinŭn saramdŭl, 2009), pp. 101–64; Youngmin Kim, "Neo-Confucianism as Free-Floating Resource: Im Yunjidang and Kang Chŏngildang as Two Female Neo-Confucian Philosophers in Late Chosŏn," in *Women and Confucianism in Chosŏn Korea*, eds. Youngmin Kim and Michael J. Pettid (Albany: State University of New York Press, 2011); Sungmoon Kim, "The Way to Become a Female Sage: Im Yunjidang's Confucian Feminism," *Journal of the History of Ideas* 75 (2014), pp. 396–16, and "From Wife to Moral Teacher: Kang Chŏngildang's Neo-Confucian Self-Cultivation," *Asian Philosophy* 24 (2014), pp. 28–47.

22. Justice Cho retired in 2004, so he could not participate in the actual decision. However, this does not weaken the importance of his question because it cannot be doubted that the question, which was raised in a public hearing in the presence of all other members of the Court, was part of the Court's reasoning process.

23. For a philosophical study drawing on a similar reasoning, see D. W. Y. Kwok, "On the Rites and Rights of Being Human," in *Confucianism and Human Rights*, eds. Wm. Theodore de Bary and Tu Wei-ming (New York: Columbia University Press, 1998), pp. 83–93.

24. *Ohmynews*, December 19, 2003.

25. The reasoning at issue is not a legal reasoning, strictly speaking. However, it is impossible to think of any sound legal reasoning that does not involve a complex set of moral propositions, beliefs, and reasoning, which I call Confucian public reasoning.

26. See, for instance, Hyunah Yang, "Unfinished Tasks for Korean Family Policy in the 1990s: Maternity Protection Policy and Abolition of the Family-Head System," *Korea Journal* 42, no. 2 (2002), pp. 68–99.

27. *Chosun Ilbo*, July 21, 2005 (English edition).

28. Constitution Article 9: The State shall strive to sustain and develop the cultural heritage and to enhance national culture.

29. This provision, however, is almost negligible, because while at the beginning of the Chosŏn dynasty, the number of Confucian yangban aristocrats amounted to merely 1–3 percent of the total population, by the end of the nineteenth century, approximately 70 percent of the Korean people had become yangban. See Sangjun Kim, *Maengchaŭi ttam sŏngwangŭi p'i* [Sweat of Mencius and Blood of the Sacred Kings] (Seoul: Akanet, 2011), pp. 497–509. In contemporary Korea, most Koreans consider themselves descendants of the yangban family and many families possess their family genealogies (*zupu* 族譜), which traditionally belonged exclusively to the yangban class. Of course, whether a particular Korean family is organized through clan organization is a different story.

30. *Hangyŏrye Shinmun*, July 21, 2005.

31. For a similar suggestion, see Chang–Hyun Lee, "Chongjungŭi chayulkkwŏn'gwa kŭ han'gye [Clan's Autonomy and Its Limit]," *Kachokpŏpyŏn'gu* [Korean Journal of Family Law] 24 (2010), pp. 75–110.

32. John Rawls, *Political Liberalism* (New York: Columbia University Press, 1993); Stephen Macedo, *Diversity and Distrust: Civic Education in a Multicultural Democracy* (Cambridge, MA: Harvard University Press, 2000).

33. Rawls, *Political Liberalism*, pp. 214–16; "The Idea of Public Reason Revisited," in *The Law of Peoples* (Cambridge, MA: Harvard University Press, 1999), pp. 129–80, at pp. 133–34. Notwithstanding Rawls's argument about "the limit of public reason," many Rawls-inspired political liberals apply public reasoning and deliberation more broadly to various cases of moral disagreement in civil society. See, for instance, Amy Gutmann and Dennis Thompson, *Democracy and Disagreement: Why Moral Conflict Cannot Be Avoided in Politics, and What Should Be Done about It* (Cambridge, MA: Belknap, 1996); Amy Gutmann, *Identity in Democracy* (Princeton, NJ: Princeton University Press, 2003); Henry S. Richardson, *Democratic Autonomy: Public Reasoning about the Ends of Policy* (New York: Oxford University Press, 2002); Gerald F. Gaus, *Justificatory Liberalism: An Essay on Epistemology and Political Theory* (New York: Oxford University Press, 1996).

34. Most clearly, Rawls writes, "Public reason is characteristic of a democratic people: it is the reason of its citizens, of those sharing the status of equal citizenship" (*Political Liberalism*, p. 213).

35. As Eamonn Callan puts it, "A powerful constraint on the background culture of liberal politics is an inevitable consequence of the education that Rawlsian political liberalism entails" (*Creating Citizens: Political Education and Liberal Democracy* [Oxford: Oxford University Press, 1997], p. 36).

36. See William A. Galston, *Liberal Pluralism: The Implications of Value Pluralism for Political Theory* (Cambridge: Cambridge University Press, 2002); Nancy Rosenblum, *Membership and Morals: The Personal Uses of Pluralism in America* (Princeton, NJ: Princeton University Press, 1998); George Crowder, *Liberalism and Value Pluralism* (New York: Continuum, 2002).

37. Michael Walzer says that "freedom requires nothing more than the possibility of breaking involuntary bonds and, furthermore, that the actual break is not always a good thing, and that we need not always make it easy. Many valuable memberships are not freely chosen; many binding obligations are not entirely the product of consent. We can think of our life together as a 'social construction' in which we, as individuals, have had a hand; we cannot plausibly think of it as something wholly made by ourselves" ("On Involuntary Association," in *Freedom of Association*, ed. Amy Gutmann [Princeton, NJ: Princeton University Press, 1998], pp. 64–74, at p. 64).

38. See William A. Galston, *The Practice of Liberal Pluralism* (Cambridge: Cambridge University Press, 2005).

39. For a detailed discussion on Confucian public reason(ing), see Sungmoon Kim, *Confucian Democracy in East Asia: Theory and Practice* (New York: Cambridge University Press, 2014), chapters 5 and 8.

40. This does not mean that liberalism has been an unchanging set of beliefs and practices. Like Confucianism, liberalism has always been contested and evolving. Thus understood, we must shed the shibboleth of essentialism in both cases. What we then are left with is the challenge of describing and perhaps joining in the ongoing negotiation between past and present on the way to the future. I am grateful to Philip J. Ivanhoe for drawing my attention to this point.

41. I introduced the term *civil Confucianism* in "The Virtue of Incivility: Confucian Communitarianism beyond Docility," *Philosophy and Social Criticism* 37, no. 1 (2011), pp. 25–48, but did not conceive of it in relation to Confucian constitutionalism. In *Confucian Democracy* (especially chapters 4 and 11), I make the constitutional dimension of civil Confucianism more pronounced, but as it stands the concept needs more articulation.

II

Liberalism, Democracy, and Confucianism: Doubts and Hopes

Chapter Five

Qualitative Defects of Korean Constitutional Democracy and Political Rationalism as a Confucian Legacy

Bi Hwan Kim

The purpose of this paper is to bring into relief an important long-term problem of Korean politics by illuminating a main cause of the qualitative defects of Korean constitutional democracy, with a special focus on the Korean political culture in which Confucianism occupies the most basal layer. The main argument of this paper has two components. One is that political rationalism as a Confucian legacy, which was established as the main political consciousness during the Chosŏn dynasty (1392–1910) by a group of orthodox Neo-Confucians called the Sarim faction or Sarimp'a 士林派 (literally, the faction of the forest of Confucian scholars) around the time of King Sŏnjo's (r. 1567–1608) accession to the throne, has been gradually and firmly occupying the bottom layer of the Korean political culture in the course of its transition through a series of political events, simultaneously shaping the character of politics and orienting the people's general perception toward politics and law. The other component of the argument is that the qualitative defects of Korean constitutional democracy in the current form might be partially explained as the result of strong political rationalism, the fundamental character of which was first introduced and established by Confucian Tohak Chŏngch'i 道學政治 (the politics by Confucian morals).[1]

It was once widely taken as a matter of fact that Korea consolidated its democracy most rapidly among the countries democratized during the third democratic wave, after its successful democratization in 1987. The assessment of Korean democracy by Freedom House and Polity IV Project has supported its apparently big success. According to new assessment methodologies introduced after the 1990s, however, Korean democracy has been generally considered an imperfectly consolidated liberal democracy, that is, a defective liberal democracy.[2] Various factors might have contributed to this, including political factors such as strong regionalism and imperial presidency, as well as nonpolitical ones such as protracted economic stagnation and serious economic bipolarization due to sustained neoliberal globalization. It is difficult, however, to view some of these factors as main determinants of the low quality of Korean politics, because, to a certain degree, they might be more properly seen as the outcomes or symptoms of Korea's defective democracy itself rather than the other way around. Accordingly, another explanation needs to be offered, one which can more persuasively shed light on the main cause of the important defects of Korean democracy. The main purpose of this paper is to identify this problem.

Rationalism, as one of the most important characteristics of Neo-Confucianism, is a special form of political consciousness, which works in conceptualizing political order, in understanding the relationship between morals and politics, and in grasping the nature of governmental activities and the legal system. It was most firmly established during the Chosŏn dynasty in its purest and strongest form, especially after the Sarim faction initiated the Neo-Confucian Tohak Chŏngch'i during the latter half of the sixteenth century. The main argument of this paper is that political rationalism, first introduced by the Sarimp'a, in the course of its struggle with the strongly hierarchical status system, has preserved and even strengthened its formal characteristics while passing through momentous political events in Korean history. It has therefore constituted the most fundamental layer of Korean political consciousness, consequently affecting the quality of Korean constitutional democracy until today.[3]

Viewed in light of rationalism, politics can be regarded as a kind of efficient social engineering by a small group of elites, in which the rule of law is deemed a necessary device mainly to punish or eradicate the deviant behaviors of the ordinary people and elections are employed as an institutional apparatus by which the majority of people delegate the political power comprehensively to elected officials. In the political climate dominated by political rationalism for a long time, especially under a hierarchical status system, it is almost impossible for politics to be viewed as a collective deliberative process through which the laws are made and revised in order to rightfully guide interactions among free and equal citizens. Nor is it possible that politicians and ordinary people can view the rule of law as a political principle effectively constraining the use of political power by governmental officials on the one hand and simultaneously providing the ordinary people with an effective means to protect their basic rights on the other. Therefore, if it can be persuasively shown that the basal layer or an essential part of the contemporary Korean political culture is occupied by strong rationalist consciousness, some qualitative defects of contemporary Korean constitutional democracy might be partly seen as the results of its influence.

The framework of the rest of the chapter is as follows. The second section explains the characteristics of political rationalism immanent in Neo-Confucianism and its historical embodiment in the middle of the Chosŏn dynasty, and the third section traces its historical process of reproduction and augmentation, with special emphasis on some important historical events before the momentous democratization in 1987. The fourth section deals with how Korean political rationalism with such a long history still strongly influences Korean politics and prevents them from progressing into fully mature democratic politics supported by the rule of law. The concluding section suggests a direction for Korean constitutional democracy, based on the appraisal of political rationalism as a dominant consciousness in contemporary Korean politics.

POLITICAL RATIONALISM OF NEO-CONFUCIANISM AND ITS HISTORICAL EMBODIMENT IN THE CHOSŎN DYNASTY

It is relatively well-established wisdom that, compared with the original Confucianism marked by empiricism,[4] Neo-Confucianism as reconstructed especially by Zhu Xi 朱熹 (1130–1200) in the Chinese Song 宋 dynasty (960–1279) can be characterized by its notable rationalism and intellectualism. Because of the difference between these two versions of Confucianism, it is sometimes hotly debated whether these two schools belong to the same tradition.[5] Without engaging in this debate, however, I take it for granted that Neo-Confucianism is a dominant branch of Confucianism, constructed especially by Cheng Hao 程顥 (1032–1085), Cheng Yi 程頤 (1033–1107), and Zhu Xi during the Song dynasty in the course of reformulating a more systematic Confucian theory of the cosmos, political society, and man, in order both to promote the moral cultivation and ethical life of the then Chinese people (especially the elite class) and to meet the challenges from Buddhism.[6] Cheng Hao, Cheng Yi, and especially Zhu Xi tried to make a serious effort to build up a coherent theory encompassing cosmology, political theory, and ethics, which could surpass the very exquisite Buddhist philosophical system that prevailed in the society in their time. Because of this reconstructive philosophical character of Neo-Confucianism, it came to exhibit a relatively abstract, rationalist, and intellectualist character rather than an empirical one, compared to the original Confucianism of Confucius and Mencius. Even though Neo-Confucianism was pursued in the course of meeting the practical challenges by offering a new interpretation of early Confucianism, its heavily metaphysical system made it virtually impossible for the ordinary

people to understand it. Despite the abstractness and logicality of Neo-Confucianism, however, Neo-Confucianism of the Song dynasty retained a certain degree of practical relevance because it was reconstructed by the then
Confucian scholar-officials who hoped to offer realistic solutions to the social and political problems of the time.

Another important point needs to be mentioned in relation to the practical
influence and the limits of Neo-Confucianism as the governmental school of
the Song dynasty. Despite its relative superiority over other schools or religions in terms of political theory, Song Neo-Confucianism neither tried to
reconstruct the whole society in line with its theories of man and political
society nor squarely pitted itself against the then flourishing Buddhism, because it accommodated many formal and substantive elements of Buddhism,
its struggle with Buddhism notwithstanding. And as traditional China entered
into the Ming 明 dynasty (1368–1644), the formalistic character of the Neo-
Confucianism of the Song dynasty was challenged by a more substantial and
empirical kind of Neo-Confucianism, called Yangmingxue 陽明學, which
was deeply influenced by Wang Yangming's 王陽明 (1472–1529) personal
experience of Buddhism and Daoism. Therefore, the Neo-Confucian aristocratic literati class of the Song dynasty neither tried nor could try to rebuild
the society out of its abstract theories. It worked as the official governmental
school only within the limited area of governmental activity, including the
recruitment of government elites.

In late Koryŏ and early Chosŏn, a group of Confucian scholar-officials
introduced Song Neo-Confucianism, especially the version developed by
Zhu Xi, to Korean society and studied and further tried to utilize it in reforming the political and legal system. Around the time of the dynastic change
and even before the establishment of the institutional arrangement of
Chosŏn's fundamental legal code during the reign of King Sŏngjong (r.
1469–1494), however, Korean Neo-Confucian scholar-officials still had to
fight against strong Buddhist elements deeply permeating every nook and
corner of the Korean society, including the court.[7] In founding the new
dynasty and establishing necessary institutional and legal systems, Neo-Confucian scholars first criticized the injustices and corruptions of the preceding
dynasty while struggling to rebuild the political and legal systems in accordance with Neo-Confucian principles. As soon as they succeeded in these
tasks, especially by virtue of some key Neo-Confucian scholar-officials'
(such as Chŏng Tochŏn 鄭道傳 1342–1398) strenuous efforts, the Sarim
scholars, first gaining in influence in rural areas, finally entered the central
government, resulting in a violent political struggle between them and the
then ruling elites, mainly composed of meritorious subjects and their family
members, during the dynastic foundation and consolidation periods. The result was a series of literati purges by the existing ruling elites. Around the
time when King Sŏnjo succeeded to the throne and consolidated his royal

power, the Sarim faction finally came into power and strove to implement its cherished Confucian ideals.[8] A special form of Confucian politics called Tohak Chŏngch'i was established as a result, and it became the basic model of politics on which the mainstream politics during the Chosŏn dynasty were predicated.

Cho Kwangjo 趙光祖 (1482–1520), one of the most radical Neo-Confucian leaders of the Tohak Chŏngch'i, who attempted to materialize the ideal Confucian politics during King Chungjong's reign (r. 1506–1544), was very radical and idealistic, because he tried to reform politics and society fundamentally by establishing new institutions such as the Hyanggyo 鄉校 (country Confucian shrine) and Hyŏllyanggwa 賢良科 (which appoints virtuous Confucian scholars to public posts by virtue of recommendations), as the Confucian ideals dictate, without taking into much consideration the existing social and political conditions of the Chosŏn society. Thus understood, Tohak Chŏngch'i was a kind of rationalist politics, in which some rational principles guided social and political practices of the society. In other words, in Tohak Chŏngch'i, some core Confucian ideals stated in the most important Confucian books or scriptures became the foundational principles, on the basis of which rulers and ruling elites had to run the government and bring an order to the society. In this sense, Tohak Chŏngch'i looked very similar to the rule-book conception of politics that emerged as the most important political style in modern Europe.[9]

It is common wisdom that rationalism as a modern epistemological position and its political counterpart first appeared in early modern Europe, in the midst of such historic events as the Renaissance, the Scientific Revolution, and the Religious Reformation. Descartes and his disciples are considered the main founders of modern rationalism.[10] During the sixteenth and seventeenth centuries in Europe, reason, once liberated from medieval religious worldviews in which revelation was understood as the dominant form of knowledge, began to play a significant role in organizing and governing the society.[11] As reason gradually took the place of revelation, it began to be recognized as the central human faculty that could transform or reorganize the whole society according to its self-constructed principles.

According to Michael Oakeshott and Pierre Rosanvallon, rationalism refers to a particular modern epistemological position and associated social or political imaginary frameworks.[12] Rationalism is a unique modern attitude which regards only the knowledge found or constructed by reason as true knowledge and dismisses practical knowledge such as skills and other forms of non-propositional knowledge as false or non-rational. And this epistemological dimension of rationalism naturally expands into the social and political framework through which most people see the social and political world. According to Oakeshott, modern rationalism became the dominant culture of modern Europe from the sixteenth century onward and influenced the whole of European society, most strongly in politics and education. Rosanvallon also identifies a strong rationalist tendency in French politics, especially in Quesnay's and his disciples' physiocratism, since the middle of the eighteenth century.[13] Despite the coexistence of empiricism or mild forms of rationalism in England and France throughout the modern times, the influence of rationalism in politics was so strong that no government in major countries throughout Europe could escape its influence. The hegemony enjoyed by this ideological type of politics in Europe all the way through modern times is definite evidence that the rationalist attitude to politics successfully took the place of more prudential or empirical attitudes.

Of course, there are some obvious differences between the modern Western rationalism mentioned above and the Neo-Confucian rationalism, especially the one imported in late Koryŏ and early Chosŏn. For example, compared to its modern Western counterpart, Neo-Confucian rationalism was not so self-conscious about the capacity and the limit of reason itself, and accordingly it did not develop its own sophisticated epistemological theories of reason and understanding.[14] Put differently, it was far more intuitionistic than the European form of rationalism. At the center of Neo-Confucian rationalism was a mix of unjustified belief in the self-evidence of objective knowledge or norms, strong deductive tendency in practical thinking and judgment, and intransigent assertion and application of that knowledge or those norms to social and political reality. Given this dogmatic character, one might say that Neo-Confucianism cannot be understood as a kind of rationalism. In a strictly modern Western sense, it can be said, it is non-rational.

Another aspect of Neo-Confucianism, however, is definitely rationalistic in the strictly modern Western sense. Even though Neo-Confucianism neither developed a sophisticated epistemological theory of reason nor made a serious effort to rationally justify the objective truth of its findings, the strongly deductive character of Neo-Confucianism, proceeding from the first moral principles to their applications in specific situations, was wholly congenial with what we find in modern Western Europe. Once moral principles were intuitively captured and written in the holy classics by great Confucian sages, they were regarded as the first principles from which other secondary moral norms were deductively derived and taught to their disciples and ordinary people. Concerning this aspect of rationalism, Neo-Confucianism and modern Western rationalism, especially defined by Oakeshott and Rosanvallon, are very similar to each other. Neo-Confucianism and modern European rationalism have a similar formal structure in which practice follows theory. Regardless of whether the first moral principles are captured intuitively or rationally, this second aspect of rationalism stipulates that first principles derived from the Confucian canons should be directly applied to particular situations without being adjusted to the contexts concerned.

Of course, there were more practical versions of Neo-Confucianism during the Chosŏn dynasty. For instance, it is widely agreed that Yi I's (李珥, 1536–1584) interpretation of Confucianism was more empirically grounded and practically relevant than that of Yi Hwang (李滉, 1501–1570). Also, so-called "Practical Learning" (*Sirhak* 實學), emerged among a group of Neo-Confucian scholars during the seventeenth and eighteenth century, calling for a renewed interest in the version of Confucianism that can directly improve social, economic, and political conditions. Despite the intermittent appearances of more practical suggestions, however, they never challenged successfully the hegemonic authority of Neo-Confucian rationalism to the end of the Chosŏn dynasty. Throughout the Chosŏn period, the rationalist trend of Neo-Confucianism was so strong that any defiance of it was never tolerated, let alone allowed to have an influence in the government. In fact, most of the defiant schools in the later Chosŏn period were not able to escape the gripping force of the hegemonic rationalist Neo-Confucianism. Even Yulgok's practical Neo-Confucian thought and Sirhak School were deeply saturated with Neo-Confucian rationalism.[15]

The overly rationalistic character of the Neo-Confucianism of the Chosŏn dynasty, compared to the classical Confucianism of Confucius and Mencius, was, I think, due to two main factors specific to the particular situation during the formative stage of the Chosŏn dynasty. First, power elites in early Chosŏn needed a new system of political philosophy and ideology, on the basis of which they could criticize the corruptions and incompetence of the Koryŏ dynasty, in which Buddhism offered a spiritual backbone for the society, as well as lay the groundwork for their successful management of the new dynasty in which they could play a decisive role.[16] The second element has to do with the fact that Neo-Confucianism as a new political ideology was imported from outside and imposed from above by emerging Neo-Confucian scholar-officials, without paying much attention to the specific historical circumstances of the time. The radical political transition made it relatively easy and, in a sense, inevitable for the new ruling Neo-Confucian scholar-officials to impose Neo-Confucian ideals and principles on the structure of the new government and organize governmental activities in line with them. The new ruling class tried to reconstruct the structure of the government and society solely in accordance with Neo-Confucian ideas of morality and politics from above and they did this without seeking to make a compromise with past cultural and religious legacies. They pitted Neo-Confucian ideals and principles squarely against all other religions and philosophical traditions, by making Neo-Confucianism the political orthodoxy of the dynasty.

The way the Sarim faction thought about the relationship between Neo-Confucian principles and practice was undeniably rationalist. Its members believed that it was absolutely imperative for them to reshape the practice of politics and society strictly in line with Neo-Confucian principles, without taking contextual particularity into serious consideration or applying them flexibly and prudentially. Viewed from this strong rationalist attitude, politics and law were easily regarded as merely instrumentally valuable in carrying out the most essential and fundamental Neo-Confucian morality. Politics and law were regarded as right or just only when they were in accord with core Neo-Confucian principles. Prudential compromises with circumstantial factors were condemned as a serious betrayal of their cherished ideals. In this mindset, it was practically impossible for various political forces to reach an agreement with one another by mutual concession and compromise.

RATIONALISM IN THE HISTORY OF
KOREAN POLITICS: UP TO 1987

Throughout the nineteenth century, Chosŏn witnessed radical changes in the political landscape and consciousness. Though some revolutionary or radical movements to replace the old hierarchical status system and inefficient governmental structure with more egalitarian and efficient ones were intermittently attempted, most of them failed. Also, there were indeed some instances that showed that the dynasty was being shaken from the root. The relative ascendance of Practical Learning over traditional Neo-Confucianism and the formation of the modernization faction (Kaehwap'a) against the then dominant conservative political factions could be read as an important sign that some radical changes were occurring in political consciousness and attitude. A series of impacts from foreign forces and their aftermaths, such as the clash between the Japanese battleship and the Korean battery in Kanghwa island and the Korean-Japan treaty on the Kanghwa island (1876), accelerated ongoing social and political disturbances, pressing Chosŏn to embark on a radical reform on its traditional way of governing society in accordance with the general tendency in modern politics and economy. Together with radical social and political changes, the traditional Confucian value system was also undergoing a fundamental erosion.

It does not mean, however, that the traditional cultural and political structure undergirding the Chosŏn dynasty was fundamentally transformed during the nineteenth century. Even if there had been a significant shift in the political paradigm during this period, be it gradual or radical, the most fundamental layer of the political structure and its underlying cultural foundation remained largely intact.

It is undeniable that the modernization of politics and its culture was the main objective of the time and political ideals and values were also undergoing a fundamental change from traditional Confucian to Western- or Japanese-modern ones. Amid this seemingly irreversible modernizing trend, however, the rationalist consciousness toward politics and law remained unchanged. Political rationalism was even more reinforced in the course of a series of historical political events, as mentioned above.

It is important to emphasize here that my argument that political rationalism remained largely unchanged during the latter half of the nineteenth century was focused on its formal rather than substantive aspect. That is, despite some drastic changes in the contents of political values or policies, the formal aspect of rationalist attitude toward politics still remained the same. Readers should be reminded that the substance of political values and policies can vary according to political and legal systems, but the formal character of political consciousness through which people see and understand political and legal affairs can remain the same.

The persistent formal characteristic of political rationalism can be explained in a following way. Let's suppose that a traditional monarchical regime has been abruptly substituted with a more democratic regime by a revolution, like the French Revolution in 1789. All past important political values and ideals have been abandoned altogether by a new democratic regime. In this case, the political change is so radical and profound that the newly established democratic regime tries to regulate society in line with new policies and legislations totally different from the ones regulating the previous regime. Despite the radical changes, however, the style of governing by the new democratic regime can remain the same. In other words, the revolutionary democratic regime can see politics and the legal system as the most efficient and comprehensive instruments to govern or shape the society according to some predetermined political values or ideals as the previous regime did. The fundamental difference between the two political regimes lies in the substance of political values or ideals, rather than in the formal character of political consciousness. In the newly found democratic regime, the way political power is legitimated and the political values are pursued might have dramatically changed. However, the current and the preceding regimes can share the rationalist consciousness or attitude toward politics and the legal system, if they understand politics and the legal system as an efficient means for social engineering by a handful of political elites. The Jacobin government after the French revolutions is the case in point. The newly established Jacobin government attempted to revolutionize the whole society according to its predetermined ideals and plans when the Jacobin party seized political power. Once the Jacobin regime was convinced that people delegated the political power to its leaders, it used its power as their exclusive and monopolistic means for controlling and managing the society. Politics, policies, and legislation were all considered efficient instruments they could utilize at their discretion. In short, they tend to see politics and legislation as a technique for comprehensive and efficient social engineering according to certain preconceived political ideals and values, rather than as self-limited

activities that coordinate diverse interests, thereby repairing and better maintaining the existing social order.

In the newly democratized political regimes, it is commonly found that
political leaders and high officials elected through free and equal elections
tend to regard democratic politics as a delegation process through which they
can receive political power from the people. Thus, Guillermo O'Donnell
once dubbed such democratic regimes as "delegative democracy," in which
the democratic election and some authoritarian elements are combined to
form a hybrid regime. [17]

Even in the West's firmly consolidated democracies, strong rationalist
tendencies in politics can be easily found, as Michael Oakeshott identified
many salient cases in his *Politics of Faith and the Politics of Scepticism*. [18]
He shows that the main paradigm of modern European politics was rationalist in that it tried to guide or shape practice one-sidedly with some preconceived rational ideas, without being conscious of the fact that the preconceived ideas themselves were abstracted from the very practices on which
they are going to be imposed. [19] As mentioned earlier, Pierre Rosanvallon
also points out that French politics before and after the French Revolution
had a strong rationalist tendency as clearly demonstrated in Quesnay's and
his disciples' physiocratism and Bonapartism. For them, "politics is . . . an art
of observation and a science of deduction: it creates nothing original and
institutes nothing novel" but only brings the laws or the general will found by
reason into society in order to reshape it. [20]

All the cases mentioned above show evidently that, regardless of whether
the political regime is traditional or modern, or authoritarian or democratic, it
can have a rationalist attitude toward politics and law, searching for an efficient means or an instrument to carry out the laws or principles preconceived
by reason. As noted earlier, the substances of laws or political principles that
a rationalist political regime brings into the society can be different from
those in other regimes, but as far as the regime's formal characteristics are
concerned, different political regimes can share the same rationalist feature.

If it is granted that political rationalism can be separated into two constitutive aspects—formal and substantive—my earlier argument can be vindicated that, despite some radical changes in the political structure and its
underlying culture, political rationalism as the most fundamental layer of the
political culture of the Chosŏn dynasty remained largely intact, or even reinforced. In the remainder of this section, I lay out, though briefly, an overview
of modern Korean political history up to 1987, the year of democratization,
in terms of the unfolding of political rationalism as the most salient formal
feature of Korean political culture. In particular, I focus on the important
influences of some historical political events in modern Korea on the political consciousness of the Korean people, instead of describing in detail how
political rationalism in modern Korea has evolved.

In nineteenth-century Chosŏn, several important political events shook the foundation of the old regime. Two features of such events are worth special attention—as an internal sign of the radical unrest of the traditional hierarchical status system and as a sign of the externally coerced transformation of the traditional society and politics. One is Tonghak 東學 (The Eastern Learning) and the other is the Kaehwa movement (the modernization movement) upon the Western impact. They both called for radical changes in the people's way of thinking and judging, as well as a total rearrangement of the entire social, political, and legal system. Nevertheless, as I have argued repeatedly, the two movements' modes of approaching political and social problems had striking similarity with traditional Neo-Confucian rationalism initiated by the Sarim faction and solidified by its political and philosophical descendants.

Despite the radical difference in values and ideals between the traditional Tohak Chŏngch'i on the one hand and the modern Tonghak and Kaehwa movements on the other, the two modern movements were equally, even more, rationalist in the traditional sense. Because they were radical or at least very progressive in the fundamental sense that everything in the old regime must be changed according to new egalitarian or liberal values, they could not avoid the traditional mode of political rationalism. For both movements, the traditional closed social system needed to be wholly replaced by a more egalitarian or liberal system and accordingly their approaches were inevitably rationalist. In other words, some specific preconceived values and ideals were absolutely needed to guide their revolutionary or reformative practices and, therefore, practices had to follow a theory one-sidedly without allowing the former to influence or alter the purity of the latter. In the case of the Kaehwa movement in particular, most ideas and values it upheld were from abroad and its participants, who were mostly educated in Japan or obtained Western-style education, attempted to impose such ideas and values on Korean society and politics from above. Therefore, the rationalist consciousness and attitude of the Kaehwa group was arguably even more salient than that of traditional Neo-Confucianism, despite the radical difference in content between the two.

The rationalist mindset of Sarimp'a and its political successors was inherited by later generations and consolidated and further strengthened during the colonial period. Japanese imperial dominance over the Korean Peninsula was undeniably rationalist. Throughout the colonial period, the Japanese imperial government worked out many plans to make the best of its dominating status and power over the Korean people. They imposed their will on Korean society and people, without paying any consideration to particular social, economic, and political conditions Koreans found themselves in. The imperial government was under no institutional or political constraints and therefore it could pursue its preconceived plans and make various experiments, including those involving human beings. The warring situation of the time made it much easier to strengthen rationalist instrumentalism in the Japanese colonial domination over the Korean Peninsula, because every war tends to induce the countries involved to mobilize and utilize all possible means and human resources in order to win the war.

Even though the first Korean government was established after the country's independence from Japanese imperial rule, it did not and could not drive off the whole legacy of the Japanese occupation. The first Korean government adopted some colonial legacies because nothing traditional was left to be put to an immediate practical use in reordering society. Main police and government organizations managed by the Japanese imperial government were maintained and reused,[21] together with their rationalist mindsets and attitudes toward politics and the legal system.

Moreover, the Korean government led by the first president of Korea, Yi Sŭngman (1875–1965), strongly championed the liberal democratic values and tried to impose liberal political values, especially anti-communist Cold War liberal values, on Korean society. Because of the relative lack of nationalist legitimacy, compared to Kim Ku (1876–1949), his political rival and the famous nationalist leader, Yi Sŭngman and his regime tried to legitimize its rule by means of a strong anti-communist ideology, instead of relying on nationalism. The Cold War anti-communist liberalism pursued by the Yi Sŭngman regime strongly resembled McCarthyism in that it was utilized mainly to eliminate leftist political opponents. For the Yi Sŭngman regime, politics and the legal system were instinctively regarded as indispensable instruments for eliminating political opponents, controlling the people, and managing the society. Yi Sŭngman and his regime's attitude toward politics and the legal system was unarguably rationalist: they instinctively presumed that political practices should follow a political theory and so politics should strive to impose an anti-communist Cold War liberal ideology on the society regardless of its particular traditions and concrete situations. This was just the same style of rationalist politics dubbed a rule-book conception of politics by Oakeshott, as it revealed a strong tendency to mechanically impose certain preconceived ideas or plans clearly expressed in an ideological rule-book on social and political practice, without considering the historically complex nature of an existing reality. The Korean War seemed to help greatly in strengthening the rationalist tendency in politics because the war mobilized all material and human resources of the society to win the war and made politics and the legal system its indispensable means, thereby encouraging more rationalist attitudes toward politics and law.

The governing style of Pak Chŏnghŭi's regime was never less rationalist in its formal character than Yi Sŭngman's. In fact, Pak Chŏnghŭi's developmental policy was a typical case of political rationalism. Throughout Pak's regime, politics was mainly considered a job of drawing up comprehensive economic plans and efficiently carrying them out for the nation's economic welfare. The main focus of politics during the period of Pak's reign was to sustain the high economic growth rate necessary for maintaining his authoritarian regime. Politics and the legal system were viewed expediently in terms of how they could contribute to the simultaneous attainment of the two interrelated objectives and, as a result, strengthen their rationalist characters. Accordingly, for the vast majority of the ordinary people, politics and law were understood as a necessary and compulsory means by which political leaders and high officials could impose their ideas and policies on the whole society and punish the deviant behaviors of the ordinary people that were considered to be obstructive to the harmonious pursuit of the ideas and policies they imposed.

This rationalist mindset, deeply shared by the elites and the ordinary people during the Third and Fourth Republic, remained essentially intact and became more consolidated after Pak's regime was succeeded by Chŏn Tuhwan's more merciless authoritarian regime. The military regime led by Chŏn and his subordinates operated according to strategic thinking and therefore tended to regard all political problems as concerned with how to attain particular goals preconceived by political leaders and their technocrats. Their goal-oriented strategic mindset plus their self-confidence in using military forces at their discretion caused them to regard politics and law as their private means for achieving personal objectives, further motivating them to control the economy and society in an arbitrary and coercive manner. The Chŏn Tuhwan regime seems to have believed that everything was possible with political power and military forces, as it occasionally employed many unusual measures, such as the coerced regeneration education program and a strict control of the press and the media through guidelines for news coverage.

Chŏn's military dictatorship marked the highest point in the long tradition of political rationalism in Korean history, in the sense that it tried to combine the strategic and instrumental aspect of political rationalism with the extreme privatization of public resources and assets in order to create and sustain the worst kind of authoritarian regime. In this regime, the legal system was merely a necessary means to control and punish the deviant behaviors of the people. The rule of law (including constitutionalism) principle was not actually different from the rule by law because Chŏn Tuhwan, a dictator, could change the laws as he wished.

DEMOCRATIZATION AND POLITICAL RATIONALISM

The year of 1987 was a historic moment for the Korean people because they succeeded in making the dictator Chŏn Tuhwan and his authoritarian regime surrender to the people's demand for constitutional reform, the most important element of which was to choose the president by direct election. The historic success of the democratization movement was preceded by a series of democratic resistance movements that broke out in June of the same year, and so the Korean people became confident in their democratic capacity and came to have a very optimistic prospect for a democratic future.

During this period, the prospect of Korean democracy seemed to be very well-grounded because Korean democracy after the historic event of 1987 continued to function reasonably well, recording two peaceful turnovers of political power between two main political parties. President No T'aeu made a great effort to earn legitimacy among the nation because, although he was elected president by a democratic election, his regime could not erase entirely the traces of the past illegitimate usurpation of political power as well as the authoritarian legacies inherited from the Chŏn Tuhwan regime. No's preoccupation with diplomatic relationships with foreign countries, which made him sideline internal affairs, was an important part of the strategy in securing his otherwise weak political legitimacy. What is ironic, though, is that insecure political legitimacy notwithstanding, No's regime made a contribution to consolidating the democratic confidence of the people because he was forced to pay great attention to the response and evaluation from the people.

Although No T'aeu was elected president by a free election, people's democratic commitment at the time was still very weak and unstable. In this regard, political leaders, including the president himself, were not very distinguished from ordinary people because they also tended to think that politics was a kind of premodern lordship through which political elites merely take care of the people's wellbeing, not necessarily by consulting with the people themselves. For them politics was no different than managing a corporation; they believed that the main task of politics (led by political elites) is to merely feed the people and control the society according to the political ideas and judgments of the ruling elites.

This rationalist attitude toward politics and law continued during the succeeding regimes, from Kim Yŏngsam to the current President Pak Kŭnhye, although some meaningful measures for improving Korean democracy were (and are being) undertaken. For example, President Kim Yŏngsam tried to consolidate democracy by both eliminating the private military faction (called Hanahoe), which had improperly exerted an enormous degree of political power, and introducing the real-name financial transaction system. Presidents Kim Taechung and No Muhyŏn made an attempt to introduce some preliminary welfare systems by imitating the Third Way policy initiated by Blaire in Britain. In particular, No's initiatives to weaken the imperial power of the president and his simultaneous attempt to give political independence to the judiciary were very notable experiments in modern Korean politics, which could open the door to the rule of law in the truest sense.

Although his experimental governing style was very fresh and meaningful in the short history of modern Korean politics, it revealed fundamental limitations as a democratic initiative because it was neither synchronized with the efforts of other governmental organizations nor given strong support from the majority of Korean citizens. In fact, his attempt to reduce his own political power by giving independence to the judiciary was totally new and strange in the dominant political climate of contemporary Korea and thus only caused unintended political confusion and economic uncertainty, which resulted in the ruling party's loss in the subsequent national elections.

In a sense, No Muhyŏn's new political experiments, the gist of which was to reduce imperial presidential power and to boost the judicial power and the independence of the prosecutors, seemed to have an anti-rationalist aspect because political rationalism tends to encourage political leaders to increase rather than decrease their political power. Concentration of power can be seen as an essential requirement for political rationalism, because the rational reconstruction of society or rational pursuit of preconceived social goals needs a considerable amount of political power. The more political power political leaders have, the more efficient the pursuit of the plan and idea might become.

It seems, however, reasonable to say that the overall political style of No Muhyŏn falls under the category of political rationalism because he tended to think that he could reconstruct the political landscape of that time and reform governmental organizations and the power structure as he wished, without taking into serious consideration the complex relationships among the established political, social, and economic interests. He seemed certain that he could manage to resolve most of the deep-rooted political, social, and economic problems with his plans and strategies. The result, however, was his crushing failure to achieve the reforms and the no less terrible defeat in the next presidential election of the ruling party. The majority of the Korean people around the time of the next presidential election had already become very disappointed with the confusion President No caused through his rough and unrefined governing style, without patiently waiting for the fruits of the reforms that his government could bring to them. And for the vast majority of the middle-class people, a direct selection of their president and representatives by regular elections at national and local elections was good enough for Korean democracy, because they were more interested in greater incomes than consolidating democracy and making democracy more economically substantive.[22] With minimal electoral democracy already at hand, Korean citizens would not proceed to deepen the meaning of democracy and democratize their society and economy beyond institutional politics because their commitment to democracy itself was only limited to the electoral regime. Only some progressive groups wanted more democracy and tried to democratize society and the economy, without securing any visible success.

Behind this weak commitment to democracy by the vast majority of Korean people, I think, lies a common political consciousness that carved their political commitment to and judgment on important political things and phenomena. The political consciousness called political rationalism provided the people with an essential political vision through which they could see and evaluate political life and public affairs.[23] Moreover, because the political consciousness was still combined with traditional, strong authoritarian social and political legacies, it functioned as a fundamental element that restricted the scope and content of democratization only to an electoral process. For most Korean people, politics was naturally viewed as an essential function of ruling elites they elected as their representatives through a democratic election, and the legal system as an essentially coercive institution by which political leaders can manage and control the society and the economy according to their preconceived plans. The rule of the professional political elites and the rule by law, instead of the popular control of the political power and political process and the rule of law, were the corollaries of this very political vision called political rationalism. Not surprisingly, some kind of delegative democracy was an inevitable informal consequence of political consciousness, often justifying an authoritarian style of politics predicated on a nominal democratic process.

It is widely observed that as soon as more democratic regimes were replaced with more overly conservative and authoritarian ones, a delegative form of democracy was more securely established through democratic elections. According to some international evaluation agencies, such as Freedom House and World Bank, the level or quality of democracy and the rule of law in today's Korea has declined, compared to two previous progressive regimes under Kim Taechung and No Muhyŏn. Despite some sporadic democratic protests against the authoritarian tendency of the two consecutive conservative regimes under Yi Myŏngbak and Pak Kŭnhye, most of the middle-class people do not show much antipathy toward them and even give sincere support. This is a real disappointment for more progressive democrats in Korea but it is quite understandable, considering the overall political consciousness through which the majority of Korean people see and evaluate their political situations and public affairs.

Of course, the comprehensive delegation of political power to political leaders through a democratic election is found in many new democracies after the third wave of democratization, and the causes are diverse, including political apathy of the ordinary people and lingering authoritarian legacies. In Korea, however, many factors that have contributed to democratic retrogression or defects, I think, can be explained in terms of political rationalism because this particular mode of political consciousness has been so deeply entrenched in the Korean political culture since the middle of the Chosŏn dynasty. Other seemingly more direct factors seem to have been influenced by Korea's long political rationalism and to that extent have only indirectly to do with the qualitative defects of Korean constitutional democracy.

Especially, the most disastrous effect of rationalism in contemporary Korean politics needs to be illuminated apart from those mentioned above. It is the viewpoint from which politicians see the political life and space and its concomitant extreme form of ideological politics in which main competing political forces deal with each other as irreconcilable enemies, reducing the democratic political space to only a live-and-let-die space of war. The tendency of a rationalist mentality toward an extreme form of ideological politics can be explained in terms of the deductive reasoning characteristic of political rationalism. Because the rationalist form of politics tends to approach political and social problems in terms of a deductive application of some fundamental political principles to particular situations, two opposing political factions with competing ideas or values inevitably clash with each other, with only the smallest chance of reaching an agreement or compromise.

In this vein, the role of the ideology of anti-communism since the beginning of the Cold War needs to be stressed in relation to its disastrous effects on Korean politics. Politics in modern Korea have fundamentally been shaped by the ideology of anti-communism one-sidedly imposed from above by the U.S. Army and political, economic, and military sympathizers from inside. As its corollary, the political consciousness of the vast majority of Korean people since Korea's independence was largely shaped by the dichotomous friend/enemy worldview. The U.S. Army and the Korean government in the formative stage of the Republic of Korea strove to infuse an anti-communist, antagonist, dichotomous political worldview into the people's minds, in the midst of the rapid spread of the Cold War across the world. This view, in combination with the rationalist legacy of the traditional Neo-Confucian political culture, took deep root in the consciousness of the contemporary Korean people and has largely determined the character of modern Korean politics. The result of this has been an arbitrary interference with social life by ruling elites, the brutal elimination and exclusion of political enemies, the mutual persecution by competing social and political factions, and strict cultural and press censorship. In this political climate, it is natural that politics is mainly viewed as a zero-sum game between irreconcilable enemies, and legal and other institutions as a necessary means for repressing political enemies, effectively controlling the people's behavior in line with collective objectives and punishing deviating behaviors.

CONCLUSION

Constitutionalism, which was systematized first by John Locke in the late seventeenth century, by Montesquieu of France in the eighteenth century, and by the founding fathers of America in the late eighteenth century, is the political principle stipulating that the government must be restricted and that it may only earn legitimacy when there are consistent legal and institutional restrictions.[24] The legal and institutional restrictions mentioned here are expressed through the constitution, the supreme law of a political society. Therefore, constitutionalism is a normative political theory that justifies the mechanism of the political system governed by the constitution.

Constitutionalism and democracy, two essential elements of modern politics, are intimately integrated to establish the most realistically desirable political form, as has been generally acknowledged. Constitutionalism is expected to restrict the arbitrary use of political power by political leaders and public officials by forcing them to strictly follow the rules and principles specified in the constitution of a country, so minimizing the possibility of tyranny by the majority. Although, superficially viewed, it looks like an anti-democratic principle that constrains the power of democratic majority, it can also be viewed as perfecting the democratic morality of equality in the sense that it protects equal democratic rights of the majority and minority.[25] Without both the restrictive and protective functions of the constitution, democracy might degenerate into the most malignant form of political domination. Because of the dual functions that constitutionalism performs in modern politics, it has been rightly viewed as one of the two essential pillars constituting a legitimate form of liberal democracy.

However, in a newly democratized society in which there has been no established tradition of constitutionalism (or more comprehensively, the tradition of the rule of law), the task to establish a sound form of constitutionalism supportive of democracy raises a very thorny problem for democratic forces, because they have to pursue two seemingly contradictory tasks at the same time. On the one hand, they have to concentrate all their efforts on consolidating the democratic regime, and on the other hand they have to make every effort to establish a stable constitutionalism that can constrain the democratic power of the majority to protect the equal democratic rights of the minority. This is a troublesome situation commonly found in newly democratized countries and it makes the future prospect of democracy very unstable and unpredictable. In this situation, some powerful political elites who were very reluctant to make concessions to democratic forces in the transition period can be easily tempted to manipulate the constitutionalist pillar of the newly established political regime in order to nullify the democratic rule of the people and secure their vested interests.[26]

As has been widely argued, democracy might become very unstable and even retreat into an electoral authoritarianism or illiberal electoral democracy without being consolidated after a dramatic success in democratization, unless the rule of law or constitutionalism is relatively securely established soon after the democratic transition.[27] In not a few cases in which there has been no tradition of established constitutionalism, however, a certain kind of coalition among political and economic elites tried to skillfully incapacitate democracy, not by directly dismantling it, but by manipulating some aspects of the rule of law and so indirectly debilitating democracy. They tend to prefer this strategy to other directly anti-democratic measures, because they can achieve their goals satisfactorily without taking the risk of being criticized as anti-democratic by the people and international society. So, to establish the rule of law not long after a successful democratization becomes an urgent task for consolidating nascent democracies. But this time, in Korea, political rationalism occupying the most basal layer of the Korean political culture prevents constitutionalism from effectively working by covertly enforcing most people to view politics, political power, and law as efficient means for governing elites in pursuing collective goals and controlling the society and the economy as they wish. In order to consolidate Korean constitutional democracy in the long run, therefore, the strong rationalist attitude toward politics must be somehow checked or moderated by a totally different kind of political consciousness, simultaneously taking other necessary measures for democratic promotion such as devising a more power-sharing form of democratic politics. In other words, a more flexible empirical mindset geared to a more proper form of politics needs to be gradually fostered through tenacious collective efforts. This suggestion sounds very paradoxical because it needs a rationalist attitude toward politics, too. But it would be a final form of rationalist politics, one that needs to be used to replace the extreme form of political rationalism with a more moderate one.

Finally, I would also like to emphasize that this effort must be accompanied by a continuous effort to overcome negative political consciousness and attitudes such as an antagonistic dichotomous worldview (i.e., the enemy/ friend worldview), mutual hatred and exclusion, and intolerance and a live-and-let-die attitude, and simultaneously foster positive political consciousness and attitudes such as mutual respect, toleration, and live-and-let-live attitudes and make them unshakably established in Korean political culture. Viewed from this perspective, it is a very interesting irony indeed that Korean constitutional democracy seems to need Confucian virtues in order to improve its democratic quality.

NOTES

* This work was supported by the National Research Foundation of Korea Grant funded by the Korean Government (NRF-2012S1A3A2033775).

1. In this paper, the term "political rationalism" is used in the way that Michael Oakeshott and Pierre Rosanvallon define in their major works. That is, it means primarily an attitude or consciousness that views politics as a kind of technique to apply preconceived rational principle(s) mechanistically to specific situations without considering their contingent character. This rationalist attitude is, of course, thought to be based on its own rationalist epistemology. In the second section of this chapter, the precise meaning of (political) rationalism for Oakeshott and Rosanvallon will be explained.

2. Hyug-baeg Im, "Faltering Democratic Consolidation in South Korea: Democracy at the End of the 'Three Kims' Era," *Democratization* 11, no. 5 (2004), pp. 179–98; Hyug-baeg Im, "Better Democracy, Better Economic Growth? South Korea," *International Political Science Review* 32, no. 5 (2011), pp. 579–97; Doh Chul Shin, Chong-Min Park, and Jiho Jang, "Assessing the Shifting Qualities of Democratic Citizenship: The Case of South Korea," *Democratization* 12, no. 2 (2005), pp. 202–22.

3. However, this is not to deny the possibility that Confucianism can be interpreted in a way that can improve the quality of Korean democratic politics. In that sense, I think, Confucianism has an ambivalent relationship with democratic politics.

4. This empirical attitude can be characterized by its emphasis on the concrete meaning of a general principle in specific context rather than the abstract principle itself.

5. For example, see the following. Jae-hoon Jung, *Chosŏnjŏn'gi Yugyochŏngch'isasang Yŏn'gu* [A Study of Confucian Political Thought in Early Chosŏn] (Seoul: Taehaksa, 2005), p. 39; Wm. Theodore de Bary, "The Uses of Neo-Confucianism: A Response to Professor Tillman," *Philosophy West & East* 43, no. 3 (1993), pp. 541–55.

6. Some scholars point out that there was also an important political intention behind their efforts to develop a sophisticated Neo-Confucian philosophical system, which was to justify and support the Confucian scholar-officials' leading role in ruling the then Chinese society. For example see Liu Zehua, *A History of Chinese Political Thought* (Zhejiang: People's Publishing House, 1996) [in Chinese].

7. Sang-kyu Kang, *Chosŏn Chŏngch'isaŭi palgyŏn* [A Discovery of the Political History of Chosŏn] (Seoul: Ch'angbi, 2013), p. 115.

8. The politics by Confucian morals was once tried by Cho Kwangjo but failed during King Chungjong's reign.

9. Michael Oakeshott, *Rationalism in Politics and Other Essays* (Indianapolis, IN: Liberty Fund, 1991), pp. 5–42; Martina Deuchler, *The Confucian Transformation of Korea: A Study of Society and Ideology* (Cambridge, MA: Harvard University Press, 1992), pp. 25–26.

10. Oakeshott, *Rationalism in Politics*, pp. 18–22; Michael Oakeshott, *Politics of Faith and the Politics of Scepticism*, ed. Timothy Fuller (New Haven, CT: Yale University Press, 1996), pp. 52–57.

11. This general description does not deny the existence of some important exceptions that had put no less weight on the role of reason than revelation, as can be identified in the Scholastic philosophy of Thomas Aquinas and the Islamic and Judaic rationalist philosophy of Al Farabi and Maimonides. On this, see Leo Strauss, *What Is Political Philosophy? And Other Studies* (Chicago: University of Chicago Press, 1988), pp. 134–69.

12. Oakeshott, *Rationalism in Politics*, pp. 99–131; Pierre Rosanvallon, "Political Rationalism and Democracy in France," in *Democracy: Past and Future* (New York: Columbia University Press, 2006), chap. 6.

13. Rosanvallon, "Political Rationalism and Democracy in France," pp. 128–31.

14. However, there is an interesting study on the epistemology of Neo-Confucianism, which argues that Neo-Confucianism has a very well developed epistemological system. See Haiming Wen, "Continuity Heart-mind and Things-events: A Systematic Reconstruction of Neo-Confucian Epistemology," *Asian Philosophy* 21, no. 3 (2011), pp. 269–90.

15. They were more practically and empirically disposed in their approach to politics and social management than the then most orthodox Neo-Confucians. Nevertheless, it has been

widely accepted that they also shared and frequently showed strong deductive tendencies in their political thinking.

16. Deuchler, *Confucian Transformation of Korea*, p. 101.

17. Guillermo O'Donnell, "Delegative Democracy," *Journal of Democracy* 5, no. 1 (1994), pp. 55–69. See also William Case, "Low-quality Democracy and Varied Authoritarianism: Elites and Regimes in Southeast Asia Today," *Pacific Review* 22, no. 3 (2009), pp. 255–69.

18. Oakeshott, *Politics of Faith and the Politics of Scepticism*, pp. 45–67.

19. Oakeshott also identifies some important anti-rationalist political trends called "politics of skepticism" in modern European political history.

20. Rosanvallon, "Political Rationalism and Democracy in France," p. 128.

21. Wang-shik Kim, "Mikunjŏngŭi chŏngch'ijŏk wisang" [The Political Status of the U.S. Military Government], in *Hyŏndae han'gukchŏngch'isa* [Modern Political History of Korea], ed. Korean Political Science Association (Seoul: Pŏmmunsa, 1995), pp. 76–114; Woon-sung Baek, "Yi Sŭngman chŏnggwŏn ritŏswipŭi kiwŏn'gwa chawŏn" [The Origin and Resources of Yi Seungman's Regime], in *Hyŏndae han'gukchŏngch'isa*, pp. 209–40; Eun-bong Choi, "Mikunjŏnghaŭi chŏngch'isahoepyŏndonggwa kyoyukchŏngch'aek" [Political and Social Changes and Education Policy under the U.S. Military Government], in *Hyŏndae Han'gukchŏngch'isa*, pp. 115–58.

22. Leonardo Morlino, Björn Dressel, and Riccardo Pelizzo, "The Quality of Democracy in Asia-Pacific: Issues and Findings," *International Political Science Review* 32, no. 5 (2011), pp. 501–8.

23. This does not mean that the vast majority of the people consciously adopted a rationalist political attitude. It is more correct to say that their political attitudes and consciousness have been unwittingly and gradually permeated by political rationalism.

24. Scott Gordon, *Controlling the State: Constitutionalism from Ancient Athens to Today* (Cambridge, MA: Harvard University Press, 1999), pp. 7, 15.

25. Ronald Dworkin, *A Matter of Principle* (Oxford: Oxford University Press, 1986), pp. 196–98.

26. Amy C. Alexander, Ronald Inglehart, and Christian Welzel, "Measuring Democracy: A Defense," *International Political Science Review* 33, no. 1 (2011), p. 59.

27. O'Donnell, "Delegative Democracy"; Guillermo O'Donnell, "The Judiciary and the Rule of Law," *Journal of Democracy* 11, no. 1 (2000), pp. 25–31; Juan J. Linz and Alfred Stepan, "Toward Consolidated Democracies," *Journal of Democracy* 7, no. 2 (1996), pp. 14–33; Larry Diamond and Leonardo Morlino, "The Quality of Democracy: An Overview," *Journal of Democracy* 15, no. 4 (2004), pp. 20–31; Alexander, Inglehart, and Welzel, "Measuring Democracy."

Chapter Six

Confucianism and the Meaning of Liberalism in the Contemporary Korean Legal System

Junghoon Lee

Recently, some scholars have begun to advocate the revival of Confucian authority and Confucian political philosophy as a solution for the problems of materialism, anomy, and egoism in Korean society.[1] On the other hand, some scholars champion communitarian liberalism, a political theory that acknowledges the importance of both individual liberty and community.[2] These scholars seem to want to complement liberalism with Confucian values.

In their view, one important part of Confucian values is to cherish community, so Confucianism is seen as an alternative solution in overcoming the problems arising from Western liberalism. The view is not unfamiliar in Korean society. Moreover, Koreans tend to deprecate individualism as being selfish, and they instead value the sacrifice of individual rights or the giving up of individual claims on behalf of the interest of the community.

In this chapter, by examining a series of legal disputes and political events, I will show that Buddhism and Christianity, which appear to be incompatible with Confucianism, take on quite strong Confucian values in Korea. Furthermore, I will argue that Confucianism, which has exerted tremendous influence on Korean society, is politically strongly statist rather than communitarian, and that Korean statism is closely related with Korean-style totalitarian fascism. My analysis of the legal precedents concerning conscientious objection to military service later in this chapter will attest to this claim.

It might be puzzling to Westerners who understand certain forms of Buddhism (particularly, those Westerners who are familiar with Southeast Asian

Buddhism or Tibetan Buddhism) that Korean Buddhists would try to force the government to acknowledge their existence and their religious body (this is a different matter from the case in which Buddhism is a state religion). This is because Korean Buddhists have a particular view of the state: their identity as a member of the state has a certain kind of priority over their identity as a member of Buddhism. And for them, their identity as Buddhists is inseparable from their identity as citizens of the state. This particular view of Korean Buddhists originates from their understanding of Confucianism, which gives primacy to the state over individuals.

Such dual memberships are certainly not historically unique. For example, there were cases in Germany of people who were Christians as well as Nazis. However, the case in Korea is slightly different and it is Confucianism that accounts for this difference. For instance, the way Korean Christians understand the relationship between the church and the state, as well as the individual and group (including the way to recognize the church as a group) is very Confucian. What is more important is that if the Korean judiciary takes this kind of attitude, it is quite apparent that the rights of minorities can be easily violated. Therefore, by examining the legal precedents of conscientious objection to military service, I will criticize strong statism implicated with the jurisprudence of the Korean courts.

In contemporary Korean society, Confucianism is the main source of strong statism, from whose grip even the Korean judiciary is not free, and a key idea that allows us to understand the Korean conception of the relationship between the individual and the group.

Before I argue this point, I would like to raise a question: Has liberalism ever existed in Korea as a sociopolitical reality and not merely as a political slogan or a political rhetoric? In this chapter, I will give a historical account arguing that in Korean politics Western political liberalism has never taken a central position. Accordingly, it is unconvincing that liberalism, which has never been fully implemented in Korea, is the major causal factor of the dissolution of Korean community, the breakdown of the family, the collapse of the educational system, the alienation of individuals, the destruction of the environment, and so on.

The problems of collectivism and family-egoism, often identified as the side effects of liberalism, have existed long before, even in the last period of Chosŏn and the colonial and post-colonial periods (the post-colonial period refers to the period between the Japanese government's surrender to America and the establishment of the Korean government). Liberalism did not exist in those years. Therefore, liberalism cannot be the cause of those societal problems. The conception of liberalism for reformists (Kaehwap'a) of the late Chosŏn period was different from Western liberalism as we understand it.

The independent movement party, which is commonly categorized as a liberal camp, did not embrace Western liberalism, either. After the establishment of the Korean government, liberalism was used as a synonym for anti-communism, and under the military dictatorship, which called itself liberal, the democratic movement was criticized by the regime as anti-liberal. Moreover, since the National Security Law exerted a quasi-constitutional authority by making the Korea Constitution a dead parchment, there was only a limited period in modern Korean history in which basic liberties, such as freedom of religion, thought, and conscience, were fully respected as constitutional rights.

I strongly object to the view that attributes the social problems of collectivism or excessive focus on individual rights simply to liberalism. In this chapter, I will discuss how Confucianism was transformed into a form of statism during Korea's Japan-driven modernization and how Confucianism, thusly transformed, still exerts a strong influence on the Korean legal system and politics. In particular, I will focus on how Confucian statism is still influencing the Korean judiciary by examining some legal cases.

THE HISTORICAL ANALYSIS OF CONFUCIAN STATISM

The Confucian Notions of the Public, the Private, and Statism

As mentioned before, it has been frequently argued that communitarianism is not an unfamiliar concept to Koreans because the Confucian tradition and Confucian values have a close affinity to communitarianism rather than individualism or liberalism.[3] The very expression of "Confucian communitarianism" has been under discussion, especially concerning its social relevance in Korea. With respect to the claims on Confucian communitarianism, I raise two questions. The first is whether Confucian political thought is indeed a communitarian idea and the second is whether the Confucian tradition still functions in contemporary Korean society. My opinion is that even though the Korean society is still under the heavy influence of the Confucian tradition, there is no firm ground for arguing that Confucianism is communitarian. This is because in Confucian political thought there is no concept of liberal individuals, a premise of communitarianism.

In the 1980s when American scholars engaged in the so-called liberal-communitarian debate, the main target of communitarianism was liberal individualism because it was believed that liberal individualism had considerably eroded the value of community and communal life. Accordingly, communitarianism was proposed as a way to deal with the contemporary problems of American society by reviving the republican tradition. The proponents of communitarianism maintained that the crisis of liberal democracy was caused not so much by excessive democracy but by the loss of civic virtues.[4] Therefore, communitarianism is theoretically infeasible without assuming the existence of liberal individuals.

As a matter of fact, the term "communitarianism" is employed by groups of scholars—diverse both ideologically and philosophically—so that it does not refer to a single, systematic school of thought. What brought these diverse groups into one philosophical movement was their shared attempt to find an alternative to the abstract theories preoccupied with the principles of justice or human rights derived from some universal morality. Instead of individual rights, communitarians found their theoretical basis in the notion of the common good as a way to achieve the political ideal of the democratic system. They claimed that the absence or deficiency of the concept of the common good is the defining characteristic of liberalism because liberalism tries to be value-neutral.[5]

In order to tackle the question of Confucian communitarianism in the context of Korean society, let me first investigate the Confucian ideas of the public and the private. In the Han dynasty of China, the term "public" (*kong* 公) referred to ethnical community (*kong* 共) and instead of referring to the whole world it implied, as in the famous case of the sage-king Shun, the ruler's impartial (*kong*) way of handling the world. Therefore, the concept of the public (公) was understood essentially as the ruler's virtue and the public and private distinction was predicated on the assumption that a minister should give priority to the state over his family and forsake his private interest on behalf of the public good.[6] This is how the ideas of the public and the private were understood in East Asia throughout history, albeit with regional variations. Most notably, Liang Qichao 梁啟超 (1873–1929), one of the modern Chinese thinkers, claimed, "Freedom is the freedom of the community, not the freedom of individuals. In barbaric times, there was only the freedom of individuals, not the freedom of the community. In a civilized age, the freedom of the community flourishes and the freedom of individuals disappears."[7] Even when East Asian countries adopted Western thoughts, the adoption was mediated largely in Confucian terms, thus preventing their full acceptance in Korea.

The Confucian ideas of the public and the private are defined in opposition to each other—good and bad or right and wrong. Accordingly, private opinions of individuals are often considered wrong, contrary to the rightness and vastness of the world. Thus individual opinions have to be considered ethically wrong and each individual is supposed to be subsumed under the Confucian ritual-based order of social status. Some scholars argue that since communitarianism respects each individual as a moral agent in social relationships, Confucian political philosophy is also communitarian.[8] However, in my view, Confucian political philosophy does not presuppose the idea of the liberal individual as a moral agent. The Confucian ideas of the public and the private understood in this way not only affected the establishment of political institutions and political thought of the early Chosŏn dynasty, but they also permeated the minds of the reformists from the late period of the dynasty to the colonial and post-colonial periods. Presidents such as Yi Sŭngman (1875–1965) and Pak Chŏnghŭi (1917–1979) were also deeply influenced by this dichotomous understanding of the public and the private and this situation has not dramatically changed to the present day. In Korea, "liberal individuals" did not exist, as individuals were there only as the members of a particular family and families existed only to serve the state.

Furthermore, law was regarded largely as an instrument to govern subordinates rather than as a universal law. Particularly, by late Chosŏn, the Confucian judiciary laws had degenerated into an oppressive tool by the ruling elites and in the course of reforming and modernizing this system Japan exerted an enormous influence. Let us examine how law was understood under modern Japan's patriarchal political structure.

Explaining the nature of the law under the Japanese statistic system, Maruyama Masao argues, "That which dominates the attitude of governmental officers and soldiers is at least not the sense of legitimacy, but the awareness that they are in a superior position and closer to the absolute value. The law does not constrain those who govern and those who are governed in equal terms. Rather, it is merely a specific instrument to control the people under the authoritarian system, at the peak of which lies the Japanese Emperor. Therefore, observance of the law is only applied to those who are subordinated."[9] According to Maruyama, factionalism in the Japanese military, marked by the idea that the army is at the top of the military and the infantry army is at the top of the army, cannot be explained by archaic feudalism, but only by the conviction that one is connected directly to the ultimate authority in the hierarchical order.[10]

Given that Korean military elites were trained in the Japanese military system and it is they who led the modernization of Korean society after the liberation from Japan, it is not difficult to infer that the Korean perception of the law as the backbone of the patriarchal political order and as a tool for political control was profoundly influenced by Japan. Moreover, all kinds of factionalism prevailing in Korea, especially centered on school or regional connections, have a great deal to do with Japanese statism, which directly influenced the modernization process of the Korean state and society.

There might be some objections that Maruyama's criticisms, focused on moral Confucian rhetoric, are not directly related to Confucianism as such. Nevertheless, apart from the rhetorical questions, the Confucian connection is not far-fetched if we examine how the Confucian legal system and political structure were indeed created during Meiji Japan and Chosŏn Korea (and Korea after liberation).

At the heart of Japanese statism is the idea that the public authority is superior to the people and its role is to educate the people. Likewise, the most important purpose of Chosŏn Confucian politics was to edify or educate the ignorant masses through the use of Confucian scholar-officials. In fact, one of the reasons that NGO movements had been so indistinct in Korea until the democratic movement in 1987 has to do with this strong statism tradition in Korea. It was Confucianism, deeply entrenched in the minds of the Korean ruling elites, that enabled them to facilitate, with relative ease, the adoption of Japanese statism during the modernization process.

Korean dictators, who grew up under the influence of Japanese statism, played an important role in its reinforcement in Korea society, and in turn, the Korean judiciary system served the military dictatorship.

Another attribute of Japanese statism is the notion that even scholarship and arts should serve the truth, goodness, and beauty of the political body of the state, and anything private should be tabooed as evil. According to this notion, the pursuits of personal love and individual profit are bad; only the pursuit of the state's goal is considered good.[11] These ideas were adopted and reinforced by Korean leaders with a Confucian background. I now turn to how Japanese statism influenced Confucianism.

The Influence of Japanese Statism on Korean Modernity

One of the reasons that Japanese statism does not presuppose the idea of the liberal individual is the influence of Confucian political philosophy. While trying to implement the modern reformation, the Meiji government simultaneously suppressed the development of civil rights by reviving Confucianism.[12] As can be seen in the very title, "Kientai 欽定" (Compiled by the Royal Order), the Meiji Constitution intended to be the law and a constitutional order for the edification and government of the ignorant masses.[13] In a sense, Japanese statism combined Confucian political philosophy as its basis and Western modernity as its supplements.

According to Sŏ Chungsŏk, Confucianism offered a philosophical foundation for Yi Sŭngman's Korean-style fascism. As noted, the political culture that prioritizes the state over the people derives from Confucian political philosophy.[14] Though Sŏ is reluctant to associate Chosŏn Neo-Confucian political ideology with Yi's principle of One-People (*ilminjuŭi* 一民主義),[15] I think that we should understand Yi's One-People principle, Neo-Confucian political ideology, and Japanese statism all under the rubric of East Asian "Confucian statism." Yi's Confucian conception of imperial rulership and One-People principle is very similar to Japanese patriarchal statism. Though he was a modernized man who converted to Christianity and received an American education, Yi was a Confucian to the bone.

Many Korean reformists embraced the theory of social evolution, which was in vogue in Japan. From the outset, the theory was adopted in Japan in close relation to the political mission of Japan's modernization. The person who introduced the theory of social evolution in Japan was Edward S. Morse, an American professor at Tokyo University. After the proclamation of the

Meiji Constitution in 1889, the Japanese government adopted the German theories of social evolution. These theories were employed to justify the social order of class distinction and an elite class; to value national community, at the core of which lies the social organism of the national culture, over technological and materialistic civilization; and to criticize liberal individualism as in conflict with national community. In the 1880s of Japan, therefore, the key ideas of social evolution, such as the struggle for existence or the survival of the fittest, were prevalent. In combination with a theory of the organic nation, the Japanese theory of social evolution was transformed into a unique form.[16]

Thus understood, it can be said that the elitism and the class-consciousness of the Korean reformists, who studied in Japan, were derived from the Confucian worldview and ethical system and reinforced by the theory of social evolution. The main goal of Confucian political philosophy is the edification of the people and the Confucian worldview is predicated on Sinocentrism, according to which the world is divided between civilized China and barbarians. For Korean reformists immersed in the Confucian worldview and way of thinking, it would not be difficult to replace China (as the Middle Kingdom) with the West and embrace an imperative to develop their nation modeled after the West.[17]

In the beginning of the twentieth century, the Research Society of Constitutional Order established by Korean reformists announced its views on the Meiji Constitution in a series of articles entitled "Articles on Constitution and Constitutionalism" (*hŏnchŏng swaetam* 憲政瑣談), in the *Hwangsŏng Sinmun* (皇城新聞) from June 12 to June 21 in 1905. These articles, submitted by a Japanese name, Rirusi 利龍子, explained the constitutional order through the traditional theory of substance and function.[18] The theory of substance and function was originally developed in Mahayana Buddhism and later adopted by Zhu Xi 朱熹, who incorporated this theory in Neo-Confucian *li-qi* metaphysics (理氣論). The substance is the essence or principle of the existence, and the function refers to its usages or instruments. That is to say, the authors of the articles regarded the Confucian virtues of benevolence and righteousness as the substance and understood the constitutional order as an instrument to carry on this moral substance. At that time, intellectuals in East Asia were familiar with this theory of substance and function and it is for this reason that the articles employed this theory to facilitate the adoption of a Western-style constitutionalism.[19]

What is important to note here is that the content of "Articles on Constitution and Constitutionalism" is the same as that of Ito Hirobumi's (伊藤 博文 1841–1909) "Understanding of Constitution" (憲法義解). It was Ito who explained constitutionalism by means of the theory of substance and function. According to Ito, those who supervise the sovereign power constitute the substance of the sovereignty and the exercise of this power is the function of the sovereignty. He claimed that when there is only the substance without the function, it turns into despotic government, and when there is only the function without the substance, it becomes chaotic. [20]

Unlike the Chosŏn dynasty, Japan in the later period of Tokugawa did not put great emphasis on Neo-Confucianism in politics. Not surprisingly, there- fore, there are some scholars who claim that Japan's early adoption of the Western legal system and constitutionalism was due to its openness to a variety of thoughts during the late period of Tokugawa. [21] Even if Japan's intellectual atmosphere was dramatically different from that of Chosŏn (where anything other than orthodox Cheng-Zhu Neo-Confucianism was vil- ified and controlled as heresy), it must be noted that Ito paid special attention to and strove to revive Confucianism in order to establish the Meiji Constitu- tion, at the center of which lay the Emperor system and a theory of the political body of the state. When he researched the European constitutions, Ito was particularly interested in Lorenz von Stein's constitutional theory, which emphasized administration and identified party politics and democra- cy as dangerous. [22] His interest lay in his strong adherence to Confucianism.

Korean reformists like Yu Kil-chun (1856–1914) and Yun Ch'i-ho (1864–1945) were also Confucians deep down in their hearts and their Con- fucian mode of thinking led them to believe that the adoption of Ito's Meiji Constitution and constitutionalism would be the best way to reinvent Korea into a modern *Rechtsstaat*. [23] They agreed with Ito that to adopt the political systems prevailing in France, England, or America would not be feasible given the reality of Korean society at the time.

Some scholars argue that in Korea statism did not arise suddenly during Pak Chŏnghŭi's reign, but was rooted in the Neo-Confucian patriarchal state system of Chosŏn. [24] Undoubtedly, Pak was also strongly influenced by Japa- nese statism. [25] Since the mid-nineteenth century, the adoption of liberalism was discussed by people like Pak Yŏng-hyo (1861–1939) and Yu Kil-chun. However, at that time, liberalism was understood mainly in political terms such as "democracy" or "constitutional government" rather than as a philo- sophical thought. [26] As we cannot think of Korean modernization separate from Japanese statism, I think we cannot think of East Asian statism separate from Confucianism.

Furthermore, we should reexamine whether it is valid to identify political leaders and political lines and factions in modern Korean history in terms of liberal democracy. What is obvious is that the Confucianism that affected the thoughts of key political leaders such as Yi Sŭngman and Kim Ku (1876–1949) in the early twentieth century was indeed statism, rather than communitarianism as an alternative to liberal individualism.

Ultra-nationalism, which emerged in the process of the modernization of the Japanese state, was a right-wing totalitarianism, which sacrificed individ- uals on behalf of the state. Korean statism, most salient during Pak

Chŏnghŭi's reign, was profoundly influenced by Japanese ultra-nationalism.[27] Korean political leaders adopted and reinforced Japanese statism in mediation of the patriarchal state system of Chosŏn.

Political factions of the late Chosŏn period tried to overcome the national crisis caused by Western imperialism and rebuild the Korean state as a member of the modern international community. Such political factions include the reformists (the main agents who drove Kapsin'gaehyŏk in 1884, Kabogaehyŏk in 1894, and the Independence Association movement in 1896), who regarded modernization as civilization and pursued the modernization reform; the conservative regime of the Kwangmu (光武) government established in 1897, which tried to reinforce the authority of the Korean emperor; and reformative Confucians, who tried to solve the current problems through the reformation of Confucianism. To these people, the two most powerful political theories were statism and liberalism (as a form of governmental system).[28]

The discourse on statism in particular became the major trend, further developing into the theory of "enriching the state and strengthening the military" (*puguk kangbyŏng* 富國强兵) on the one hand and the theory of state organism on the other. In the beginning, the theory of "enriching the state and strengthening the military" was spread by reformists and prevailed in the intellectual community, providing the theoretical basis for promotion of industries and increase of production, as well as the strengthening of military provisions. However, as the reformist movement ended in failure in 1905, the theory of state organism started to gain prominence through various independent movements to protect national sovereignty. At that time, the theory of "state organism" was widely shared by various political factions, including reformative Confucians. Up to democratization in 1987, autocratic governments in modern Korea violated the liberal democratic constitutional order by constructing a political system which combined statism with extreme right-wing anti-communism.

While in the West a liberal democratic constitutional order was created through independent developments of liberalism, constitutionalism, and democracy and their dialectical interactions, in Korea, the distinction between these philosophical traditions was not clear from the beginning because upon the foundation of the Republic of Korea liberal constitutionalism was suddenly embraced.[29] Since the time of the modern enlightenment, liberalism in Korea was developed not by a certain group of classes sharing the same interests, but by political groups sharing a common ideological aim and political goal.[30] As a result, liberalism in Korea did not undergo individual developments of liberalism, constitutionalism, and democracy and was, therefore, unable to develop each political theory thoroughly. Rather, a liberal democratic constitutional order was simply given as a form of governmental institution at the time of independence and foundation of the Republic.

For this reason, there is a significant gap between the liberal democratic constitutional order and the actual Korean legal reality.

In conclusion, Confucian communitarianism did not exist in Korean history. Therefore, instead of promoting Confucian communitarianism as an alternative to liberal individualism, we should remove the dark shadow of statism and try to build a legal system that is congruent with the liberal democratic constitutional order. In what follows, I will continue my discussion by examining some important legal cases regarding the freedom of religion.

CONFUCIAN STATISM AND THE INFRINGEMENT
OF THE FREEDOM OF RELIGION

Government's Intervention in Religious Issues

In 2008, Korean Buddhists carried on anti-government demonstrations, raising their voice against the government's religious bias. According to their claim, one indication of the government's religious bias was that the information system on transportation set up by the Ministry of Land and Maritime Affairs includes detailed information on Christian churches, but not on Buddhist temples. In addition, the protestors took issue with the fact that the chief of the National Police Agency appeared in the advertisement on behalf of a particular religion. In order to pacify Buddhists' protests, the government and the ruling party established the Report Center for Religious Discrimination by Public Officials and proposed a revised bill on the National Public Service Law, enabling punishment for officials who discriminate against a particular religion. The Report Center caused a social commotion when it advised not to place the Cross on top of the Christmas tree set up in front of the City Hall of Seoul during the Christmas season.

Even in the United States, a heated public debate ensued over whether to include the Nativity scene for Christmas decorations at city halls. For example, in the city of Pawtucket, Rhode Island, Christmas decorations were set up only in a park owned by a nonprofit organization and this park was located in the heart of the city's shopping district. The Christmas decorations include a Santa Clause house, a Christmas tree, a banner that reads "Seasons Greetings," and a crèche or Nativity scene. However, the federal district court and federal appellate court upheld the challenge and enjoined the city from including the crèche on the Christmas display. Later, in the 5-4 verdict, the Supreme Court, led by Chief Justice Burger, rejected this ruling by the lower courts on the basis of the Wall of Separation principle, permitting the city's inclusion of a crèche on its annual Christmas display. The key point of the judgment is in the following:

The city has a secular purpose for including the crèche in its Christmas display and has not impermissibly advanced religion or created an excessive entanglement between religion and government. The display is sponsored by the city to celebrate the Holiday recognized by Congress and national tradition and to depict the origins of that Holiday; these are legitimate secular purposes. Whatever benefit to one faith or religion or to all religions inclusion of the crèche in the display effects, is indirect, remote, and incidental, and is no more an advancement or endorsement of religion than the congressional and executive recognition of the origins of Christmas, or the exhibition of religious paintings in governmentally supported museums. [31]

In this judgment, the Court concluded that the city's inclusion of the crèche on the Christmas display was not to promote Christian religion. A majority opinion held that the main purpose of the Christmas display is the celebration of the public holiday and the inclusion of the nativity scene was only to symbolically show the historical origin of the Christmas holiday, therefore having only secular purposes. The Court also used the three-part test articulated in the *Lemon v. Kurtzman* case of 1970 as a guide for this case. The Lemon test is: first, whether the governmental action in question has a secular purpose; second, whether its principal or primary effect is to advance or inhibit religion; and third, whether it creates an excessive entanglement of the state with religion and thus has violated the Wall of Separation principle. Nevertheless, the Court made clear its unwillingness to judge any sensitive cases by any single test or criterion of the Lemon test.

In my view, the above case can give us useful guidance for the paradoxical situation of the separation between the state and religion in Korean society. Of particular importance is the U.S. Supreme Court's decision that the Lemon test should not be applied blindly; the religious domain should not be controlled by the government and the laws, but regulated autonomously by civil society. What I mean by the paradoxical situation of the separation between government and religion in Korea is that the government intervenes in the religious sector by arbitrarily or selectively implementing the principle of the separation between the state and religion. The Korean government's recommendation to Seoul, that the Santa Clause ornament is permissible but the Cross is not, is the case in point.

As a matter of fact, it is difficult for the judiciary to clearly delineate the boundary between historical/cultural value and religious value of the Nativity. [32] It is extremely difficult for the courts in Korea to provide an unambiguous standard to decide in what case the Cross symbolizes its religious meaning and under what circumstances it acquires *only* a historical and cultural meaning. Given that the boundary between the cultural and religious phenomena is extremely murky in the Korean societal context, some religions have begun to appeal for an active involvement of the state in religious matters in the name of the Wall of Separation principle. The situation is quite ironic because the active involvement of the state is demanded by religious organizations in order to maintain the stark separation between the state and religion. Of course, what I am criticizing here does not involve the cases in which a person whose religious freedom has been violated is protected by the judicial procedures.

When governmental officials infringe on the right of individuals by religious discrimination, the legal system as well as the National Human Rights Commission of Korea can rectify these cases. Despite these legal protections, however, both the government and the ruling party adopted the claims made by some religious groups by enacting the law that punishes officials who discriminate against a person based on his or her religious background.[33] The attitude of these religious groups which attempted to secure their status and profits through state intervention is the byproduct of statism that is pervasive in Korean society. Such desire for recognition by the government is another aspect of statism and it is widely found in Korean civil society. This is not true only of the religious sector. In Korea, most NGOs take support from the government for granted and understand such support as the state's official recognition of them.

Thus understood, we should be critical of both the government and the ruling party, which conveniently resort to criminal punishment in the difficult cases involving religious discrimination, and religious groups and religion-related NGOs that subscribe to statism. It is a critical problem that religious groups and NGOs are denying their own autonomy and thereby shrinking the realm of civil society. Korean civil society has been and still is under the heavy influence of Confucianism, which gives primacy to the public (especially the state) over the private.

In reality, religious groups and NGOs urge the government to intervene in religious matters and demand budget support from the state. They also actively participate in the legislation process. Of course, it is natural that the government's infringement on the freedom of religion is subject to judicial scrutiny. However, Korean society is obviously far from liberal, in that the government often creates some new branches to take control over social (including religious) affairs in civil society, and the civil society for its part prefers active governmental intervention in the hope that the government can prevent a problematic situation from happening. All the more problematic is the reality that criminal punishments are easy options for the state in the name of the effectiveness of legal enforcement (of religious freedom).

Seen in this way, the problematic situation in Korea in which the state frequently intervenes in religious matters is caused not only by a government that fails to delineate its proper boundary and overconcerns itself with the internal affairs of civil society but also by religious groups and NGOs themselves who demand a more active state intervention. This leads to the paradoxical situation in which state intervention is justified on the basis of the separation of the state and religion.

Even the political reform initiated by the first civilian government under President Kim Yŏngsam's leadership was sometimes criticized because of strong statism implicated in it. [34] From the Chosŏn dynasty to the present, the influence of statism has been immense and its dark shadow still spreads over the areas of politics, economics, society, and culture. The realm of autonomy in civil society is extremely narrow and there is a strong belief among religious groups and NGOs that social problems can be solved only by means of the state's active involvement in civil society and more proactive lawmaking activities.

Religious groups demand active intervention and support from the central and local governments. When religious groups and NGOs fail to receive the governmental subsidies, almost "customarily" given, they start to complain of the state's religious bias. But when they see the state subsidize other religions, they attack it for the violation of the separation between the state and religion. Under these circumstances, the state policy cannot be consistent: in the name of the principle of the Wall of Separation, the government makes itself an object of ridicule by saying "Lotus flowers are permitted but not the baby Buddha" (on Buddha's birthday) or "Stars are permitted but not the Cross" (on Christmas).

Another point to be noted is that this kind of governmental intervention does more harm than good for the socially beneficial functions of religion. For instance, one of the ward offices in Seoul initiated a program for mutual cooperation between the ward (*tong* in Korean) office and churches within its district. The core objective of this program was to remove blind spots of the welfare system and to facilitate a systematic and enduring support system for low-income families by coordinating the individual efforts by various Christian religious groups. This program carried out various projects, such as medical support, supply of daily necessities, delivery of lunch boxes to senior citizens, support of scholarship for children in charge of the household, and so on. [35]

However, Buddhist groups immediately held a demonstration against the allegedly religiously biased ward chief, forced him to make a public apology to them, and ultimately caused the annulment of the program. [36] In this case, Buddhist groups grounded their claim on the principle of the separation of the government and religion. This is one of the cases in which religious groups took the principle of the separation between the state and religion to their petty private advantages and obstructed an otherwise productive and salutary relationship between the local government and religious groups. What could have been the socially beneficial function of religion was seriously undercut.

In the case of the city of Pawtucket in the United States, the major point was that the inclusion of the crèche in the Christmas display on private land could be seen as the promotion of a certain religion, which could be felt by some people, say Jews or other non-Christians, as discrimination. In contrast, and quite ironically, what was at stake in the case about Korean Buddhists was the exclusion of them from the alliance between the state and religion. Religious groups in Korea take governmental support for granted and they consider governmental support an emblem of state recognition. Even though Buddhist groups argue for the constitutional principle of the separation of the state and religion, the gist of their complaint lies in the close connection between the state and other religions. They never demand a real separation between the state and religion; they only wish the state to form a closer relationship with themselves. This paradoxical situation has a deep connection with Korea's entrenched statism.

Thus far, my discussion has been focused on Buddhist groups who push the state over religious autonomy but the same is true of Christian groups. For instance, some Christians claim that their religious belief is for the nation and pressure politicians and public officials, irrespective of their individual religious faiths, to attend their prayer meetings. These cases cannot be made sense of from a liberal perspective. In my view, this problematic feature of religious civil society in Korea is deeply connected with the strong influence of Confucian statism, in which the state and the ego are massively fused. Neither Christians nor Buddhists are immune from the influence of Confucian statism in Korea.

Both the statism deeply entrenched in religious groups and the state intervention in religious organizations by means of the law are problematic. However, more problematic is the statism expressed by the judiciary through legal interpretations because here individual and minority rights are on the line. In the next section, I will investigate the problem of statism by analyzing legal cases with regard to religion.

The Cases

In the 1970s, the Korean Supreme Court ruled that it was legitimate for a school to expel a student who had refused to salute to the national flag because she thought it the idolatry of a nation, an act which was against her personal religious faith. [37] This case demonstrates the strong influence of nationalism on the court in Korea.

Perhaps the judiciary's anti-liberal statism is best shown in the cases concerning conscientious objection to military service. Conscientious objection refers to the denial of mandatory military service because of one's moral or religious beliefs. The Korean Supreme Court judged that conscientious objection is not a basic right of freedom of religion guaranteed by the constitution. Accordingly, the Court ruled that even if the Establishment of Homeland Reserve Forces Act includes provisions that could possibly suppress conscientious objections, it does not necessarily violate Articles 18 and 19 of the constitution (stipulating the freedom of conscience).[38]

Moreover, even though the Ministry of National Defense permits military officer-clergies to conduct their duties unarmed, reserve officer-clergies are required to take part in all kinds of military training programs, including marksmanship, without exception. However, unlike the court in the 1980s, which ruled to apply the law mechanistically to all Koreans without considering their personal religious faiths, in the 2000s, courts started to change as the society became more democratic. The process of ruling became less anti-liberal. Regardless of the change in legal procedure, however, the legal judgment still remained anti-liberal. Following is the summary of the Supreme Court's decision on conscientious objections:

> The freedom of conscience includes the freedom to make a conscientious decision through omission. This means that citizens have a freedom not to be forced, directly or indirectly, to do things against their conscience and have a right to demand the state to protect this freedom. The fundamental purpose of Article 19 of the Constitution, which protects the freedom of conscience, is to uphold the ideal of liberal democracy by protecting individual dignity and each individual citizen's distinctive identity and by tolerating minorities who hold different ethical values from the majority. Nevertheless, the freedom of conscience is a relative freedom which can be qualified in case by the second clause of Article 37 of the Constitution. (See the Supreme Court. Decided July 13, 1982. 82to1219).[39] Moreover, the mandatory military service provision stipulated in the first clause of Article 39 of the Constitution is a basic national obligation necessary for the existence and security of the nation. The Military Service Law, which has been applied to the defendant, is also the embodiment of the legislative intention with regard to the constitutional duty of national defense.[40]

What is worth noting is that in the same verdict, the Court conceded that the U.N. Commission on Human Rights had recommended repeatedly that there should be no discrimination against those who refused to hold weapons on the basis of their conscience and the government should allow them to do alternative mandatory services without punishing them, including and especially imprisonment. The Court also noted that the European courts, too, had been upholding the constitutional right to conscientious objection. More importantly, the Court submitted that the introduction of alternative mandatory services could be immensely conducive to the enhancement of the nation's liberal democratic legitimacy by tolerating minorities who have different views and values than the majorities. In the end, however, the Court did not accept the defendant's request.

While acknowledging that Article 18 of the International Covenant on Civil and Political Rights is basically the same in its content and scope as the freedom of conscience and the freedom of religion guaranteed in Articles 19 and 20 of the constitution, the Court maintained that the defendant cannot be exempted from the Military Service Law. This shows that Korea's strong statism overshadows universal human rights and the values advocated by the international human rights regime.

Furthermore, the Court claimed that the legislators have extensive legislative discretion to decide whether to impose punishment on the defendant or allow him to do alternative service. Even if the Korean Military Service Law has various "special conscription measures" (for those who have disabilities, special talents, and other legally valid reasons) such as a public service program, a special research agents program, and an industrial agents program, the Court, rather than finding a way to allow the conscientious objector to fulfill his military service duty by alternative means, held that the imposition of punishment on them does not violate the principle of excessive prohibition, the principle of proportion, or the principle of nondiscrimination.

What does this case tell us? Apparently, the Court acknowledges that the introduction of alternative services could enhance the cause of liberal democracy. However, why does the Court still impose punishment on conscientious objectors given that the law does offer citizens with special reasons (health or talent) alternative conscription programs? Some scholars argue that this kind of attitude reflects the judiciary's anti-liberalism[41]; in the totalitarian system, the very concept of the prisoner of conscience is inconceivable and all crimes are considered immoral behaviors against the national community. In this scheme, conscientious objectors are treated as criminals who deny the solemn duty of military service because of their misguided belief in heresy.[42] From the Confucian perspective, any claim that goes against the sacred interest of the state is a sort of blasphemy.

All the more ironic is that those who are enrolled in the public service program, special research agents program, and industrial agents program to fulfill their mandatory military service are paid more than regular soldiers in the mandatory military service, but this inequality has rarely been the subject of an active public debate. But then why the inequality for conscientious objectors, whose difference from those enrolled in special conscription programs is merely whether they hold the weapon in the training camp? Thus understood, it is undeniably discriminative that the state allows conscientious objectors no option for an alternative service and even punishes them.

Let us turn to another troubling case. Against the claim that the state has discriminated against the defendant's freedom of religion by holding the state bar examination on Sundays, the Constitutional Court ruled that, unlike Western countries with a Christian background, in Korea Sundays are understood as secular public holidays rather than special days for religious ceremony. Accordingly, the fact that the state holds the state bar examination on Sundays should not be regarded as religious discrimination. [43]

The Court's judgment here, however, is inconsistent with its reasoning with regard to the question of whether missionary activities should be treated as misdemeanor. That is, the courts are inconsistent in their interpretations of the standard of the freedom of religion. This is not merely the question of administrative expediency. In my view, there is a strong tendency toward statism in the way the Korean courts are balancing the interests of the state and private individuals because they never allow the latter to obstruct the former, however justified the latter is in terms of private interests or even rights. Underlying the courts' decisions is the Confucian notion of the public and the private, which values the public and devalues the private.

However, I think that a more serious problem than the statism permeating the courts' public reasoning is the inconsistency in their legal interpretations. The following is a summary of the Court's judgment with regard to missionary activities in public space.

> The freedom of religion guaranteed by the first clause of Article 20 of the Constitution includes the freedom to do mission activities to promote one's religion and recruit new believers. Given that spreading a religious doctrine in the public place is an integral part of the missionary activity, it should be cautioned in applying the Minor Offence Law to cases involving missionary activities in order not to infringe on the right of the individuals. This is the legislative purpose of Article 4 of the Minor Offense Law. Therefore, in imposing the punishment on certain missionary activities—which often involve raising voices or using an amplifier for the purpose of drawing attention of the people and propagating one's opinions—on the basis of the 26th clause of the Article 1 of the Minor Offense Law, specific details of the exact place, period, object, and method of the missionary activity should be taken into account and decide whether the activity has gone beyond the boundary of the conventional mission activity and thereby violated other legal interests. [44]

The above judgment acknowledges the importance of individual freedom and decides that mission activities involving some noises should not be punished without any specific evidence of the disturbance of the public order simply on the basis of the importance of a public order in the public space. The problem is that there is no coherence in legal interpretations regarding individual freedom—religious freedom in particular—between cases deeply connected to the interests of the state such as the military service case and cases that have no such implications.

One may argue that the apparent incoherence is due to the *difference of balancing* arising from the differences between the weight of the values under balancing and the situation in which the object of balancing is located. However, as seen in the case of the conscientious objection above, it seems self-contradictory that while upholding the liberal principle of rights protection, the courts do not apply the very principle to the cases that they deal with. In the next section, I will review the meaning of liberalism.

THE MEANING OF LIBERALISM IN THE
KOREAN LEGAL SYSTEM

According to Will Kymlicka, what makes Rawls's theory great is not necessarily that everybody finds it convincing but that most alternative theories have been presented as some form of objection to it.[45] Let me also begin with Rawls. Some scholars criticize liberalism because it does not present us with the ultimate value worth human pursuit, so that it can easily fall into relativism or nihilism. Others say that this very fact of liberalism is not a disadvantage but a strong advantage because it enables cultural pluralism, essential for a civilized society.[46]

As I have shown, from a utilitarian perspective, the government can easily infringe on the rights of the minorities or of the social underdogs in the name of the value that the state pursues. It is why in Korean society, where Confucianism has reinforced the prominence of the public interest over private interest, the court should be fully committed to liberalism. To make matters worse, when the utilitarian perspectives heavily entrenched during the process of industrialization are combined with military culture, minority voices and interests can be easily oppressed. In my view, what is important in Korean society is not so much the overcoming of liberalism but the struggle to realize the Western tradition of respect for an individual person in an effective way.

The golden rule of Jesus of Nazareth is implicit in John Stuart Mill's idea of equality: "To do as you would be done by, and to love your neighbor as yourself." Mill argued that this golden rule upholds the perfect spirit of utilitarian ethics.[47] Now, let us discuss the advantages of political liberalism, which applies the golden rule of Jesus to a liberal democratic constitutional order in a systematic philosophical way. With respect to the protection of the freedom and rights of minorities, political liberalism can offer the best solution.

Rawls defined justice as fairness in terms of a shared sense of justice derived from a political consensus voluntarily agreed upon by citizens by means of reason. The "reason" here refers to public reason. In Rawls's view, for a sense of justice to be undergirded by public reason, it must be freestanding from moral, philosophical, or religious comprehensive doctrines, which are often in conflict.[48] Deeply concerned with the construction of political society as a system of mutual cooperation given that pluralism is marked by moral conflicts, Rawls was convinced that the very source of political conflicts consists of the collisions of comprehensive doctrines that are mutually incommensurable as well as all kinds of discriminations based on social status, class, gender, and race.[49]

At the heart of Rawls's political liberalism is reasonable pluralism. In the pursuit of political liberalism based on reasonable pluralism, including religious pluralism as well as non-religious pluralism, the critical political question is how to formulate the principles of justice in a liberal constitutional polity that can undergird reasonable pluralism.[50] Of course, this is not to argue that we should accept Rawls's theory of justice uncritically.

Religious pluralism and religious tolerance can only start from mutual understanding. In most cases, religious intolerance is caused by mutual ignorance. If people only argue for their own religious beliefs and do not tolerate those of others, religious pluralism is impossible.

Political liberalism presupposes the existence of individuals who subscribe to diverse religious doctrines such as Buddhist or Christian doctrines but rely on public reason as citizens who thereby can tolerate different values. What this means is that a pluralist society is possible only when a majority of its citizens are predisposed to voluntarily agree on the sense of justice underpinning a liberal democratic polity.

Even if there is such a majority, a problem remains: there is always the possibility of social injustice committed by the majority. In this case, it is difficult to solve social injustice by means of moral and rational arguments. As Reinhold Niebuhr aptly observes, what is lacking among all the moralists, whether religious or rationalist, is an understanding of the brutal character of human community and the power of collective self-egoism.[51]

An owner of a slave might be a moral person but he is also a member of a community that accepts slavery as justified. Even in a society where each individual accepts religious pluralism, there is always a possibility of the unjust suppression of the minority by the majority.

Moreover, the sociological presupposition of the liberal individuals who are predisposed to agree on the principles of democratic constitutional justice is the result of a series of political struggles. For example, the U.S. civil rights movement started from a political struggle to gain public recognition that black people were equal human beings and equally entitled to civil and political rights. The movement did not start from an abstract agreement among the members of American society on the hypothetical assumption that "I could have been black." The change in the attitude of the U.S. Supreme Court would not have been possible without the long process of political struggle. The case of *Brown v. Board of Education* in 1954, in which the court declared that the separation of public schools for black and white students is unconstitutional, powerfully shows that individuals ready to agree on the principles of liberal constitutional democracy can only be made to comply through political struggles.

Moreover, I am convinced, agreeing with Niebuhr, that we cannot entrust the establishment of a democratic constitutional order to the personal morality of liberal individuals. The achievement of a democratic constitutional order depends indispensably on the proper functions of the judiciary and the judicial process of relief. As I pointed out, even in a society composed of individuals with political reason, social injustice can be brought by the social majority. This is why the judiciary should function as a bulwark for a liberal constitutional democratic order. Only when the judiciary plays its role as the guardian of individual rights can liberal constitutional democracy be stably sustained.

If we apply what I have argued in this section to the cases examined in the previous section, the conclusion becomes clearer: in a Korea still under the strong influence of Confucian statism, individual and minority rights can be effectively protected only if the courts are fully committed to liberalism.

CONCLUSION

During the modernization period, most leading figures in Korean politics were strongly influenced by Confucianism. Some were educated in America and some were converted to Christianity, but they were not wholly free from Confucian influences. Japan tried to modernize its state by establishing the Meiji Constitution, but Ito Hirobumi, the leading figure of Meiji Japan, was able to bolster Japanese statism through the revival of Confucianism. Many Korean reformists pursued Ito's Meiji constitutionalism and thus were affected strongly by Japanese statism. In addition, the theory of state organism and the theory of social evolution imported from the West were combined with Confucianism, giving rise to a unique form of Confucian statism, which exerted a tremendous impact on modernizing Japan and Korea. Even in the present day, Korean courts are under the influence of Confucian statism.

In the second and third sections, I demonstrated that even Buddhists and Christians in Korea are not free from Confucian statism. Also, I interpreted the way the Korean state intervenes in religious matters in civil society from the perspective of Confucian statism. And by examining legal cases with regard to conscientious objections to mandatory military service, I revealed that the Korean courts are still under the heavy influence of Confucian statism. Finally, my brief sketch of liberal legal and political philosophy enabled us to understand the tremendous importance of the Korean courts' liberal commitment to individual and minority rights.

In this chapter, I argued against the claim that Koreans are familiar with communitarian values through Confucianism and therefore that Confucian communitarianism can be an alternative to liberalism by highlighting that Confucian communitarianism never existed in Korean society. Rather than giving rise to communitarianism, Confucianism became the source of statism.

NOTES

1. Chaibong Hahm, *Yugyo chabonjuŭi minjujuŭi* [Confucianism, Capitalism, Democracy] (Seoul: Chŏntonggwa hyŏndae, 2002), pp. 18–24.

2. Seil Pak, "Wae kongdongch'e chayujuŭiin'ga—Hoeŭirone taehan tappyŏn" [Why Communitarianism? A Response to Skeptics], in *Kongdongch'e chayujuŭi: Inyŏmgwa chŏngch'aek* [Communitarian Liberalism: Ideal and Policy], eds. Seil Pak, Sŏng-rin Na, and Doh Chull Shin (Seoul: Nanam, 2008), pp. 17–21.

3. Hyojong Pak, "Kongdongch'ejuŭie taehan sŏngch'al" [A Reflection on Communitarianism], in *Kongdongch'e chayujuŭi*, p. 127; Sangik Yi and Tong-hyŏn Son, "Yugyo kongdongch'ejuŭiwa simin kongdongch'e" [Confucian Communitarianism and Civil Community], in *Kongdongch'e chayujuŭi*, p. 175.

4. Tongsu Kim, "Hyŏndae kongdongch'ejuŭiŭi sasangjŏk kich'o: Chayujuŭijŏk kaeinjuŭi pip'anŭl chungsimŭro" [The Philosophical Foundation of Contemporary Communitarianism: Its Critique of Liberal Individualism], *Han'guk chŏngch'ihakhoebo* [Korean Political Science Review] 26, no. 3 (1993), p. 8.

5. Tongsu Kim, "Minjujuŭiwa kongdongch'ejuŭi: Chayujuŭi, kongdongch'ejuŭiŭi nonjaengŭl nŏmŏsŏ" [Democracy and Communitarianism: Beyond the Liberal-Communitarian Debate], *Han'guk chŏngch'ihakhoebo* [Korean Political Science Review] 26, no. 1 (1993), pp. 278–80.

6. Yuzo Mizoguchi, *Chunggukŭi konggwa sa* [The Public and the Private in China], trans. T'aesŏp Chŏng and Yongch'ŏn Kim (Seoul: Shinsŏwŏn, 2004), pp. 18–19 (originally, Yuzo Mizoguchi, *The Public and the Private in China* [Tokyo: Tokyo University Press, 2001], pp. 35–43) (in Japanese).

7. Reprinted from ibid., p. 86.

8. Yi and Son, "Yugyo kongdongch'ejuŭiwa simin kongdongch'e," p. 177.

9. Masao Maruyama, *Hyŏndae chŏngch'iŭi sasanggwa haengdong* [Ideas and Actions in Modern Politics], trans. Sŏkkŭn Kim (Seoul: Han'gilsa, 1997), p. 56. Maruyama pointed out that we cannot attribute the absence of guilt in some war criminals to the corruption of individuals. It was primarily the systematic problem of one nation. In a similar vein, I think we can understand the insensibility and shallowness of the Korean despotic government and the Korean judiciary which supported such a government.

10. Ibid., p. 59.

11. Ibid., pp. 50–51.

12. Samsŏng Yi, *Tongasiaŭi chŏnjaenggwa p'yŏnghwa*, vol. 2 [War and Peace in East Asia 2] (Seoul: Han'gilsa, 2009), p. 223.

13. For the theory of the political body of the state and the constitution, see Ryuichi Nagao, *Constitutional History as Intellectual History in Japan* (Tokyo: Shinzansha, 1997), pp. 1–4, 87–101 (in Japanese); for the process of formation of the Kintei Constitution and its meaning, see Akihiro Kwaguchi, *Constitutional History of Meiji Japan* (Sapporo: Hokkaido University Press, 2007), pp. 5–18, 42–76 (in Japanese); and for the Meiji Constitution and the Japanese emperor's right stipulated in it, see Saburo Ienaga, *Research on the History of Japan's Modern Constitution* (Tokyo: Iwanami Press, 1998) (in Japanese).

14. Chungsŏ Sŏ, *Yi Sŭngmanŭi chŏngch'i ideollogi* [Political Ideology of Sŭngman Yi] (Seoul: Yŏksabip'yŏngsa, 2005), pp. 167–95.

15. Korean scholars are reluctant to connect anything negative to the Chosŏn period. Even those historians who criticize statism often lose an objective attitude when it comes to the nation as a blood-related community.

16. Pokhŭi Chŏn, *Sahoe chinhwaron'gwa kukka sasang* [The Theory of Social Evolution and National Thought] (Seoul: Hanul Ak'ademi, 2010), p. 45.

17. Some Western readers might not agree with my view because they consider Zhu Xi's thought to be close to postmodernism. However, rhetoric differs from reality, which requires the application of politics and law. The elements of postmodernism are only found in the Confucian classics, just like the warfare of the Crusades did not necessarily accord with the general teachings of the Bible.

18. It is still unknown who Rirusi was.

19. Shozo Huzida, *The Principle of the Emperor's Rule and the State* (Tokyo: Misuzu Press, 2012), pp. 16–19 (in Japanese). Ito Hirobumi devised the Meiji Constitution of the emperor system and the theory of the nature of nation based on Neo-Confucianism.

20. Hirobumi Ito, *The Understanding of the Constitution* (Tokyo: Iwanami Press, 1989), pp. 175–82 (in Japanese).

21. Kazuziro Koga, *The Pattern of Modernity: A Comparative Study on the Rule of Law between Japan and China* (Tokyo: Shunzu Press, 2014), pp. 3–12 (in Japanese).

22. Concerning Ito Hirobumi's research on the constitutions in Europe and his view, see Takii Kazuhiro, *Ito Hirobumi—Japan's First Prime Minister and Father of the Meiji Constitution*, trans. Takechi Manabu (London: Routledge, 2014).

23. Chŏnghun Yi, "Myŏngch'i hŭmchŏng hŏnbŏp sŏngnipkwa Han'guk kaehwap'aŭi ch'ujong" [The Enactment of the Meiji Constitution and Its Influence on Korean Reformists], *Pŏpch'ŏrhak yŏn'gu* [Korean Journal of Legal Philosophy] 15, no. 2 (2012), pp. 7–50.

24. Ch'ansŭng Pak, "20 segi Han'guk kukkajuŭiŭi kiwŏn" [The Origin of 20th-century Korean Nationalism], *Han'guksa yŏn'gu* [Journal of Korean History] 117 (2002), p. 200.

25. Cho Hŭiyŏn, *Pak Chŏnghŭiwa kaebal tokchae sidae—5.16 esŏ 10.26kkachi* [Pak Chŏnghŭi and His Era of Despotism and Development, from 5.16 to 10.25] (Seoul: Yŏksa pip'yŏngsa, 2008), p. 32.

26. Chŏngin Kang et al., "Chayujuŭi: Ch'eje suhowa minjuhwaŭi ijung kwaje saiesŏ" [Liberalism: Between the System Protection and Democratization], in *Han'guk chŏngch'iŭi inyŏmgwa sasang* [Ideology and Thought of Korean Politics] (Seoul: Humanit'asŭ, 2009), p. 125.

27. Pak, "20 segi Han'guk kukkajuŭiŭi kiwŏn," pp. 200–43.

28. Hyŏnch'ŏl Kim, "Kaehwagi man'guk kongbŏpŭi chŏllaewa sŏgu kŭndae chugwŏn kukkaŭi insik: 1880 nyŏndae kaehwap'aŭi chuwŏn kaenyŏmŭi suyongŭl chungsimŭro" [The Introduction of Public Law of All Nations and the Awareness of the Western Modern Sovereign Nation in the Time of Korean Enlightenment: Centering on the Acceptance of the Concept of Sovereignty by the Reformists in 1880s], *Chŏngsin munhwa yŏn'gu* [Journal of Spirit and Culture] 28, no. 1 (2005), pp. 127–45; Tohyŏng Kim, "Taehanjeguk ch'ogi munmyŏng kaehwaronŭi palchŏn" [The Development of the Theory of Civilization in the Beginning of Korean Empire], *Han'guksa yŏn'gu* [Journal of Korean History] 121 (2003), pp. 175–90; Yŏngmo Kim, "Kaehwagi chŏngchi kaehyŏkkaŭi sahoejŏk sŏnggyŏk: Kaehwa kwallyoŭi paegyŏng punsŏke ŭihan chŏpkŭn" [The Social Characteristics of Political Reformers in the Time of Korean Enlightenment: Through the Analysis of the Background of the Reformist Bureaucrats], *Han'guk chŏngch'i hakhoebo* [Korean Political Science Review] 10 (1976), pp. 100–18; Kŭnho Yu, "Kaehwa sasangŭi kaedanjŏk koch'al: Chogi kaehwap'aŭi sasangchŏk t'ŭkchilŭl chungsimŭro" [The Study of the Korean Enlightenment Thought: Centering on the Characteristics of the Early Reformists' Thought], *Han'guk chŏngch'i oegyosa nonch'ong* [Journal of Korean Political and Diplomatic History] 1 (1985), pp. 15–28; Unt'ae Kim, "Hanmal kaehwa sasanggwa kŭ undongŭi chŏngae" [The Development of the Korean Enlightenment Thought and Its Movement in the Late Period of Chosŏn], *Han'guk chŏngch'i oegyosa nonch'ong* [Journal of Korean Political and Diplomatic History] 4 (1987), pp. 150–60; Hyŏnch'ŏl Kim, "Che 1ch'a ilbon mangmyŏng sigi Pak Yŏnghyoŭi hwaldonggwa kapsinjŏngbyŏn kadam kaehwap'a" [The Activities of Pak Yŏnghyo and the Reformists Participating in the Kapsin Coup during the Period of the First Asylum in Japan], *Han'guk chŏngch'i oegyosa nonch'ong* [Journal of Korean Political and Diplomatic History] 21 (2000), pp. 35–50; Hŭihwan Yi, "Yun Ch'i-hoŭi kaehwa sasang" [The Reformist Thought of Yun Ch'i-ho], *Han'guksa yŏn'gu* [Journal of Korean History] 44 (1984), pp. 140–55.

29. Yŏngil Kim, "Miwanŭi p'ŭrojekt'ŭrosŏŭi Han'guk chayujuŭi" [Korean Liberalism: An Unfinished Project], in *Kongdongch'e chayujuŭi*, p. 84.

30. Chiyŏng Mun, "Han'guk chayujuŭiŭi yŏksa" [History of Korean Liberalism], in *Kongdongch'e chayujuŭi*, pp. 67–68.

31. Lynch v. Donnelly 465 U.S. 668 (1984).

32. The Constitutional Court. Decided Feb. 7, 2006. 2006heonma20: Most symbols or patterns used by the government and the local government has a close connection with our traditions, and one source of such traditions is religious tradition. In this case, it is unclear whether the usage of traditional religious symbols is to approve of a certain religion or not. For example, some of the banknotes of Korean won use the portraits of the prominent Confucian thinkers and one could ask whether this case violates the separation between government and religion. It is not an easy task to judge the religiousness of each concrete case. The Constitutional Court ruled that the symbol of Taegeuk circle of yin-yang used in the 5000-won note does not violate the principle of the separation between government and religion, because the symbol of Taegeuk is no longer recognized as an object of religious worship or believed as a center of religious practice.

33. According to Article 84 of the revised bill of National Public Service Law proposed by Congresswoman Kyŏngwon Na, a public servant who has perpetrated religious discrimination should either be jailed for up to one year or fined five million won (approximately US$5,000). However, since this article on penalty caused a controversy over the violation of the constitution, the National Public Service Law was revised into an advisory form to prohibit religious discrimination.

34. Yunki Hong, "Kaehyŏk kukkaŭi chagit'ujaeng: Kukka kaehyŏkkwa sahoe kaehyŏkŭi pyŏnjŭngbŏp" [Reformist Nation, Struggle for Itself: Dialectic between National Reformation and Social Reformation], *Tangdae pip'yŏng* [Contemporary Review] 6 (1999), pp. 37–40.

35. Yŏnghap news, 2006, 11, 22.

36. *Pŏppo Sinmun*, 2006, 12, 14.

37. The Supreme Court. Decided Apr. 27, 1976. 75nu249.

38. The Supreme Court. Decided July 23, 1985. 85do1094; The Supreme Court. Decided July 15, 2004. 20043do2965. Particularly, in the latter case, the court offers an opinion that there should be a revision on the cases of anti-liberal precedents. This change of the court was made possible by the democratic movement.

39. Article 37(2): The freedoms and rights of citizens may be restricted by law only when necessary for national security, the maintenance of law and order, or for public welfare. Even when such restriction is imposed, no essential aspect of the freedom or right shall be violated.

40. The Supreme Court. Decided July 15, 2004. 2004do2965.

41. Chaesŭng Yi, "Pyŏngyŏk kŏbue taehan panŭng yangsang" [The Forms of Response to Conscientious Objection], *Pŏpkwa sahoe* [Law and Society] 32 (2007), p. 268.

42. Ibid., p. 269.

43. The Constitutional Court. Decided Sept. 27, 2001. 2000heonma159.

44. The Supreme Court. Decided Oct. 9, 2003. 2003do4148.

45. Will Kymlicka, *Contemporary Political Philosophy* (New York: Oxford University Press, 2002), p. 10.

46. Kŭnsik Yi, *Sangsaengjŏk chayujuŭi: Chayu, p'yŏngdŭng, sangsaenggwa sahoe palchŏn* [Symbiotic Liberalism: Liberty, Equality, Symbiosis, and Social Development] (Paju: Tolbege, 2009), p. 124.

47. Kymlicka, *Contemporary Political Philosophy*, p. 33.

48. John Rawls, *Political Liberalism* (New York: Columbia University Press, 1993), pp. xx–xxi.

49. T'aeuk Chŏng, *Chayujuŭiŭi pŏpch'ŏlhak* [Liberal Legal Philosophy] (Seoul: Hanul ak'ademi, 2007), pp. 48–49.

50. Rawls, *Political Liberalism*, pp. xxi–xxii.

51. Reinhold Niebuhr, *Moral Man and Immoral Society: A Study of Ethics and Politics* (Louisville, KY: Westminster John Knox Press, 2013), p. xxxiv.

Chapter Seven

Confucius for Our Time

Reflections on Politics, Law, and Ethics

Fred Dallmayr

In his famous essay "The Clash of Civilizations?" Samuel Huntington curiously invoked the notion of a "Confucian-Islamic Connection" as one of the prominent features of the new millennium. As he wrote, in the global arena a "Confucian-Islamic Connection" is emerging or has emerged "to challenge Western interests, values and power." Despite the ostensible emphasis on "civilizations," Huntington in his essay was not concerned with the differences between Islam and Confucianism, nor with their distinctive cultural and religious character; the accent was basically on power. The connection, he wrote, has come into being "designed to promote acquisition by its members of the weapons and weapons technologies needed to counter the military power of the West." At least in the case of East Asia, military ambition was allied with economic advances. Citing an expert on Chinese development, the essay noted that "the Chinese-based economy of Asia is rapidly emerging as a new epicenter for industry, commerce and finance" because it contains "substantial amounts of technology and manufacturing capability (Taiwan), outstanding entrepreneurial, marketing and services acumen (Hong Kong)," and "very large endowments of land, resources and labor (mainland China)."[1] Given the focus on military power and economic might, it appears that the question mark behind the essay's title could readily be dropped, seeing that, under the cited auspices, a "clash of civilizations" is virtually inevitable.

No matter his academic expertise, Huntington's portrayal of the looming global scenario was basically anti-educational. When people confront each other as clashing opponents, they can fight and perhaps demonize each other, but they cannot learn from each other. If parents and children or teachers and pupils always clashed with each other, no education or learning could happen. However, education, maturation, and transformation are precisely at the heart of "civilization" seen as a civilizing and humanizing process. Perhaps no other philosophy in the world has been more committed to this civilizing and humanizing goal than East Asian Confucianism (I leave aside here the Islamic component in Huntington's fictitious "connection"). The emphasis on humanizing education is evident in such central Confucian notions as *ren* 仁 (humaneness), *li* 禮 (rite or ritual), and *dao* 道 (proper way of being). In the words of philosopher Tu Weiming, "learning in the Confucian perspective is basically moral self-cultivation. It is a gradual process of building up one's character by making oneself receptive to the symbolic resources of one's own culture and responsive to the sharable values of one's own society."[2] To be sure, Confucian education is not conceived under anthropocentric or ethnocentric auspices. As Tu writes at another point, the process of humanization is manifested in four dimensions: "cultivating personal life (*xiushen* 修身), regulating familial relations (*qijia* 齊家), ordering the affairs of the state (*zhiguo* 治國), and bringing peace to the world (*ping tianxia* 平天下)." He also cites a crucial insight from "The Doctrine of the Mean" (*Zhongyong* 中庸): "Unless one can realize the nature of all things to form a trinity with heaven and earth, one's self-realization cannot be complete."[3]

If these statements pinpoint—at least to some extent—the character of the Confucian tradition, it is clear that Confucianism provides an enormous resource for learning and educational cultivation, not only for East Asian people, but for people around the world. The erection of geopolitical barriers and "clash" scenarios impedes this learning process and thus impoverishes the civilizing potential of humankind. Unfortunately, impediments can be fostered not only by geopolitical strategies, but also by intra-civilizational processes. As it happens, the Confucian legacy (curiously) has itself become involved in a clash, namely, a clash of interpretations among Confucian scholars. In a way, the situation in East Asia can be compared to developments in Western countries where, in recent decades, traditional religion has made a comeback in the teeth of modern secularism—sometimes with a vengeance. Having suffered severely from marginalization and oppression during the "Cultural Revolution" and beyond, East Asian Confucianism likewise is experiencing a resurgence or revival, inspiring at least some of its practitioners with a sense of cultural triumphalism hostile to all the features characterizing Western modernity.

As it seems to me, one can distinguish today at least three modes of Confucian revival: a minimalist, a maximalist, and a hybrid or in-between mode. In the first type, Confucian teachings are limited to private family life without intruding into social and political domains. In the second type, Confucianism is erected into an all-embracing or totalizing ideology governing politics and society. In the last type, the focus is on limited constitutional reform coupled with personal and civic education or transformation. In the following discussion, I shall concentrate on the second and third type (since the first elicits little or no public debate). My argument here will basically be in support of the third type.

CONFUCIANISM AS STATE IDEOLOGY

In its long historical evolution, Confucianism has always been in close contact with ruling (dynastic or imperial) powers—though not always in full harmony. Like everywhere else, political rulers in East Asia have not always been amenable to ethical or philosophical pedagogy, even when relying on Confucian teachings to bolster their legitimacy. Theodore de Bary refers to the Chinese tradition of the "classics mat" (*qing-yan* 慶筵), a place from which Confucian sages were able to instruct and even reprimand imperial rulers when they engaged in dubious policies; but he also points to situations when such attempted instruction backfired, exposing Confucian sages to mortal danger.[4] In this respect, Confucian teachers often suffered the same disappointment that Plato experienced during his visits to the tyrant of Syracuse. On the whole, however, Confucian sages were less willing to antagonize imperial power than to accommodate themselves to its whims—thus overindulging, perhaps, in the celebrated Asian virtue of "harmony." The most frequent accusation leveled against Confucian scholars in the past has been not their daring but their timidity, and their often pliant surrender to the imperial or feudal status quo. In this respect, a Western parallel can again be found: namely, the traditional formula of "throne and altar" where the "altar" (or religion) was too often instrumentalized to bestow its blessings on the "throne."

To a large extent, it was precisely this subservience to imperial and feudal traditions which caused Confucianism to fall into disfavor during the twentieth century, especially in China. In mainland China, the communist revolution and later the "Cultural Revolution" insisted on making Confucianism a byword for feudal domination and exploitation. In due course, however, the excesses of these upheavals engendered a counter-movement evident in either the slow and tentative or the robust and muscular restoration of Confucianism in many parts of East Asia. Curiously, the most muscular and uncompromising restoration occurred early on in a city on the margin of East Asia: Singapore. As is well known, after splitting away from Malaysia in 1965, the city-state experienced a rapid political and economic rise under the leadership of Lee Kuan Yew (prime minister or senior minister consecutively from 1959 to 2004), a politician wedded firmly to the old-time ideas of "top-down" authority and discipline. One of the main sources of legitimation relied on by Lee was traditional Confucianism focused on filial piety, clan loyalty, and respect for established rulers. Given the multicultural character of Singaporean society, this preferred accent on Confucianism was bound to lead the government into repeated friction with alternative worldviews, especially with Muslims, Christians, and other traditions. Still more pronounced was the friction between Lee's authoritarianism and progressive tendencies in Western democratic politics; it was in this area that, in conjunction with other leaders, he launched the idea of the "Asian values" seen as an antidote to, and replacement for, Western-style "human rights."[5] For present purposes, however, the most important repercussion was in the field of Confucianism itself, which, compressed into a state ideology, was in danger of losing its reflective and humanizing qualities.

Although perhaps tempted by the economic advances, none of the leading East Asian countries have chosen to follow whole-heartedly the Singaporean model. This is true of both Taiwan and South Korea, despite strong Confucian leanings in both countries. For a number of reasons, especially its ambivalent and strongly contested rule, Confucianism in mainland China rarely inspired its followers to espouse the Singapore model or to advocate a return to pre-revolutionary dynastic conditions. Yet, in a modified and somewhat subdued form, historical nostalgia is evident in some mainland Confucian trends or perspectives. The major goalpost of these trends is the restoration of old-style authoritarianism, sometimes coupled with the erection of Confucianism into a state religion. Two main Chinese intellectuals are prominently associated with these trends: the philosopher Jiang Qing and social theorist Kang Xiaoguang. The former is well known to Chinese audiences for his restorative sentiments and his strong opposition to Western-style modernization in any form. What matters to Jiang primarily is the preservation of traditional Chinese values which are threatened by the onslaught of Westernization and globalization—trends which in their combination are bound to undermine "Chineseness" or the traditional fabric of Chinese "identity." For the philosopher, Western modernity is nothing but a collection of moral blemishes or defects; the basic core of modern Western life is said to be egocentrism and rampant, even subhuman selfishness. As he writes: "In the guise of modernity, men become animals full of desire. . . . My understanding of (Chinese) tradition is antithetical to modernity in that human desire must somehow be restricted by heavenly law."[6]

Jiang's critique of modernity carries over into his assessment of Western democracy, especially liberal democracy, which (in his view) ushers in a Social Darwinism which, in the end, "will destroy the human race." The contrast between this kind of democracy and Chinese tradition could not be clearer, because "Confucianism puts its ultimate wager of human salvation on the reemergence of a sage king"—a ruler who, though benevolent, would be absolutely supreme.[7] More recently, Jiang has stepped forward with an ambitious proposal designed to anchor Chinese political life firmly on Confucian grounds, in opposition to both Marxist communism and Western liberal democracy. The proposal is contained in a book whose title already announces its program—*A Confucian Constitutional Order: How China's Ancient Past Can Shape Its Political Future*—and to which Jiang contributed core chapters. The book grew out of a workshop held in Hong Kong in 2010 and assembles, together with Jiang's chapters, a number of rejoinders by Chinese intellectuals. Despite the public clamor surrounding the book, Jiang's proposal is somewhat less authoritarian or anti-democratic than might have been expected. Basically, the effort is to defend a multi-dimensional and balanced public scheme—although the aspect of democratic will-formation is relatively marginalized or decentered. As in his previous writings, Western democracy is the main target of critique. "The major flaw of democracy," he writes, "is the uniqueness of the legitimacy of the popular will. This exaggerated importance given to the will of the people leads to extreme secularization, contractualism, utilitarianism, selfishness, commercialism, capitalization, hedonism, mediocrity, neglect of ecology, lack of history, and lack of morality." As he adds: "In a democratic system, the authority and legitimacy of the government are determined by a formal will but not a substantive will of the people." The concern is with majority opinion "with no respect for the quality of the opinion."[8]

In Jiang's view, popular will is not a sufficient basis for the legitimacy of a political regime but needs to be supplemented by two other forms of legitimation: namely, a sacred-transcendent and a cultural-historical type. In his words: "Sacred legitimacy (transcendent), cultural legitimacy (historical), and the will of the people (human-centered) restrain each other; . . . each contributes in its own way to the work of checks and balances, contributing to the whole through what is different in each." All three types properly balanced constitute what Jiang calls the "Way of Human Authority"; in classical language, they represent the balance of "heaven, earth, and the human." In view of the ongoing process of Western-style globalization, he considers the cultural-historical type of legitimacy particularly important because it can "help non-Western countries to develop politically without obliterating all their cultural traditions." In terms of constitutional design, he proposes a parliamentary system composed of three houses, each reflecting a distinct source of legitimation. Thus, sacred legitimacy is embodied in the "House of Ru (*Tongruyan*)" or House of Scholars, cultural legitimacy in the "House of the Nation (*Guotiyan*)," and popular legitimacy in the "House of the People" (*Shumin yuan*)." Scholars (*Ru*) are chosen by recommendation and nomination; their leader is a great scholar or sage proposed by other Confucian scholars (perhaps paralleling the Iranian supreme Ayatollah). The members of the "Nation" are selected by hereditary criteria and by assignment; their leader is to be a direct descendant of Confucians and he selects other members who are descendants of other great people. The members of the "House of the People" are chosen by universal suffrage and by election from functional constituencies. To become a law, legislative proposals must pass all three, or at least two of the chambers; but the "House of Ru" has a permanent veto power. The chief executive of the system—who may be a monarch, but not necessarily so—is chosen by the consensus of all three houses. [9]

As one can see, Jiang's proposal is an elaborate design reflecting a desire for maximal balance among constitutive elements. Yet, although recognizing other historical perspectives, Chinese tradition is definitely paramount and Confucianism occupies the position of a dominant ideology or (what John Rawls called) a "comprehension worldview." To this extent, the valuable ideal of "harmony" is evidently slanted in one direction. In a less elaborate way and with less concern for harmony, a Confucian public order is also championed by Kang Xiaoguang in several of his works. As in Jiang's case, the chief objective for Kang is to rescue or salvage Chinese tradition from the onslaught of Western modernity; together with the former, he finds the chief means to accomplish this objective in the erection of Confucianism into a public ideology and even into a "civil religion" permeating social and public life. Fashioned as a religion, Confucianism for Kang can provide substantive legitimacy for the Chinese government (perhaps even a "sacred legitimacy"), that is, a source of legitimation lost or badly tarnished in recent decades. More specifically, it can supply justification for (what he calls) "benevolent government" or a benevolent authoritarianism wielded by eminent Confucian scholars (*ru*); only such scholars, he insists, can properly rule the country because they alone know "the Will of Heaven." More clearly than Jiang, Kang identifies the main target of constitutional reform (or rather revolution): the prevailing structure of Chinese government. As he boldly states, his project involves two simultaneous agendas: "to Confucianize the Chinese Communist Party and to Confucianize Chinese society. When Confucianism replaces Marxism-Leninism as state ideology and Confucian scholars replace the communist cadres, the process of creating benevolent government is complete." [10]

MODERATE CONSTITUTIONAL REFORM

The proposals discussed so far are certainly impressive in their subtle complexity and restorative zeal. They might even be ideal frameworks for a society some three or four hundred years ago. However, the proposals are formulated by contemporary writers and meant to apply to society (or societies) existing today. This means they emerge in a modern context—or as a response to this context—and thus cannot escape some modern political expectations. It so happens that the modern state is indeed conceived as a "nation-state" and thus is meant to reflect (at least to an extent) the historical-cultural background of a given nation (or collections of nationalities). However, the same state is also meant to be a "rule-of-law" state (*Rechtsstaat*), that is, a state whose rules and constitutional principles apply equally to all inhabitants of its territory, to majority as well as minority populations, to indigenous people as well as immigrants, to supporters as well as non-supporters of a dominant worldview or faith. In contrast to the asymmetry of rules and legal statuses prevailing in traditional societies, the modern state necessarily injects an equalizing and universalizing tenor into public life which puts pressure on "national identity." [11] To this extent, the insertion of a "House of the Nation" and a "House of Scholars"—in Jiang's sense—into the constitutional design cannot be reconciled, or can be reconciled only with the greatest difficulty, with the modern principles of personal freedom and equality before the law.

Most of the Chinese scholars participating in the Hong Kong workshop reflected on this issue and found Jiang's proposal flawed if not entirely untenable. In a wide-ranging rejoinder, political theorist Joseph Chan charges the proposal with extremism and anachronism. "Today," he writes, "the forces of modernization have demolished the main pillars of traditional Chinese society, and so Confucianism faces a challenge that never occurred before. . . . They cannot simply try to revitalize the traditional values once cherished by people, without considering if these values are socially relevant at all in modern society." What renders this relevance dubious is the great diversity and cultural pluralism prevailing in contemporary societies, including Chinese society. Foisting Confucianism as a "comprehensive doctrine" on a pluralistic society is for Chan both undesirable and futile; more importantly, the attempt to foster ethical maximalism or "perfectionism" turns out to be itself ethically flawed. Promoting this goal, he states, is undesirable in the main "because it damages civility"; but in a pluralistic society, "civility is of crucial importance" because it reflects a "common bond" among citizens despite different opinions and interests. By riding roughshod over differences, Jiang's proposal for Chan discloses an "ideological politics" that "destroys the common bond of citizens and rejects civility." Despite these strong criticisms, Chan is by no means an enemy of Confucianism or a devotee of ethical neutrality of the state (in the Western liberal sense). Rather, his recommendation is for a "moderate perfectionism" and a moderate Confucian constitutionalism, coupled with the promotion of Confucian values in civil society. [12] (I shall return to this point later.)

The charge of an excessively "perfectionist" or maximalist design is also leveled against Jiang by philosopher Chenyang Li. What particularly irks Li is the religious dogmatism or heavy "transcendentalism" present in Jiang's structures. He does not deny that the notion of "heaven" is an integral part of Confucianism, but finds that Jiang's usage of the notion elevates it beyond human and political reach. As he shows on the basis of historical study, it was already in the early stages of Confucianism that "the notion of 'heaven' was transformed from one that is primarily a transcendent and personal deity into one that is in the triad of 'heaven-earth-humanity.'" In line with his return to a primeval transcendence, Jiang also maintains that Confucian constitutionalism is or should be "transcendent and sacred, that is, religious in character." For Li, this accent flies in the face of the necessarily mundane, human, and practical character of a political constitution. The fact is, as Jiang concedes, that "heaven" cannot manage human affairs directly, but to do so has to be "brought down to earth, to human society"—and is effectively brought down by Jiang to the rule of Confucian sages or scholar-officials. However, if this delegation happens, what use then is the invocation of transcendent heaven, besides playing the role of "aesthetic adornment"? Like Joseph Chan, Li is not an opponent or detractor of Confucianism but wishes it to play the role of an ethical resource counterbalancing secular authority rather than that of a religious "establishment" or ruling power. As he writes, instead of merging Confucianism and politics, including democratic politics, "we should keep them in a relationship of checks and balances in the same society." As a shorthand formula for this relationship, under contemporary democratic auspices, he proposes the label "Confucian content with democratic form."[13]

In a more complex and nuanced manner, a similar argument was advanced by philosopher Tongdong Bai in the Hong Kong workshop. Bai's complaint focuses mainly on the excessively religious and dogmatic character of Jiang's proposal, a feature which is in conflict both with the inner spirit of the Confucian tradition and with the pronounced pluralism of contemporary social-political life. As he points out, the term "Confucian" in Jiang's usage refers to Confucianism "as a form of state religion (*rujiao* 儒教) and not as a school of philosophy (*rujia* 儒家)." Basically, what Jiang wishes to revive is a constitutionalism where "Confucian" means a form of religion and where religion refers to "a transcendent, sacred, religious, and metaphysical system." Actually, Bai agrees with Jiang's effort to launch a "political Confucianism" as opposed to an abstract moral ideal; however, they differ radically in the way this launch is conceived. For Bai, Confucianism is indeed a "political philosophy," and to take it as such means that it deals with perennial values and problems—but problems which always "express themselves at a special time, in a special place, and in a special form." What political philosophers need to do in order to grasp both the permanent problems and their concrete contexts is to "go to the spirit of the tradition (its 'old state')" and then recontextualize its teachings, thereby achieving the goal of "interpreting the 'old state' and give it a new mandate." By contrast, what Jiang does is take Confucian teachings (as formulated at one time in the past) as dogma or "sacred" legacy and transfer it to today's world. Thus, he imposes an "old mandate" on a "new state" or pours "old wine into new skins."[14]

What renders this procedure dubious and unappealing is both the fixed character assigned to "old-state" Confucianism and the inability of this kind of traditionalism to come to terms with the contemporary pluralism of perspectives and life forms. It is particularly the latter aspect which robs Jiang's proposal of its claimed comprehensiveness and balance. In Bai's words: "At a time when pluralism is inevitable, such a system cannot be universally adopted by everyone. Therefore, Confucian constitutionalism (the religious kind) cannot even be a constitutionalism for all Chinese, but only for a cult that follows a particular reading of Confucianism." Together with Li, Bai holds that Jiang's construal of "heaven" is "independent of, and higher than, the way of human beings"—a treatment which makes it possible for heaven to repress "the well-being of human beings," thereby opening the door to "the form of totalitarianism that has appeared in the West." In order to counter this danger, Bai—while still upholding the importance of Confucian teachings—opts in favor of a "thinner" or less maximalist form of constitutionalism. As he argues, in light of the prevailing pluralism, it is not possible "to attain even a common understanding of Confucianism among a large number of Confucians without resorting to oppression." Somewhat along the lines of Chenyang Li, he prefers to see Confucianism more as a watchdog and counterbalance to political rulers than as an established regime. His conclusion is that, in order to defend the contemporary significance of Confucianism, "we will need to go back to the living spirit of Confucianism and not to the dogmatic system of a certain era." If this is done, we shall be able to "face the political reality of today, showing how, following the Confucian spirit, we can answer questions from today's reality."[15]

The Hong Kong workshop was not the only forum or venue where questions of Confucian constitutionalism were discussed. The issue has a broader relevance and has been approached from different angles by numerous intellectuals. In many cases, the issue merges or overlaps with another prominent concern; namely, the desirable role of merit or "meritocracy" in East Asian public life. All the writers previously discussed share this concern to a certain degree, sometimes prominently, sometimes in a more reserved fashion. Clearly all who support a maximalist Confucian order and the rule of Confucian "sages" are committed to a form of public authority rooted, wholly or prominently, in exceptional merit or privilege. However, even writers with less pronounced maximalist leanings often attach a positive estimate to meritocracy. A good example is Chenyang Li. As he states in the text mentioned before, he endorses the Confucian triad of "heaven-earth-humanity"—where heaven and earth clearly limit the principle of popular sovereignty in favor of alternative types of authority. Recently, Li co-edited a book with political theorist Daniel Bell which discusses the challenge presented by "political meritocracy" for democracy in East Asia. The basic outlook of the book is succinctly put forth in its introduction (authored by Bell). As we read there:

"The democratic idea that power must flow from the people is deeply embedded in contemporary political discourse and practice." However, can some cultures and societies not embrace a "mixture" or synthesis of meritocracy and democracy? Relying on opinion surveys, the text finds support for such a solution in at least three out of six East Asian "Confucian" countries—which leads the author to this conclusion: It surely cannot be adequate to use "liberal democratic norms as they emerged from Western political history to judge the rest of the world's political development. Given the centrality of political meritocracy in Chinese political tradition . . . , China's rise will almost certainly mean that meritocracy will also serve as a reference point to political development."[16]

As one should note, Bell himself has come forward with a constitutional design for China—a design moderately reformist (or hybrid) in character despite distinct meritocratic leanings. Bell's proposal is for a bicameral legislature composed of a democratically elected lower house (*Shumin Yuan*) and a meritocratic upper chamber, called "House of Virtue and Talent" (*Xianshi Yuan*), selected on the basis of special merit or accomplishment, and possibly the result of an examination system. The proposal clearly reflects a moderate outlook averse to fundamentalism of any kind. Moreover, Bell tends to leave open the question whether the lower or the upper chamber should be given preference—although indicating that the second option might be preferable in the Chinese context.[17] A similarly "synthetic" model has been proposed by Tongdong Bai, whose critique of Jiang's maximalism has been cited before. Basically, Bai endorses Bell's bicameral structure and thus seeks to combine Confucianism in some way with modern democracy—especially a model of democracy indebted to liberal thinkers (like John Rawls) and the liberal notion of a "thin" constitutionalism. Notwithstanding its indebtedness, Western democracy for Bai is deeply flawed, and hence needs to be reconstructed or re-focused. His own preferred regime—which he calls "Confu-China"— would protect the rule of law and human rights and include a democratic "House of the People," allowing people's voices to be heard. However, on important or long-range issues, the latter would bow to a strong upper chamber selected on the basis of superior ability and virtue. As he states at one point: "The Confucian hybrid regime is a government for the people, but not purely by the people; rather it is partly by the people and partly by the competent people."[18]

CONSTITUTIONALISM AND CIVIC VIRTUES

Constitutional orders are legal frameworks from which domestic legislation is derived and to which it is supposed to conform. For this reason, they are often also called "basic laws." In this capacity, constitutional stipulations share the advantages and deficits of laws as such: they provide an orderly framework within which social life can operate, but they do not provide (or provide only to a limited extent) a safeguard against manipulation, evasion, and outright defiance. Differently put: laws by themselves do not assure lawfulness or law-abidingness. It is mainly for this reason, I believe, that in the long Confucian tradition there has always been a tension between legalism and ethics, between "rule by law" (*fazhi* 法治) and "rule by virtue" (*dezhi* 德治), and a decided tendency in favor of the latter. In the words of Stephen Angle: "The proper role and content of *fa* were matters of debate throughout the Confucian tradition. Law and legal codes were not seen by Confucians as having any special place within the larger universe of institutions" and "Confucius's own discomfort with litigation is well-known." In more recent times, the tension between law and virtue (or human disposition) has erupted in virulent form, and not directly under Confucian auspices. During the Cultural Revolution, Maoism was claimed to rely on the "rule by man" (that is, the Great Helmsman), and not on "rule of or by law"—a formula which gave aid and comfort to arbitrary despotism. Largely due to arbitrary excesses, the post-Mao era saw a slow return to legalism and lawfulness—though without a complete dismissal of ethics. Angle quotes a speech by Chairman Jiang Zemin of 2001 in which he said: "In the administration of a country, rule of law (*fazhi*) and virtue politics (*dezhi*) complement and promote each other. Neither should be overemphasized to the neglect of the other."[19]

This is surely sage advice; however, it does not entirely settle the issue of the relation between law and ethics. Contemporary Confucian thinkers can hardly forget the long history of tension, and sometimes antagonism, which has dominated Chinese life for so many centuries. And they can also hardly forget the underlying reason behind the tension. The fact is that law or legislation tends to be in the hands of political leaders who may or may not be virtuous and who have the power to enforce their ambitions; moreover, even initially virtuous people may be corrupted by power (and be more corrupted the more power they wield). Constitutional or legal orders do not by themselves provide safeguards against these dangers—which is precisely the reason for a certain distrust of *fa* among Confucian thinkers and their preferred emphasis on moral education. The writers (cited before) propounding moderate constitutional reform are all more or less enamored with meritocracy; but as good Confucians they must also realize that merit and virtue are not created by constitutional or legal provisions but have to be fostered independently or at least in tandem with social or public institutions. For those who are forgetful of this fact I need only remind them of the "classics mat" mentioned at the beginning and the fortunes and misfortunes associated with this institution.

The argument here is not that law and ethics are necessarily at odds with or antithetical to each other, but simply that they are not identical (although perhaps compatible) and endowed with their own integrity. Collapsing the two removes a possible restraint on political power, and especially on the abuse of power. To put it simply: Even the best political rulers—as long as they are human—are fallible and need to remain accountable not only to themselves but to the people they rule, especially to all those people directly affected by their policies. This, of course, is the basic insight of democracy, and Confucians should not be too ready to dismiss this insight as a "Western" import. To be sure, Confucians also want to make sure (to the extent feasible) that political rulers are meritorious, that is, that they hold their position not only on the basis of popular election but on the basis of their virtue and ethical disposition. But the way to accomplish this is not through self-selection or top-down imposition, but through broad-based civic education which enables people to make wise and informed public choices. As Aristotle said long ago: the quality of a meal cannot be left to the judgment of the cooks alone. This underscores the important—in fact all-important—role of civic education in a social or political body conceived as an ethical community. But education is not a process of manipulation, dictation, or inculcation, but of persuasion, patient learning, and guidance by good example.

To repeat: With these comments I did not wish to dismiss constitutional reform but only assign it to its proper place. As it happens, most of the proponents of constitutional reform previously mentioned seem to agree with this point. Thus, Joseph Chan distinguishes between Confucianism as an ethical and educational outlook and Confucianism as a public doctrine. As he writes: "Although as a moral or religious philosophy Confucianism may develop its conception of the good life as comprehensively and rigorously as possible, as a normative basis of political action it should present a noncomprehensive conception" compatible with democratic practices. And he adds: "Supporting moderate perfectionism [on the level of public order] not only does not require ideological control by the state but in fact demands a high level of freedom of speech, so that citizens can freely assess Confucianism and discuss policy in a rational manner." Pushing this point a bit further, Chenyang Li envisages a system exhibiting "Confucian content with democratic form." Using slightly different vocabulary from the one I used before, he proposes that ethics and politics or "Confucianism and democracy" are "two independent value systems and should be treated as such. Instead of integrating them into one system—which would result in a significant loss of some core values in both systems—we should keep them in a relationship of checks and balances in the same society." As we know, checks and balances sometimes operate in a complementary or harmonious way, sometimes in a more critical or agonistic way.[20]

Perhaps some of the most pointed and helpful remarks on the issue of Confucianism and democracy are those offered by Tongdong Bai at the Hong Kong workshop. Reacting to Jiang's religious model, he notes that its distinctive elitism is based on the assumption "that the popular will—due to the poor educational, moral, and political quality of the populace—cannot be trusted." He counters: "But is it not a Confucian tenet that the government and the Confucian elite have the duty to educate the common people and that, if we follow Mencius and Xunzi, every human being is educable and can become a sage through education?" Bai actually does not completely reject Jiang's institutional proposals, as long as they operate—here I interpret him freely—on the level of civil society rather than the state. "These institutions," he writes, "can play a role of watching over the rulers, and, when the rulers have to think about the long-term consequences of their policies, . . . they may have an incentive to plan policies beyond mere short-term interests." This is another way of phrasing the notion of checks and balances. In another context, Bai emphasizes that, in his model of "Confu-China," "participation is still preserved" and that Confucians "can happily acknowledge the civilizing role of mass participation." More specifically, Confucians "may even see the practical and psychological benefit of making people feel politically involved through mass participation in the age of democracy."[21]

Some concluding remarks. Although helpful, comments of this kind in my view need to be amplified and fleshed out. As it seems to me, proposals for constitutional reform (whether maximalist or reformist) tend to fall short by taking too lightly a basic premise of any viable constitutional order: the promise of ethical and civic education. More generally, I find that the move from a philosophical or metaphysical Confucianism (in previous decades) to a "political" Confucianism (of today) may sometimes be made too rapidly, as if it were a move from idealism to realism, from perfection to political compromise. This assumption violates the integrity of both Confucianism and modern democracy. The point is that the latter cannot simply be identified with a "liberal," interest-based model (not even the Rawlsian variety), but embraces a very different version according to which democracy (in John Dewey's memorable phrase) is "a form of moral and spiritual association."[22] If we take this version seriously, then civic education is crucial not only for Confucians but for Western democrats as well. What, from this angle, renders significant the contemporary upsurge of Confucianism is not so much the invigoration of "Confu-China" but its contribution to uplifting the moral fiber of public life in the East and the West. Here, the "humanizing" quality of education, stressed by Tu Weiming, comes to the fore again. For clearly, education and learning do not stop at borders; properly cultivated, they can serve as crucial antidotes to looming "clashes of civilization," bending them gently in the direction of "peace for the world" (*ping tianxia*).

NOTES

1. Samuel P. Huntington, "The Clash of Civilizations?" *Foreign Affairs* 72, no. 3 (1993), pp. 28, 45, 47. The citation is from Murray Weidenbaum, *Greater China: The Next Economic Superpower?* (St. Louis, MO: Washington University Center for the Study of American Business, Series 57, 1993), pp. 2–3.

2. Tu Weiming, *Confucian Thought: Selfhood as Creative Transformation* (Albany: State University of New York Press, 1985), p. 68.

3. Tu Weiming, *Humanity and Self-Cultivation: Essays in Confucian Thought* (Berkeley, CA: Asian Humanities Press, 1979), pp. 27–28, 97.

4. See Wm. Theodore de Bary, *Neo-Confucian Orthodoxy and the Learning of Mind-and-Heart* (New York: Columbia University Press, 1981), pp. 14–15, 28–29; also his *Nobility and Civility: Asian Ideals of Leadership and the Common Good* (Cambridge, MA: Harvard University Press, 2004), pp. 6, 12.

5. On the issue of "Asian values" compare my "'Asian Values' and Global Human Rights: Tensions and Convergences," in *Achieving Our World: Toward a Global and Plural Democracy* (Lanham, MD: Rowman & Littlefield, 2001), pp. 51–69; also see Jack Donnelly, "Human Rights and Asian Values: A Defense of 'Western' Universalism," in *The East Asian Challenge for Human Rights*, eds. Jeanne R. Bauer and Daniel A. Bell (Cambridge: Cambridge University Press, 1999), pp. 60–87; and Sumner B. Twiss, "A Constructive Framework for Discussing Confucianism and Human Rights," in *Confucianism and Human Rights*, eds. Wm. Theodore de Bary and Tu Weiming (New York: Columbia University Press, 1998), pp. 27–53.

6. See Jiang Qing and Sheng Hong, *To Nurture Virtue with Virtue* (Shanghai: Jointly Press, 2003), pp. 56, 59, 184 (in Chinese).

7. Ibid., p. 161. Compare also Jiang Qing, *Political Confucianism* (Beijing: Jointly Press, 2003) (in Chinese).

8. Jiang Qing, *A Confucian Constitutional Order: How China's Ancient Past Can Shape Its Political Future*, eds. Daniel A. Bell and Ruiping Fan and trans. Edmund Ryden (Princeton, NJ: Princeton University Press, 2012), pp. 33–34.

9. Ibid., pp. 37–41. For a similar perspective see Ruiping Fan, *Reconstructionist Confucianism: Rethinking Morality after the West* (Dordrecht: Springer, 2010).

10. See Kang Xiaoguang, *Benevolent Government: The Third Road to China's Political Development* (Singapore: Global Publishing Co., 2005), pp. vii–xlix (in Chinese). On Kang's "Institutional Confucianism" compare Stephen C. Angle, *Contemporary Confucian Political Philosophy* (Cambridge: Polity Press, 2012), pp. 41–47.

11. For the tension between nationalism and rule of law in the modern state see especially Alasdair MacIntyre, "Is Patriotism a Virtue?" in *Theorizing Citizenship*, ed. Ronald Beiner (Albany: State University of New York Press, 1995), pp. 209–28; also my "Transnational Citizenship? Paths beyond the Nation-State," in *In Search of the Good Life* (Lexington: University Press of Kentucky, 2007), pp. 188–204.

12. Joseph Chan, "On the Legitimacy of Confucian Constitutionalism," in Jiang, *A Confucian Constitutional Order*, pp. 99–100, 102–4.

13. See Chenyang Li, "Transcendent Heaven? A Critique of Jiang Qing's Grounding of the Right to Rule," in Jiang, *A Confucian Political Order*, pp. 130–1, 135–37.

14. See Bai Tongdong, "An Old Mandate for a New State: On Jiang Qing's Political Confucianism," in Jiang, *A Confucian Political Order*, pp. 114, 117.

15. Ibid., pp. 118, 122, 125, 128.

16. Daniel A. Bell, "Introduction: The Theory, History, and Practice of Political Meritocracy," in *The East Asian Challenge for Democracy: Political Meritocracy in Comparative Perspective*, eds. Daniel A. Bell and Chenyang Li (New York: Cambridge University Press, 2013), pp. 17, 25.

17. See Daniel A. Bell, *Beyond Liberal Democracy: Political Thinking for an East Asian Context* (Princeton, NJ: Princeton University Press, 2006); also my "Exiting Liberal Democracy? Bell and Confucian Thought," in *The Promise of Democracy: Political Agency and Transformation* (Albany: State University of New York Press, 2010), pp. 205–12; and Bell, "Toward

Meritocratic Rule on China? A Response to Professors Dallmayr, Li, and Tan," *Philosophy East and West* 59 (2009), p. 556.

18. Tongdong Bai, "A Confucian Version of a Hybrid Regime: How Does It Work, and Why Is It Superior?" in Ball and Li, eds., *The East Asian Challenge for Democracy*, p. 73.

19. Angle, *Contemporary Confucian Political Philosophy*, pp. 60, 67.

20. Jiang, *A Confucian Constitutional Order*, pp. 102, 111, 137.

21. Ibid., p. 125; Bell and Li, eds., *The East Asian Challenge for Democracy*, p. 74.

22. See John Dewey, "The Ethics of Democracy," in *John Dewey: The Early Works, 1882–1898*, vol. 1, eds. George E. Axtelle et al. (Carbondale: Southern Illinois University, 1969), pp. 239–40. As he adds there: "Democracy, in a word, is a social, that is to say, an ethical conception, and upon its ethical significance is based its significance as governmental." Compare also my "Democratic Action and Experience: Dewey's 'Holistic' Pragmatism," in *The Promise of Democracy*, pp. 43–65.

III

Epilogue

Chapter Eight

On Confucian Constitutionalism in Korea

A Metacommentary

Hwa Yol Jung

> Don't bleach language, savor it instead. Stroke it gently or even groom it but don't "purify" it.
>
> —Roland Barthes, *The Neutral*

This commentary aims to interpret other interpretations, that is, provide a commentary on commentaries. The term *metacommentary* is taken from the prize-winning essay by the young American literary critic Fredric Jameson.[1] For Aristotle *metaphysics* is that philosophical discipline which comes *after* (post) physics. So does metacommentary follow commentaries. It is used here as the hermeneutical principium which embraces the Confucian concept of the "rectification of names" (*zhengming*)[2] to which Confucian scholars today—both Eastern and Western—have yet to pay more serious attention. The Confucian "rectification of names" goes well side by side with another passage also in the *Analects* which states that "without knowing [the *power* of] language, it is impossible to know humanity."[3] For Heidegger, language is the mother of all human relations. In my metacommentary I intend to emphasize that hermeneutical method which does not forget the interpreter's own self-reflection of his or her being-in-the-world both theoretical and experiential. It also involves at least a partial effort of deconstruction in the original sense Heidegger uses the term. Deconstruction, however, is often mistakenly likened to a demolition derby, which denotes destruction for the sake of destruction with no reconstruction or no appropriation of tradition whatsoever. As its etymology intimates, construction follows destruction. In the present metacommentary on "Korean/Confucian constitutionalism," I will take heed of the French literary savant or *meijin* Roland Barthes's words of caution issued in his epigraph above for the use of language in interpreting other interpretations: not to "bleach" or "purify" but to "savor" and "stroke it gently" or "groom" it, if needed. For Barthes, I should add, the Eastern sinographic cultures of Japan and China, whose daily linguistic diet has been wholly or partly sinography, were not at all foreign. Following his visit for several months to the sinographic culture of Japan, he wrote the most fascinating and captivating *oeuvre* entitled *L'Empire des Signes*, that is, of sinograms (*kanji* in Japanese) in 1970. The work thoroughly and delightfully exhibits and "savors" his *Japonisme* or his love of things Japanese from haiku and bonsai to Zengakuren.

In sum, my metacommentary does not pretend to perform a "purification ritual" or "rite" for or against "Korean/Confucian constitutionalism." It is no accident that China's growing wealth and increasing power, I think, are connected to the increasing popularity of sinology, including sinography, which is the most difficult phenomenon to learn, according to one Western commentator, in the evolution of the universe. So was the increasing popularity of Japanology including Zen a few decades ago in the United States. In this light, we should slightly modify Foucault's nexus of power and knowledge, which is also the motivating and underlying thesis of Edward Said's *Orientalism*, to the nexus of wealth/power and knowledge.[4]

THE CONSTRUCTION OF "CONFUCIAN CONSTITUTIONALISM" IN EASTERN AND WESTERN CONTEXTS

The Cambridge History of Twentieth-Century Political Thought, edited by Terence Ball and Richard Bellamy (2003), carried Bhikhu Parekh's contribution called "Non-Western Political Thought," in which he cites the slogan "Down with Confucianism" (written by a Western observer in 1949), which has a negative portrayal of "Confucian constitutionalism."[5] In the volume, however, no single essay discusses either Chinese or Confucian political thought. The fortune of Confucian political thought, especially "Confucian constitutionalism," has dramatically changed the world arena of comparative political philosophy because of the dedicated and energetic efforts by the Canadian political philosopher Daniel A. Bell and two Korean brothers, Chaibong Hahm and Chaihark Hahm—the older brother, Chaibong Hahm, was trained in political theory and the younger one, Chaihark Hahm, in jurisprudence at law schools, both in the United States. In this essay I will focus on the work of Chaihark Hahm, who has written more than anyone else I know in Korea on the question of "Korean-Confucian constitutionalism" based on the Confucian concept of *li* (in Chinese) or *ye* (in Korean), which is translated by Chaihark Hahm into English as "ritual," "rite," or "ritual propriety."[6] He asks the question of whether "Confucian constitutionalism" is a "foreign transplant" or "indigenous" or native to the culture of Korean soil. I say it is an odd question because Confucianism, like Buddhism and Christianity in Korea, is a foreign transplant. The rite of ancestor worship (*chesa* in Korean) is, I think, a hybridization of Confucianism and shamanism, which, I think, is more indigenous than Confucianism.

Chaihark Hahm's innovative and constructive work on "Confucian constitutionalism" based on the concept of *li* or *ye* deserves a celebratory accolade: it is well-conceived, well-documented, well-argued, and well-executed in details. I "savor" it—to use Barthes's precious word.[7] Because it is the *crossing* (X-ing) of Eastern and Western ideas as well as the crossing of two disciplines, jurisprudence and political science, it puts another nail in the coffin of Rudyard Kipling's famous or infamous separatist idea that East is East and West is West, and the twain shall never meet. In the age of globalizing or the glocalizing world of multiculturalism, Kipling's separatism is outmoded and, to use a stronger language, it should be "out-lawed."[8] Glocalization rather than globalization implies the judicious idea that today the global without the local is vacuous and the local without the global is myopic. This radically new phenomenon of globalization is prophetically exemplified in the thinking of one of the wisest and greatest minds of the West: Johann Wolfgang von Goethe (1749–1832), who coined the felicitous and mind-opening phrase *world literature* (*Weltliteratur*) or "worlding" of literature, as Heidegger would put it, which alone makes him a true visionary: as he expresses, he who knows himself and the other will also recognize that East and West cannot be separated. His most poignant philosophical expression is "In the beginning was the Deed!" (*Im Anfang war die Tat!*), reminding us of the quintessence of Sinism, especially of Confucianism, as will be shown in the second section of this essay. Goethe was most audacious to lash out at the most sanctified canon of Western philosophy, the Delphic/Socratic oracle— "Know thyself." On account of it, I would call Goethe a "dare devil." Socrates, according to Goethe, seduced man from activity in the outside world and sought to draw him into "a false inner contemplation." Goethe contended rightly or ritely that man knows himself insofar as he knows the world, and man only comes to know himself in the world.

Chaihark Hahm's work exemplifies what I call a transversal approach. By transversality, to put it simply, I mean the *crossing* (X-ing) of DIFFER-ENCES which results in hybridity by way of confluence, that is to say, intercultural, interdisciplinary, interspecieistic, intersensorial, and inter-racial (bi-racial or mixed race). From the very start here, it must be made clear that the logic of my transversal approach is an emulation of the Sinic logic of yin and yang, which is twofold. First, the yin-yang logic is radically different from the Hegelian and Marxian dialectics in that historical transformation has no final synthesis which is called by Maurice Merleau-Ponty "hyper-dialectic" and by Mikhail Bakhtin "unfinalizable dialogism."[9] Consequently, the transversal approach results in hybridization, the process of which has no final end in intercultural matters, that is, hybridization goes on endlessly as the hybridization of hybrids. Second, yin and yang as two opposites are based on the principle of complementarity rather than antagonist violent confrontation as in the Marxian proletarian revolution. There is complementarity in the yin-yang logic and thus in the transversal approach; what is lacking or absent is complemented by the other. Therefore, what is lacking in the West (yang) is complemented by the East (yin). Thusly viewed, the East no longer remains a *negative mirror* but becomes a *parallax* to the West.

Let me say that Chaihark Hahm's jurisprudence and politics of constitutionalism are firmly rooted in culture. I would agree wholeheartedly with him when he pinpoints culture as the bedrock of everything we do and think, including jurisprudence and politics. *Li* or *ye* is a cultural phenomenon. Thus nothing we do or think can escape from the parameter of what I call cultural hermeneutics. So-called philosophical hermeneutics provides us with the general principles of hermeneutics, whereas cultural hermeneutics is, as we might say, an "applied hermeneutics" without any pejorative adage. The late noted cultural anthropologist Clifford Geertz, with a phenomenological proclivity judiciously or, to use his own expression, "most bluntly," states:

> [T]here is no such thing as a human nature independent of culture. Men without culture would not be the clever savages of Golding's *Lord of the Flies* [or, I might add, Hobbes's war-mongering men in the state of nature] thrown back upon cruel wisdom of their animal instinct; nor would they be the nature's noblemen of Enlightenment primitivism [perhaps Geertz has in mind Rousseau]. . . . Without men, no culture, certainly; but equally, and more significantly, without culture, no men.[10]

This is the reason why I use the phrase "Korean/Confucian constitutionalism."

My "grooming" of Chaihark Hahm's re/Orient/ation of "Korean/Confucian constitutionalism" based on *ye* or the "right/rite stuff" of constitutionalism as a transversal approach is rather one-sided, that is, the adjective "Confucian" weighs more heavily than (democratic) "constitutionalism," at least the concept itself is a Western invention. In my "grooming," I will focus on the American presidential constitutionalism simply because Korean constitutionalism is patterned after the American presidential political system. Democracy or the rule of the *demos* is a Western invention, in Periclean Athens in ancient Greece. The rhetorical skills of Pericles the Olympian, such as the "Funeral Oration," are heroic and legendary. Thucydides (we might call him the Sima Qian of the West), the author of *The Peloponnesian War*, lionized

Pericles as a great statesman able to tame and control "the wild beast of democracy."[11] In the modern West, we must begin with the *Magna Carta* or the Great Charter in the Anglo-American world, which is a revolt against the allegedly monarchical misrule, which Aristotle called "tyranny," that is, the "illegitimate" form of monarchy. Thereafter, the French Revolution's slogan of *vox populi* (the voice of the people) was *"liberté," "egalité,"* and *"fraternité."*[12] In the United States, the democratic constitutionalism is well expressed by President Abraham Lincoln as the government *of, by,* and *for* the people. However, to define the concept of democracy, the government *of* and *by* the people is far more important than *for* the people because even authoritarian rulers can declare that they are *for* the people. In today's British parliamentary political system (i.e., its democratic constitutionalism), the *vox populi* is reflected in the House of Commons, whose legislation is the supreme law of the land since it, unlike the United States, has no single document called a "constitution."

In the American presidential political system, the function of the Supreme Court is most significant since Chief Justice John Marshall delivered the decision in *Marbury v. Madison* in 1803. "Judicial review" in the United States exemplifies what we might call jurisprudential hermeneutics, the subject of which has rarely been discussed in the European tradition of hermeneutics as a philosophical discipline. Be that as it may, the Supreme Court is not just a legal institution but, more importantly, it is regarded as a *political* institution, that is, it must be seen in terms of the political climate. Because it is a political institution, it has been controversial. In the twentieth century, Chief Justice Earl Warren's (1953–1969) writing of the controversial opinion in *Brown v. the Board of Education* (1954), where school segregation was declared to be "inherently unequal" and thus "unconstitutional," is unquestionably a *political* judgment. This is one clear piece of evidence that the Supreme Court of the United States is a *political* rather than just a jurisprudential *institution*.

In order to understand the workings of American constitutionalism, it is imperative to know the idea of the separation of powers (i.e., the legislative, the executive, and the judiciary) and their checks and balances. In this context, there is the twofold assumption which underlies (democratic) constitutionalism. First, Lord Acton's principle or even truism that power *tends* to corrupt and absolute power corrupts absolutely. Second, the institutional mechanism of preventing the abuse of power is not the concentration of power in any one institution of government but the separation of it. This principle of the separation of powers is enunciated and formulated by the French Baron de Montesquieu (1689–1755) in his magnum opus *The Spirit of the Laws* (*De l'Esprit des Lois*, 1748) of which James Madison, one of the framers of American constitutionalism and one of the authors of *The Feder-*

alist Papers, was well aware.[13] Chaihark Hahm mentions Montesquieu with no serious discussion.

THE EUTROPHICATIONAL RHETORIC OF "RIGHTS TALK"

"Lockeanism," Louis Hartz declares, is "Americanism" or American exceptionalism. The Harvard law professor Mary Ann Glendon, to whom Chaihark Hahm acknowledges his indebtedness for "guidance, inspiration, and critical comments" in his 2001 published essay entitled "Conceptualizing Korean Constitutionalism," identifies American Lockeanism with "rights talk." It launches a "reality check" on the Lockean tradition of "rights talk" as "possessive individualism"—to use the Canadian political theorist C. B. Macpherson's phrase (cf. R. H. Tawney's "acquisitive society").[14] "Possessive individualism," the British Marxist literary critic Terry Eagleton elegantly puts it, "abandons each subject to its own private space, dissolves all positive bonds between them and thrusts them into mutual antagonism."[15] Interestingly, "rights talk" as "possessive individualism" advances what we might call "asocial sociability" of humans. Furthermore, Sheldon S. Wolin attributes the decline of political philosophy to the ascendancy or primacy of *homo oeconomicus* over *homo politicus* since the Greek political philosophies of Plato and Aristotle.[16] It was Aristotle who defined the humanity of humans in terms of their lives in a *polis*, that is, if the human is not a political animal, he or she would be either a god or a beast. To sum up: my critique of "rights talk" as possessive individualism with an accent on Sinism is another way of going "beyond liberal democracy" based on what Heidegger calls "fundamental ontology" or the ontology of humans as embodied social process.

For Locke, the sole function of civil government under social contract is to protect and preserve individual property which is a composite of life, liberty, and estate or, as Thomas Jefferson rephrased it, "the pursuit of happiness." Since estate is nothing but the product of labor, labor is central to Locke's structuration of property (i.e., labor theory of value). Locke meant to create a society of acquisitive individuals. For Locke, wilderness or the untoiled or uncultivated land is called "waste" (his own word). Locke's labor theory of value has a blind spot, which would be called "Wilderness-Attention-Deficit Syndrome" (WADS). It is often taken for granted and thus worth noting that with Locke's "possessive individualism" there comes a literally earth-shaking shift in the history of Western political thought from the ascendancy of political categories to that of economic ones, which marks the difference between the premoderns and the moderns, including Karl Marx.[17] Hence is the "decline of *political* philosophy." If Locke's liberalism is characterized as "possessive individualism," then Marx's socialism is "possessive collectivism." In this light, the importance of Hannah Arendt's work, *The Human Condition*, lies in her effort to retrieve the premodern (e.g., Aristotelian) ascendancy of the political (the public affairs of the *polis*) over the economic (the private affairs of households), whose center is labor, that is to say, its end is to restore *political* philosophy as philosophy of political *action* distinct from labor (*homo laborans*) and work (*homo faber*).[18]

The United States is indeed the land of "rights talk." It is the mark of American exceptionalism. The historian of American political thought Louis Hartz observed that "Locke dominates American political thought, as no thinker anywhere dominates the political thought of a nation."[19] Francis Fukuyama's controversial thesis of the "end of history," despite his later denial, was a kind of fulfillment of Locke's prophecy that America would be the future of the world.[20] Amy Gutmann also observes that most prominent political philosophers are rights theorists. The depth of Locke's "possessive individualism" in the American psyche is intimated by Mary Ann Glendon in *Rights Talk* when she says, "The American rights dialect is distinguished not only by what we say and how we say it, but also by what we leave unsaid."[21] Today rights talk has invaded and colonized even the nonhuman world of nature: many if not all speak without reservation of the "rights of nature" and "animal rights" as well as "civil rights" and universal "human rights." We are possessed by and obsessed with "rights talk." A call for the "reclamation" of responsibility by opponents of "rights talk" is also misguided because responsibility has never assumed conceptual prominence or strategic equity with rights in Western modernity.

Ethics and politics are inseparable: politics begins with ethics and ends in ethics. The purpose of this proposal is to ascertain the thesis that responsibility as first ethics is a viable *alternative* to and inclusive of freedom, that is, freedom to labor, work, and acquire or own estate, which is presupposed by "rights talk." It is not enough to say, however, that freedom and responsibility are correlative for the simple reason that we can be free without being responsible but we cannot be responsible without being free. Freedom may be the first word, but it cannot be the last word. In other words, this proposal entertains the idea of "taking responsibility seriously" in contradistinction to Ronald Dworkin's idea of "taking rights seriously" in the tradition of Hobbes, Locke, John Austin, and William Blackstone. "If someone has a right to something," asserts Dworkin, "then it is wrong for the government to deny it to him even though it would be in the general interest to do so."[22] Thus, Dworkin endorses the inviolable sovereignty of an acquisitive individual.

The conceptual career of responsibility has been stagnant and dismal. It has become infused and confused with a person's "accountability" for his or her own conduct ever since it was first introduced in English and French in 1787. Having been associated with personal, political, and legal reward and punishment, responsibility has by and large become and still remains merely a sublimated correlative of rights even for those who care for the concept. Taking responsibility means standing behind, backing, or giving support to the substantive idea of rights. Anthony Downs is most extreme when he unequivocally asserts that if you are not selfish, you are not rational.[23] Indeed, there is a paramount and urgent need for the clarification and rectification of responsibility as a deconstructive critique of "rights talk." Carol Gilligan, for whom "rights talk" is by and for men, sums up women's moral orientation as follows:

> [T]he moral problem arises from conflicting responsibilities rather than from competing rights and requires for its resolution a mode of thinking that is contextual and narrative rather than formal and abstract. This conception of morality as concerned with the activity of care centers moral development around the understanding of responsibility and relationships, just as the conception of morality as fairness ties moral development to the understanding of rights and rule.[24]

Like Gilligan, I take the concept of responsibility as a corrective antidote for "rights talk" seriously.

SINISM AS RELATIONAL ONTOLOGY

The term Sinism was coined by the American sinologist H. G. Creel to characterize the *Weltanschauung* of the Chinese, which is this-worldly, practical, concrete, and particular rather than other-worldly or transcendent, theoretical, abstract, and general.[25] By it I include the geographical region of Korea and Japan in addition to China, where sinography is used wholly or partly as their steady daily linguistic diet. Sinism includes Confucianism, Daoism, and the hybrid or transversalized religion Chan/Sŏn/Zen Buddhism in Korea and Japan as well as in China, and it exemplifies a species of relational ontology. Since 1985, I have been using the neologism *relational ontology* to characterize Sinism. The relational thinking of Sinism signifies the idea that everything is related to everything else in the cosmos and nothing can exist in isolation.

In the beginning was the word, and the word was embodied Relation. To modify the poetic expression of the Chinese Daoist Zhuangzi, the Dao of Relation was born before Heaven and Earth, and yet you cannot say it has been there for long; it is earlier than the earliest time, and yet you cannot call it old. Relation is prior to the existence of the self or the other. It is *between*, or the interface of, the self and the other, humanity and nature, mind and body, masculinity and femininity, reason and the sensorium, the East and the West, and so on (see especially Watsuji's magnum opus).[26] There is now the religious order called "Interbeing" which the Vietnamese Zen Buddhist Thich Nhat Hanh has founded. Furthermore, it is interesting to note that there is the empirical evidence shown by the American cultural psychologist Richard E. Nisbett in *The Geography of Thought* that relational thinking is the hallmark of the East Asian peoples.[27] In short, Sinism as relational ontology is centered in what French social philosopher Pierre Bourdieu has elegantly phrased "the *performative* magic of the social."[28]

The first principle of relational ontology is: to be alone is not to be. Social existence is characteristic of the humanity of humankind. As French sculptor Auguste Rodin's *Cathedral* where two right/rite hands are coming together, we may call it the "sacrament of coexistence." Good or bad, we are condemned to coexistence. Insofar as we are born of mothers, we are always already socially situated. The religious myth of immaculate conception is most miraculous of all miracles because it defies the biological mandate of human coexistence. There is no self unencumbered by the surrounding milieu both social and natural. As Arendt writes: "No human life, not even the life of the hermit in nature's wilderness, is possible without a world which directly or indirectly testifies to the presence of other human beings."[29]

Let me comment on the strictly tradition-bound nature of Confucianism on account of my experience with the practicality of performing or fulfilling filial piety (*xiao* or *hyo*). The proof of filial piety is in practicing or performing it. I would call it "affective" endearing reciprocity as a Confucian rite whose function, like many other non-Confucian rites, especially religious rituals, whose *habitus* is "body-learning" rather than "head-learning" alone, brings group solidarity or creates the sense of community (*communitas, Gemeinschaftlichkeit*, or *Mitmenschlichkeit*). Filial piety exemplifies the ideal of the performative magic of primary sociality. Many years ago I came across a moving story about the nature of the (goddess) *Pietas* in reading Carl Kerenyi's work on Greco-Roman religion. It goes as follows:

> [O]n the site of this temple, so it was related, a mother had once been imprisoned and had been kept alive by the milk of her own daughter's breast. The story may have been adapted from a Greek original, though this is by no means certain. But it would have been pointless, had it not represented *pietas* in the ideal form in which it appeared to the Romans. The special thing which here stands out is something *bodily and spiritual* [italics added for emphasis] at the same time. *Pietas* here shows itself as a form of absolute reciprocity in nature, a completely closed circle of giving and receiving. In some variants of the story, the mother's place is taken by the father. But the example thus revered is always the same *natural circle of reciprocity . . . pietas* as a matter of course united those who give nourishment with those who in uninterrupted thankfulness return it, unites the source of life without its creatures from which its sources receive life.[30]

Later, I discovered one of a collection of twenty-four ivory carvings which illustrate the twenty-four exemplary acts of Confucian filial piety at the Wellcome Institute and Museum of the History of Medicine in London. I understood anew what Confucian filial piety really means: it is a "virtue ethic," which, as I define it, is neither deontological ("obligation" or "duty" in Kant's deontology), nor teleological (in Aristotelian ethics), and definitely not "utilitarian" (in Jeremy Bentham's ethics and Francis Bacon). It is a "virtue ethic" because it involves the natural cycle of generational reciprocity. It is really "thanking" for your indebtedness to your preceding generation or parents. In my short metacommentary on filial piety and the popularity of the topic in contemporary China, I urged that the rigidly tradition-bound performance must be re/formed in order to accommodate the changing times and conditions.[31] The rigidity of performing the rite of filial piety, like all rituals, makes it "ritualistic" and "ceremonious" (i.e., meaningless) in the pejorative sense of the terms.

In this connection, I should mention Herbert Fingarette's works, especially *Confucius—The Secular as Sacred*, which has been a lasting inspiration for my work on Confucianism.[32] It is a gem of a little *tôme*, which, I think, has not been discussed often enough in the scholarship of Confucianism, including "Confucian constitutionalism." The first chapter entitled "Human Community as Holy Rite" (*li*) in itself is sufficient enough to go "beyond American liberal democracy" as "rights talk."[33] Having said that, we should pay more attention to the Confucian idea of *ren* in the context of today's globalizing world in addition or in conjunction with the Confucian concept of *li*. Let me recount what Fingarette said about his learning of Confucianism. His impression of Confucius in the beginning was exactly like what Hegel said about Confucius; that is, Confucius is a "prosaic and parochial moralizer" whose philosophy has only "archaic irrelevance"—the same kind of view I hear from my close Korean philosophers who had been educated in the "modern" West. In his later years, Fingarette discovered that Confucius said things not being said anywhere else, and that those things needed to be said. When I became interested in studying East Asian philosophy, I learned Confucianism as "practical humanism" in the sense of European Enlightenment thought based on "reason" rather than medieval "faith." Now I am convinced that Fingarette's idea of "human community as holy rite" combined with *ren* in creating a world community is priceless. My current critique to "rectify" liberal democracy as "rights talk" is based on the idea of "sacrament of coexistence," which includes the sense of community or *communitas* (*Gemeinshaftlichkeit*) that needs to go beyond American liberal democracy as "rights talk," and to rectify excessively possessive individualism that carries no sense of *community* holy or unholy. Moreover, I have been inspired by Fingarette's conception of the Confucian "music of humanity" (*ren*) which, as Confucius himself was an aficionado of music whose quintessence is "harmony," that is, the performing art which has the element of infusing our harmony with not only interhuman reciprocity but also, more importantly, an interspecific one in the era when transversal geophilosophy is our *ultima philosophia* for generations and ages to come.

From the viewpoint of relational ontology, the scotoma of "rights talk" is primarily twofold. In the first place, "rights talk" is ontologically misinformed and misconceived. It does not deny sociality as such. It only reifies sociality when it defines sociality in terms of self-centeredness or egocentricity rather than the dialogics of self and other whose center is in the middle or betweenness. The British sociologist Norbert Elias calls this dialogical middle "a figuration of interdependent individuals."[34] René Girard's neologism "interviduality" or Spinoza's "transindividuality" also emphasizes the spatial and temporal inbetweenness without losing sight of individuality. However attractive and precious the terms *self-reliance, rights, autonomy,* and *independence* may be, they are disconnected to the social reality of affiliation, association, and interdependence. Interdependence, that is, interdependence cum difference, cannot and must not be anathema to the human or cosmic condition of plurality. In the second place, more importantly, "rights talk" is tantamount to the denial of the ethical in that there is no ethics involved in self-centeredness or in the pursuit of happiness as the maximization of one's self-interest. Care of the self entails no ethics. Ethics is caring of the other which is exemplified in altruism. Furthermore, possessive individualism, elegantly defined by Mary Ann Glendon as "I's have it," not only is egocentric but also identifies narrowly the pursuit of happiness with material possession or otherwise: to put it ontologically, it identifies "being" with "having," that is, the whole with one of its parts. "Having" more and more things or the acquisition of wealth is not, cannot, and must not be an end in itself. Rather, it is only a means to the happy or good life. In his discourse on "political economy," even the philosopher of classical liberalism John Stuart Mill expressed his dismay concerning the endless "tip-toeing" of economic competition in pursuit of acquiring more and more things in Great Britain in his own time.

THE ROLE OF DIFFERENCE IN RELATIONALITY

Without differences, the very idea of human plurality or multiplicity is an impossibility. Plurality is many whereas sameness or the identical is one. Thus, the concept of difference makes all the difference in the making of relationality. Human plurality means that we coexist with others in their otherness in communication, speech, and action. Difference and relation are correlatives: the former makes the latter both necessary and possible. In the same vein, Michael Walzer remarks that differences make toleration neces-

sary and toleration makes differences possible.[35] But for difference, relationality is the flatland of sameness or the identical, that is to say, there is no
relationality at all. Carol Gilligan puts it concisely: we make "connection in
the face of difference."[36] The following remarks by Cornel West are unsur-
passable in discussing Sinism in the context of globalizing a world of multiculturalism toward "a global village" (Marshall McLuhan's popular phrase):
"Distinctive features of the new cultural politics of difference are to trash the
monolithic and homogeneous in the name of diversity, multiplicity and
heterogeneity; to reject the abstract, general and universal in the light of the
concrete, specific and particular; and to historicize, contextualize and plural-
ize by highlighting the contingent, provisional, variable, tentative, shifting
and changing."[37]

HETERONOMY AND RESPONSIBILITY AS FIRST ETHICS

The idea of heteronomy—a term which is taken from the corpus of Emmanuel Levinas's writings—is most elemental and central to the ethics of
responsibility: it is the very foundation upon which the ethics of responsibility is constructed. In building the foundation of responsibility, I draw my
inspiration and direction principally from three twentieth-century thinkers
whose ideas are its building blocks, as it were: the Scottish philosopher John
Macmurray, the Russian literary theorist Mikhail Bakhtin, and the Jewish-
French phenomenologist Levinas. They all are dialogists who reject the primacy of the "theoretical" (e.g., epistemological) in favor of the "practical"
(e.g., ethical) in search of self-transcendence as opposed to self-absorption
and self-affirmation. They continue the heritage of Ludwig Feuerbach's "Copernican" discovery in 1843 of a "Thou" or the primacy of the other as the
cornerstone of the future of philosophy. His discovery may be called the
"Copernican revolution" of social and political thought for the reason that
Copernicus's cosmological heliocentrism is to Ptolemy's geocentrism what
Feuerbach's heterocentrism is to egocentrism. In the same vein, responsibility is heterocentric (other-centered), while rights talk is egocentric (self-
centered).

Levinas, who is regarded by many as the greatest moral philosopher or
ethicist in the twentieth century, spurred an interest in ethics as the primary
subject of philosophy (i.e., ethics as *prima philosophia*).[38] He, too, continues
to trek Feuerbach's "Copernican revolution" in ethical, social, and political
thought. Levinas attends directly to the question of *ethics as first philosophy*,
which, I might add, is his most important contribution to phenomenology as
a philosophical movement in the twentieth century—as a matter of fact, he
introduced phenomenology to the French philosophical audience. Parentheti-
cally, his popularity enhances and authenticates the study of Confucianism as

moral philosophy. Based on the asymmetrical relation of the self and the other in which each is different because he or she is singular, not the other way around, the other as other (alterity) is, ethically speaking, prior to the self (ipseity). To be asymmetrical, relationship cannot be a plural of the I's. Ipseity alone makes the ethical untenable: it defaces or effaces the ethical. To reiterate: the ethical is not self-centered but self-transcendent. Only by way of heteronomy or self-transcendence is an ethics possible in which the other is not only not an *alter ego* but also is primary to the ego. Thus Levinas maintains that plurality (sociality) is not a multiplicity of numbers, but is predicated upon a radical alterity of the other. The ethical is the conception of the self whose center is "elsewhere" and "otherwise."

Responsibility as self-transcendence which is neither self-affirmation nor self-negation scales the philosophical depth and plateau of Levinas's ethics as first philosophy. His meditations on the primacy of the ethical and the heteronomic ethics of responsibility were inspired by the ancient heritage of Israel. He also acknowledges that the primary importance of the ethical is the Jewish contribution to the history of Western philosophy, and he turned for illumination to Judaic texts for his heteronomic ethics of responsibility. Judaism is a parable, as it were, for the ethical. Interestingly, in Hebrew responsibility (*ahariout*) and "other" (*aher*) share the same etymological root. Contrary to "rights talk" which elevates the self to a high plateau, the ethics of responsibility elevates the other to a higher place (*altar*). The only "rights" which are worth the name are the rights of the other(s).

Levinas's heteronomy does not efface or deface freedom, individuality, or subjectivity. He contends that heteronomy enriches rather than impoverishes the social and ethical life of the individual self in resonance with Bakhtin's dialogism. As it has earlier been said, the heteronomic ethics of responsibility is not only compatible with, but also more inclusive and thus weightier than, freedom because one can be free without being responsible but one cannot be responsible without first being free. Freedom is the necessary but not sufficient condition of responsible action. Human existence is *invested as freedom* rather than condemned to it. The aim of political theory itself is to ensure spontaneity by reconciling individual freedom with the freedom of the other. In other words, individual freedom is defined relationally, not absolutely or unconditionally, in the world of coexistence. In Levinas, subjectivity itself is affirmed never for itself but for an Other (*pour l'autre*). It comes into being as heteronomic: "it is my inescapable and incontrovertible answerability to the Other that makes me an individual 'I.'" Consequently, the notion of responsibility that coincides with the ethical is the confirmation of the "I" as subjectivity. Levinas says of responsibility as the essential, primary, and fundamental structure of subjectivity because he describes subjectivity in ethical terms: Ethics, he writes, does not supplement a preceding existential base; the very node of the subjective is knotted in ethics understood as responsibility. Since each subjectivity is unique and different from others, its responsibility is, accordingly, untransferable. Not only is responsibility untransferable but it is also unreciprocal: as Levinas emphasizes in no uncertain terms, responsibility is without concern for reciprocity: I have to respond to and for the Other without occupying myself with the Other's responsibility in my regard. Thus responsibility is an unconditional concern *for others* without the forethought of reciprocation: it is truly a *gift*.

CONCLUSION

The heteronomic ethics of responsibility heralds and celebrates the dialogical principle of a consummate community where the singular self is enfleshed with the singular other. It is an imperative for the future survival and preservation in perpetuity of the earth which shelters and nurtures humanity and nature in myriad ways. It is a paradigmatic way of thinking and doing—the way of a new phoenix, as it were, rising from the ashes of the past. By cultivating the habits of the heart as well as the mind and soul, the heteronomic ethics of responsibility opens a new threshold for philosophizing politics for generations yet to come. After all is said, in conclusion, everything, however small it may be, is a vital element of what Gaston Bachelard calls "coexistentialism."[39] All we earthlings, humans and nonhumans, together form what Aldo Leopold calls "a biotic community" or "earth democracy." Thus—to evoke John Donne's reputed devotional meditation with a slight modification—no human is an island unto himself or herself: to be alone is not to be. Even the death of a small creature and the disappearance of a small thing diminish my being because I am involved in a web of relationships in the world of all living beings and non-living things, both large and small. We are all precious earthlings. If we continue to speak the same language together without a radical continental shift to "earthcare" as a household (*oikos*) word, we are surely doomed and heading toward the end of the earth as well as the death of humanity.

I would contend that Sinism as a musical album and performance of earthly wisdom holds humanity's future in the palm of its hands. In association with Leopold's conservation aesthetics and ethics in orchestrating in harmony all living beings and non-living things on the "altared" Earth, Sinism is capable of constructing globally a new ethico-aesthetic paradigm which awakens us from the deadly slumber of complacent optimism and irresponsible negligence in the hopes of the greening of the earth once again and of passing proudly the green torch of life onto our posterities in perpetuity. Optimism is not only cowardice but also blind to hope. Unlike an optimist who is oblivious to the past and obsessed with a lifetime of present moments, the pessimist is evermore mindful of the future with which hope beyond despair is a friendly ally. History *à venir* will meet a beacon of hope without falling into an abyss of fatalistic and nightmarish despair from which there is no awakening.

NOTES

I wish to express my wholehearted thanks to Sungmoon Kim for sending me Chaihark Hahm's works.

1. Fredric Jameson, "Metacommentary," *PMLA* 86 (1971), pp. 9–18.

2. See *Analects* 13.3. Unless otherwise noted, in this chapter the English translation of the *Lunyu* 論語 has been adapted from *The Chinese Classics*, vol. 1, trans. James Legge (Oxford: Oxford University Press, 1893).

3. *Analects* 20.3.

4. Edward W. Said, *Orientalism* (New York: Random House, 1978).

5. Bhikhu Parekh. "Non-Western Political Thought," in *The Cambridge History of Twenti-eth-Century Political Thought*, eds. Terence Ball and Richard Bellamy (New York: Cambridge University Press, 2003), pp. 553–78.

6. See Chaihark Hahm, "Conceptualizing Korean Constitutionalism: Foreign Transplant or Indigenous Tradition?" *Journal of Korean Law* 1, no. 2 (2001), pp. 151–96; "Constitutional-ism, Confucian Civic Virtue, and the Ritual Propriety," in *Confucianism for the Modern World*, eds. Daniel A. Bell and Chaibong Hahm (Cambridge: Cambridge University Press, 2003), pp. 31–53; "Law, Culture and the Politics of Confucianism," *Columbia Journal of Asian Law* 16, no. 2 (2003), pp. 253–301; "Negotiating Confucian Civility through Constitutional Discourse," in *The Politics of Affective Relations: East Asia and Beyond*, eds. Chaihark Hahm and Daniel A. Bell (Lanham, MD: Lexington Books, 2004), pp. 277–308.

7. *Li* or *ye* as ritual propriety is, as Chaihark Hahm has shown, a political virtue. However, *ye* as an "affective" reciprocity has a seamy side: it may lead to "gift-giving or -taking," if not outright bribery, favoritism, nepotism, and so on. See Mayfair Mei-hui Yang, *Gifts, Favors, and Banquets: The Art of Social Relationships in China* (Ithaca, NY: Cornell University Press, 1994). In the United States, it is called political "cronyism," for which Richard Daly, the mayor of Chicago in the 1950s, was notorious. In Southern states, there is or was something called the "politics of friends and neighbors."

8. I borrow the phrase *glocalization* from the *New York Times* journalist Thomas Friedman, who uses Lexuss and olive tree as mixed metaphors.

9. See Mikhail Bakhtin, *The Dialogic Imagination*, eds. and trans. Caryl Emerson and Michael Holquist (Austin: University of Texas Press, 1981) and *Problems of Dostoevsky's Poetics*, ed. and trans. Caryl Emerson (Minneapolis: University of Minnesota Press, 1984).

10. Clifford Geertz, *The Interpretation of Cultures* (New York: Basic Books, 1973), p. 49.

11. Vincent Azoulay, *Pericles of Athens*, trans. Janet Lloyd (Princeton, NJ: Princeton University Press, 2014).

12. Among the concepts of liberty, equality, and fraternity in democratic constitutionalism, fraternity is the least discussed. Wilson C. McWilliams, in *The Idea of Fraternity in America* (Berkeley: University of California Press, 1973) wrote the most comprehensive work on frater-nity as "affective reciprocity with the hopes of restoring the past,"or the way of recovering the future. It, I think, expands the range of American political thought beyond liberal democracy or "rights talk." McWilliams acknowledges the English Baronet James F. Stephen's *Liberty, Equality, Fraternity*, ed. R. J. White (New York: Cambridge University Press, 1967).

13. Baron de Montesquieu, *The Spirit of the Laws*, eds. and trans. Anne M. Cohler, Basia Carolyn Miller, and Harold Samuel Stone (Cambridge: Cambridge University Press, 1989).

14. C. B. Macpherson, *The Political Theory of Possessive Individualism: Hobbes to Locke* (Oxford: Clarendon Press, 1962); R. H. Tawney, *The Acquisitive Society* (New York: Harcourt, Brace, and Howe, 1920).

15. Terry Eagleton, *The Ideology of the Aesthetic* (Oxford: Blackwell, 1990), p. 22.

16. Sheldon S. Wolin, *Politics and Vision: Continuity and Innovation in Western Political Thought*, expanded edition (Princeton, NJ: Princeton University Press, 2004), chap. 9: "Liberalism and the Decline of Political Philosophy," pp. 257–314.

17. See Wolin, *Politics and Vision*, pp. 257–314.

18. Hannah Arendt, *The Human Condition* (Chicago: University of Chicago Press, 1958).

19. Louis Hartz, *The Liberal Tradition in America: An Interpretation of American Political Thought since the Revolution* (New York: Harcourt, Brace, 1955), p. 140.

20. Francis Fukuyama, *The End of History and the Last Man* (New York: Free Press, 1992).

21. Mary A. Glendon, *Rights Talk: The Impoverishment of Political Discourse* (New York: Free Press, 1991), p. 76.

22. Ronald Dworkin, *Taking Rights Seriously* (Cambridge: Harvard University Press, 1977), p. 269.

23. Anthony Downs, *An Economy Theory of Democracy* (New York: Harper and Row, 1957).

24. Carol Gilligan, *In a Different Voice: Psychological Theory and Women's Development* (Cambridge, MA: Harvard University Press, 1982), p. 9.

25. H. G. Creel, *Sinism: A Study of the Evolution of the Chinese World-View* (Chicago: Open Court, 1929).

26. Watsuji Tetsuro, *Watsuji Tetsuro's Rinrigaku: Ethics in Japan*, trans. Yamamoto Seisaku and Robert E. Carter (Albany: State University of New York Press, 1996).

27. Richard E. Nisbett, *The Geography of Thought: How Asians and Easterners Think Differently and Why* (New York: Free Press, 2003).

28. See Pierre Bourdieu, *The Logic of Practice*, trans. Richard Nice (Stanford, CA: Stanford University Press, 1990). Speaking of Pierre Bourdieu's conception of "the *performative* magic of the social," we can never overemphasize the phrase in describing the quintessence of Confucianism in particular and Sinism in general. In the English-speaking world of philosophy, there is John Austin, who made a splash a few decades ago in philosophy based on his innovative idea of speech as "performative utterances" which are neither prescriptive nor descriptive. However, he was analytical rather than ethical as in Confucianism. The ethical notion of *sincerity* (*cheng*), which I call the moral soul of Sinic Eastern-Asian people, governs their conduct. Etymosinologically speaking, sincerity is spelled "word-achieved." When you promise something in words, you mean to *perform* in deed whatever you promised. This is why I am fond of Goethe, whose motto was "in the beginning is the Deed," which sounds very Confucian! Or else your promise would be empty or meaningless. Wang Yangming, whose philosophy I admire, calls it the unity of knowledge and action in the everyday life-world. Later, I also learned that in the oral culture of ancient "Homeric" culture, there was *mousike* inclusive of oral poetry, drama, dance, and what we call today music. These four components are all performative. For that reason, I call *mousike* "performing arts." Moreover, the communication or therapeutic conversation between the analyst and the patient is not just informative but is performative because their spoken language is "illocutionary." Because Sinism, especially Confucianism, is a species of relational ontology as *embodied* social process, its rites (*li*) are "body-learning," not just "head-learning," especially as in learning dance.

29. Arendt, *Human Condition*, p. 22.

30. Carl Kerenyi, *The Religion of the Greeks and Romans*, trans. Christopher Holme (New York: Dutton, 1962), p. 119.

31. Hwa Yol Jung, "A Metacommentary on the Current Debate on the Problematique of Filial Piety," *Dao: A Journal of Comparative Philosophy* 7 (2008), pp. 131–34.

32. Herbert Fingarette, *Confucius—The Secular as Sacred* (New York: Harper and Row, 1972).

33. Cf. McWilliams, *Idea of Fraternity in America*.

34. Norbert Elias, *The Civilizing Process*, vol. 1: *The History of Manners*, trans. Edmund Jephcott (New York: Pantheon Books, 1978).

35. Michael Walzer, *On Toleration* (New Haven, CT: Yale University Press, 1997).

36. "Preface: Teaching Shakespeare's Sister," in *Making Connections: The Relational Worlds of Adolescent Girls at Emma Willard School*, eds. Carol Gilligan, Nona P. Lyons, and Trudy J. Hanmmer (Cambridge, MA: Harvard University Press, 1990), p. 10.

37. Cornel West, "The New Cultural Politics of Difference," in *Out There*, ed. Russell Ferguson et al. (Cambridge, MA: MIT Press, 1990), p. 19.

38. Emmanuel Levinas, *Totality and Infinity*, trans. Alphonso Lingis (Pittsburgh, PA: Duquesne University Press, 1969); *Collected Philosophical Papers*, trans. Alphonso Lingis (Dordrecht: Martinus Nijhoff, 1987).

39. Gaston Bachelard, *The Poetics of Space*, trans. Maria Joas (Boston: Beacon Press, 1964).

Acknowledgments

The editor thanks the Korean Studies Promotion Service at the Academy of Korean Studies for a generous grant in support of the conference "Confucianism, Law, and Politics in Korea: Past and Present" on December 5–6, 2013, held at City University of Hong Kong, from which this volume was generated. This project was supported by an Academy of Korean Studies Grant funded by the Korean Government (MEST) (AKS-2011-AAA-2102). The Center for East Asian and Comparative Philosophy of City University of Hong Kong provided administrative support for the conference as well as for the preparation of the manuscript. Thanks are also due to Moowon Cho, Ruiping Fan, Eirik Harris, Philip J. Ivanhoe, Jonathan Kang, Hyoungchan Kim, Youngmin Kim, Hsin-wen Lee, Jaeyoon Song, and Bulran You, for participating in the conference as well as for providing valuable comments on the papers. Special thanks are due to Richard Kim for proofreading and commenting on the chapters and Youngsun Back for doing an initial translation of Junghoon Lee's original Korean essay and romanizing the Korean (and Korean-Chinese) characters in the volume according to the McCune-Reischauer system. I am also grateful to Joseph Chan and Justin Tiwald, who reviewed and approved this book project with valuable comments—both revealed their identity in their reviews. Finally, I would like to express my deepest gratitude to Sarah Campbell, my editor at Rowman & Littlefield International, for her support for this project, and to her assistant Sinéad Murphy for facilitating the publication process.

Several chapters were published previously and the editor is grateful for permission to reproduce the original materials.

Chapter 1 originally appeared as "Conceptualizing Korean Constitutionalism: Foreign Transplant or Indigenous Tradition?" *Journal of Korean Law* 1, no. 2 (2001), pp. 151–96.

Chapter 3 originally appeared as "Locating Feminism beyond Gender and Culture: A Case of the Family-Head System in South Korea," 담론 201 10, no. 1 (2007), pp. 245–90.

Chapter 6 was published originally in Korean as "한국법체계에서 자유주의의 의의: 종교의 자유를 중심으로," 법철학연구 13, no. 3 (2010), pp. 113–46.

Index

absolute monarchy, 27, 47n35
absolute power, 4, 20–21, 47n33, 195
Accusing the Ascendants and Elders. *See Kojonjang*
administrative rules, 28–30
adoption, 60–61
aggravated penalty provisions, 75
altered judgments (*pyŏnhyŏng kyŏlchŏng*), 44n8
alterity, 202
The Analects (Lau), 122n18
ancestral precedents. *See* established laws of royal ancestors
ancient institutions (*koje*; *guzhi*), 34
ancient rituals (*korye*; *guli*), 34
Angle, Stephen, 183
anti-communism, 143, 151
Antragsdelikt, 63
Aquinas, Thomas, 47n34, 146n11
Arendt, Hannah, 197, 199
Aristotle, 184, 191, 194, 196
"Articles on Constitution and Constitutionalism," 155
association: freedom of, 115; voluntary private, 114–119
Austin, John, 197, 206n28

Bachelard, Gaston, 204
Bakhtin, Mikhail, 194, 202
Ball, Terence, 192
Barthes, Roland, 191–192, 193

Bell, Daniel, 181–182, 192
Bellamy, Richard, 192
Bickle, Alexander, 43
Bi Hwan Kim, 8–9, 12
Binli (Guest Rituals), 51n82
Blackstone, William, 197
Blaire, Tony, 140
bone rank system, 90
Book of Documents, 54n122
Book on Punishment (*Hyŏngjon*), 65
Bourdieu, Pierre, 13, 199, 206n28
Bourgon, Jérôme, 69
British constitutionalism, 24–25, 47n40, 47n41, 195
Brown v. Board of Education, 167, 195
Buddhism, 149–150, 161–162, 167, 168, 198; anti-government demonstrations and, 158; Mahayana, 155; Neo-Confucianism and, 129–130, 133
Burger, Warren E., 158

The Cambridge History of Twentieth-Century Political Thought (Ball and Bellamy), 192
Cathedral (Rodin), 199
CEDAW. *See* Convention on the Elimination of All Forms of Discrimination against Women
Chan, Joseph, 12, 179, 184
Charter of Rights and Freedom, 26
Chatterjee, Partha, 96

211

About the Authors

Fred Dallmayr is Packey J. Dee professor emeritus in the Departments of Philosophy and Political Science at the University of Notre Dame (USA). He holds a doctor of law degree from the University of Munich and a Ph.D. in political science from Duke University. During 1991–1992 he was in India on a Fulbright research grant. He is past president of the Society for Asian and Comparative Philosophy. His work has been mainly in modern and recent Western philosophy, in comparative philosophy, and in cross-cultural political thought. Among his recent publications are *Beyond Orientalism* (1996; Indian ed. 2001), *Achieving Our World* (2001), *Dialogue among Civilizations* (2002), *In Search of the Good Life* (2007), *The Promise of Democracy* (2010), *Return to Nature* (2011), *Being in the World: Dialogue and Cosmopolis* (2013), and *Mindfulness and Letting Be* (2014).

Chaihark Hahm is professor of law at Yonsei University School of Law in Seoul, Korea. He has written on a wide range of topics including the Confucian theory of constitutionalism, comparative constitutional adjudication, Korean legal culture and history, civic ideals and citizenship education, and human rights. Professor Hahm's works in English have appeared in *Journal of Democracy, American Journal of Comparative Law*, and *I•CON: International Journal of Constitutional Law*, among others. He is co-editor of *Politics of Affective Relations: East Asia and Beyond* (2004) and a member of the editorial board of *I•CON*. He is currently working on a manuscript on the constitutional founding of Korea and Japan, which will be published by Cambridge University Press.

Hwa Yol Jung is emeritus professor of political science at Moravian College in Pennsylvania and president of the North American Korean Philosophy

Association. His research interests include political philosophy, phenomenology, existential philosophy, hermeneutics, transversal philosophy (East and West), and transversal geophilosophy as *ultima philosophia*. Among his many publications are *Prolegomena to Carnal Hermeneutics* (2014), *Transversal Rationality and Intercultural Texts* (2011), *The Way of Ecopiety: Essays in Transversal Geophilosophy* (2009), *Rethinking Political Theory: Essays in Phenomenology and the Study of Politics* (1993), and *The Crisis of Political Understanding: A Phenomenological Perspective in the Conduct of Political Inquiry* (1978). He is a member of Phi Beta Kappa and recipient of the 2012 Edward Ballard Prize, which goes to an excellent achievement in phenomenology.

Bi Hwan Kim is professor of political theory at Sungkyunkwan University, Seoul, and currently president of the Korean Society for Political Thought. His research interests include the history of Western political thought, contemporary political philosophy, the rule of law and democracy, and Confucianism. He is the author most recently of *Politics and Culture in Postmodern Times* (2005), *Libertarians, Liberals and Democrats* (2005), *The Political Philosophy and Dialectical Theory of the Rule of Law: Plato and Aristotle* (2011), *This Is Democracy* (2013), and *The Philosophy and Political Thought of Oakeshott: Philosophy of Freedom and Liberation beyond Ideology and Pragmatism* (2014), all in Korean. His articles have been published in *Government and Opposition*, *Journal of Legal Philosophy*, and many other journals.

Hee-Kang Kim is an associate professor of the Department of Public Administration at Korea University. She received her Ph.D. in political science from the University of Chicago in 2005 and wrote a dissertation on the feminist theory of equality. Her research and teaching interests are in justice theory, feminist theory, and normative policy analysis. Her articles have appeared in various journals including *Public Affairs Quarterly*, *Journal of Women, Politics & Policy*, *Women's Studies International Forum*, *Asian Perspective*, and *Korea Observer*.

Marie Seong-Hak Kim is a professor of history at St. Cloud State University and an attorney at law (Minnesota Bar). Her research interests lie in comparative legal history, focusing on Europe and East Asia. She is the author of *Law and Custom in Korea: Comparative Legal History* (2012) and *Michel de L'Hôpital: The Vision of a Reformist Chancellor during the French Religious Wars* (1997). She was a fellow at the Netherlands Institute for Advanced Study (2013–2014), a fellow at the Collegium de Lyon, Institut d'études avancées, in France (2011–2012), and a Fulbright Senior Scholar in

Korea (2004–2005). Her current research deals with law and justice in modern Korea.

Sungmoon Kim is an associate professor of political theory at the Department of Public Policy of the City University of Hong Kong. His research interests include comparative political theory, democratic and constitutional theory, and the history of East Asian political thought. His research has been published or is forthcoming in journals such as *American Political Science Review, British Journal of Political Science, Contemporary Political Theory, Critical Review of International Social and Political Philosophy, History of Political Thought, Journal of the History of Ideas, Philosophy and Social Criticism,* and *The Review of Politics.* Kim is the author of *Confucian Democracy in East Asia: Theory and Practice* (2014) and co-editor of *Confucianism—A Habit of the Heart* (forthcoming).

Junghoon Lee is an associate professor of jurisprudence and legal history at the Department of Law of University of Ulsan (South Korea). His research interests include legal positivism, natural law theory, and the history of East Asian legal and political thought. He is the author of *Confucian Law and Legal Thought of Korea from the 15th Century to the 19th Century* (2011, in Korean) and his other research has been published in various Korean journals, mainly in legal philosophy and legal history. Two representative articles are "The Meiji Constitution's Influence on the Modern Korean Legal System" (2011) and "A Study of John Finnis's Practical Reasonableness" (2013), both in Korean.